Clear My Vision

A Year of Focus on Christ

Clear My Vision: A Year of Focus on Christ

A *FocusChoice Therapy* publication.

Copyright © 2013, 2017 by David C. Heebner. All rights reserved.

Please visit **www.focuschoicetherapy.com** for more about David Heebner's new and innovative therapy model, information about products and services, and to order additional copies of this title or David's other books.

David C. Heebner, LPC

| 14143 Robert Paris Court | 43129 Tall Pines Court |
| Chantilly, Virginia 20151 | Ashburn, Virginia 20147 |

ISBN: 148194746X
ISBN-13: 978-1481947466

Unless otherwise indicated, all Scripture quotations are taken from THE MESSAGE, copyright © 1993, 1994, 1995, 1996, 2000, 2001, 2002 by Eugene H. Peterson. Used by permission of NavPress. All rights reserved. Represented by Tyndale House Publishers, Inc.

Revised Edition, 2017.
Cover design: Qinisile Nkosi, Chris Eberly
Interior design: Chris Eberly
Editors: Chris Eberly, Deborah Gonzalez

First Edition, 2013.
Editor and Co-author: Sarah Deutsch

Printed in the United States of America.

This book is humbly dedicated to my family,
who support my passion to teach;
to my friends, who cheer me on;
to all the clients from the past 30 years, who taught me more
than I could ever teach them;
and to my Lord, who never stops talking to me
and who loves me more than I can even imagine.

Forward

Have you ever felt like you were living the real-life version of Bill Murray's movie "Groundhog Day"? In the movie, Murray is forced to relive the same day over and over again, with seemingly no chance of ever breaking out of this loop. If you have ever felt stuck in a habit, powerless to change, without solutions, then the book in your hand will give you hope.

In this book, author and professional counselor David Heebner has compiled a year-long journey that will help you see everything with a new clarity and focus of vision. Many books have been written on the subject of vision, but few deal with vision as David Heebner does in this book. Vision is not limited to dreaming about your future or seeing possibilities where others see impossibilities. Vision is a fundamental part of your everyday life that shapes your direction and your desires. Where is your vision focused? What captures your attention? How can you discover clarity of vision?

The book you are about to read gives you a year's supply of scriptures that show you how to keep your focus on God in every situation. Focus has a life-changing, life-directing power that can either lead you down a path of destruction or lead you into the life that God has for you. God's wonderful plan for you is not achieved through personal effort or performance. It is simply the result of choosing a God-focused life over a self-focused life.

As you read this book you will be encouraged, challenged, and instructed. So, turn the page and start the journey to clear your vision!

Curtis Cook
Ozark, Missouri
January 2013

Introduction

For over 50 years of my life, I functioned as an expert "performer" in school, at home, and at work. I wanted to please people, and I was pressured by my own need to "get things right." These performance skills worked in my favor at home on my family's dairy farm, as well as in the church I attended while growing up. However, they worked against me in my relationships, especially my relationship with God. I felt as though, no matter how hard I tried, I would never be able to win the approval and acceptance of God—or others around me.

During a very stressful period in my life several years ago, I finally gave up. I decided I could no longer depend on my own ability to perform to earn love or affirmation. This decision didn't provoke an immediate, dramatic transformation in my life—the ingrained habits of my performance mentality did not disappear. However, I did experience a steady shift in my focus as I asked God to lead me—to show me what to say and do every moment of every day. I asked God to take over my life, and I found myself repeatedly making choices that took my attention off my own effort to perform and placed it on the Lord.

Slowly, I began learning that my relationship with God is not dependent on my performance. At first, I frequently asked God in my prayers to "help me." Although asking anything of God is a part of living a life focused on Him, asking God to merely "help me" was not enough to effect a total life transformation. My prayers still had a "me" focus—as if I was asking God to be my assistant as I continued to run things myself!

Because of my addiction to perfection, I never really embraced reading God's Word. Even my efforts to excel at knowledge of the Scriptures only frustrated and discouraged me. However, on September 6th, 2011, God used a verse to change my life. I received a letter from a Christian friend in Honduras, a letter written in Spanish, quoting The Message's translation of Philippians 3:12-21. In Philippians 3:15, Paul says that if we have anything less than total commitment to Christ in mind, God will clear our blurred vision, and help us to see. This simple phrase challenged me and turned my attention to God in a way I had never could have imagined. Through it, He showed me how completely He wants to take control of my life if I only choose—not try—to focus on Him.

This revelation was absolutely transforming for me. Now I began to realize that God does not want to help me perform. How well or how poorly I live a life in obedience to His Word will never change God's love for me. As I released myself from perfectionist tendencies and control measures, God showed me that "trying to simply do the right thing" without knowing and loving God only took my focus off Him When I'm so caught up in fretting over how I'm doing, I lose sight of what He is doing in and through me. He wants me to focus on Him—and get my consideration for self out the way—so He can perform in me.

I've come to realize that all that God requires of you and of me is that we make a continual choice to love and focus on Him and then follow where He leads. We can be totally committed to following Christ—without beating ourselves up for our failures! He wants me to watch Him do it all for me, and just glorify Him in His faithfulness and love.

When God surprised me with this amazing passage from Philippians, I suddenly had a desire to explore His Word to understand how God could draw my attention to Him through His love. What is most fascinating to me now is that the more I focus on God, the more ways He has of drawing my attention to Him. The ways He gets to my heart are endless. God knows all my love languages, and His love is irresistible. He captivates my thoughts and emotions more powerfully than any addictive or compulsive pull in my life. He lifts my depression. He gives me company when I am lonely. He distracts me from my anxiety. He listens patiently when I vent my anger to Him. He fills me with joy. He even shows me what to say and do at work, and gives me new and inspiring thoughts to share with others who need encouragement and clear direction. I am just as fearful and insecure as ever, but I hardly notice or experience those feelings because I have become more and more confident in Him every day.

In these daily readings, you'll find scriptures full of God's promises that show us how to focus on Him. Through His Word, the Lord draws our attention back to Him with love and graciousness. These words are excellent to dwell on at any point in your life, but they are especially comforting during tough times. My comments after each Scripture hopefully will give you a sense of how God has drawn me to Him and held me close, in both good times and bad. As we journey onward together in faith, I pray you will know the joy and celebration that focus on His love can bring.

Clear My Vision

A Year of Focus on Christ

January 1

So let's keep focused on that goal, those of us who want everything God has for us. If any of you have something else in mind, something less than total commitment, God will clear your blurred vision—you'll see it yet!

- Philippians 3:15-16

This time of year, people craft resolutions and goals for the future. New Year's resolutions all have a couple of things in common: they typically require a lot of effort, and they typically don't last long. In his letter to the Philippians, Paul encourages his readers to "keep focused" on the goal of total commitment to Christ. Unlike many resolutions, this goal of total focus on Christ is not accomplished through effort, but through a simple choice—the choice to make God the center of our lives. It's so easy, it may seem *too* simple. Maybe it seems to you that total commitment to focus on Christ is not possible. If you feel this way, don't give up! In His timing, God will clear your blurred vision, and you'll see the simplicity of His plan. All we need to do is to keep our focus on the Lord, and He will show us the way. He will keep our vision clear as we follow Him into everything He has for us.

PRAYER: Lord, where you lead me, I will follow. Keep my vision clear, and lead me in your way, into everything you have planned for me. When I feel that total commitment to you is not possible for someone who fails as often as I do, remind me of this simple, yet profound promise. I choose to focus on you.

Personal Reflections

January 2

*But I am well on my way. . . I've got my eye on the goal.
. . I'm off and running, and I'm not turning back.*

- Philippians 3:12-14

Focusing on God is a lifetime journey, not a one-time experience. Since our human nature tempts us to focus on ourselves, this faith journey of making Christ our ultimate focus will feel strange and difficult at first. I admit that I have frequently taken my gaze off Him and reverted to my old, self-focused habits. Thank goodness life is a long race and not a sprint! God has been teaching me that the important thing is to keep my eye on the goal, and not worry about how fast I am getting there. Slowly but surely, if we continue to turn our focus back to Him without beating ourselves up for looking away, a new pattern of God-focus will develop in our hearts.

PRAYER: Lord, thank you for the example of Paul in this letter to the Philippians. Today I ask that you remind me to focus every time I get distracted from you. Continue to always draw my attention back to your loving care, especially when life gets crazy. I know I am well on my way now, even if it sometimes doesn't feel like it. Thank you for reminding me to be faithful in the little things, especially when it comes to keeping my eyes on you. I'm running toward you now, and I'm not going to turn back!

Personal Reflections

January 3

. . .I've got my eye on the goal, where God is beckoning us onward—to Jesus.

- Philippians 3:13

When I played sports as a kid, my dad was always my biggest fan. He waved more, clapped harder, and cheered louder than anyone else in the stands. Since he was a dairy farmer, he could not get to my Friday night football games until the second quarter, but when he did arrive, everyone knew it! My dad's pride and enthusiasm gave me a huge burst of energy in those football games, but it took many years for me to realize that his love was a picture of the love God the Father has for me. God loves us, takes pride in us, and cheers for us throughout our lives. He is beckoning us onward to the ultimate touchdown—running into the arms of Jesus! Sit and think for a minute about this: the Lord is your biggest fan.

PRAYER: Thank you, Lord, for cheering for me so passionately all the time. When I look your way, I can't help but notice your support. I am humbled when I think about how much you love me. Thank you so much for being my biggest fan and for helping me to keep my eye on the goal. Imagining you standing on the finish line, holding your arms out in welcome, waiting for me, I am amazed. Your love is more real and more powerful than anything I have ever known.

Personal Reflections

January 4

Do you see what this means—all these pioneers who blazed the way, all these veterans cheering us on? It means we'd better get on with it. Strip down, start running—and never quit!

- Hebrews 12:1

As a kid playing sports, I was always more passionate about the game when there were lots of fans in the bleachers. Knowing that they were there, cheering me and my team on to victory, gave us the inspiration we needed to keep going. As we Christians run the race and fight the good fight, we have the hometown advantage. There's a host of Christian heroes of the faith cheering us on from the finish line! When you get discouraged and feel tempted to take your eyes off the prize, remember that you're not in this alone—the saints are cheering for you!

PRAYER: Lord, thank you for your promise that your faithful servants are cheering for me every day until I reach the finish line and enter heaven to spend eternity with you. I may feel like a novice when I try to navigate my way through this life, but this verse reminds me that each and every one of those veterans felt the same way at one time. You helped them to reach the goal, and I believe you will help me in the same way. Thank you for the pioneers who blazed the way and showed me how to keep my eyes fixed on you. I want you to be in the center of my vision as I run this race.

Personal Reflections

January 5

Stick with me, friends. Keep track of those you see running this same course, headed for this same goal.

- Philippians 3:17

Not only do we have the saints of old cheering us on as we go, but we also have companions running the race along with us. In Philippians, Paul encourages us to spend time with others in our community of believers and benefit from their friendship along the way. How different our race is from all other races in which everyone competes for him or herself! The Lord wants us to run together to help each other to stay focused on Him. By ourselves, our human nature is to focus on ourselves and lose sight of Him. But together, we can remind our fellow runners to stay the course.

PRAYER: Lord, please bring other faithful followers into my daily life so that we can encourage each other to stay focused on you. I know when we stick together it is much easier to avoid wandering out of the way. I want to be able to reach out to others and help them to stay on course as we all head for the same goal, keeping our eyes on you. Help me to keep track of my friends, and help me know how to encourage them. Thank you again for the stories of the pioneers. They encourage me when I am tired, lonely, or afraid. Knowing that I run the same course as millions of other saints inspires me to keep running.

Personal Reflections

January 6

I'm not saying that I have this all together, that I have it made. But I am well on my way, reaching out for Christ, who has so wondrously reached out for me.

- Philippians 3:12

What a wonderful reassurance from this passage on running the race of life! Even Paul, the great apostle, admitted that he didn't have it all together. Thank goodness—I know I sure don't have it made either. I can start this race with a huge sigh of relief, knowing that the Lord only desires that I keep on reaching out for Him, my focus totally on His power to save me.

PRAYER: Lord, remind me over and over again how much you love me just the way I am, and that you put no pressure on me to perform. Thank you that you reached out to me before I ever reached out to you. Your power gives me the strength to keep running. Thinking about how you—wondrously!— reached out for me blows my mind and makes me ever more eager to make you the center of my life. I know I am well on my way to making you the chief focus of all of my thoughts and feelings. Thank you for setting me free from my old habits of shame and self-focus.

Personal Reflections

January 7

Friends, don't get me wrong: By no means do I count myself an expert in all of this.

- Philippians 3:13

Over many years, so many people have come to me looking for advice on how to live. At times I felt I had to be perfect in order to be able to help others. It gives me so much relief to know that I don't have to try to be perfect anymore. I don't need to be an expert. I don't even need to be "knowledgeable," or wise, or clever! God is so much wiser than I could ever hope to be that I am eager to have Him take over my life and my work of helping others. I can have peace knowing that He is completely capable of running my life in a way that pleases Him and brings me deep joy.

PRAYER: Lord, many times the pressure to know it all, to offer sound advice, and to perform in order to achieve success can be overwhelming. Thank you that this pressure is overwhelming, because it prompts me to turn to you in desperation and ask you to take over my life. Please continue to prompt me through your Holy Spirit to focus on your perfection, so that I don't even feel the need to try to be perfect anymore. When my heart is focused on you, I delight in just being your messenger. I want to live as your mouthpiece, and not worry about having expert words of my own.

Personal Reflections

January 8

. . . reaching out for Christ, who has so wondrously reached out for me. . .

— Philippians 3:12

For much of my life, I have tried to find my own way to Christ, straining to make Him real in my life. This verse tells me that Jesus has already reached out to me exactly where I am. If I simply stretch out my arm to Him, He will hold onto me and show me the way. No straining on my part is required. I don't even have to make the first move! Jesus has already reached out and pulled me back from the cliff of where I was tottering on the brink of self-destruction, trying in vain to make my own life work. I would have fallen over the edge if he hadn't rescued me. Now I am safe in His arms, and I can see much more clearly just how foolish I was to try to make it on my own. Surrendering to the Savior is the beginning of new life!

PRAYER: Lord, I am so grateful that you have reached out to me and will never let me fall. Remind me to focus on you and let you hold my hand. The thought that you reached out for me, when I was dead to you, buried deep in my selfish self-centered focus and my unkind words and deeds, continues to amaze me. Your love is truly wondrous! Now that I have experienced how incredible you are, I want to reflect your love in my daily interactions with others.

Personal Reflections

January 9

I've called your name. You're mine. . . I paid a huge price for you. . . That's how much you mean to me! That's how much I love you!

- Isaiah 43:2-4

The love of a father is a marvelous thing—and the love that your Heavenly Father has for you is greater still! Take a moment to reflect on this wonderful promise—you are His child. He knows your name, and you belong to Him. Just think about that: He knows your name! In fact, He knows you intimately, everything about you. He knows your past, with all its scars and struggles, joys and fears, triumphs and failure. He knows your present, with every thought and feeling and every momentary experience. He knows your future, with all its opportunities and possibilities, hopes, and dreams. He loves and values you so much that He paid a huge price for you—gave His own life to save you! That's how much He loves you.

PRAYER: God, remind me every day that I belong to you. I am a needy child and I rely on your constant assurance of how much you love me. The thought that you not only know my name, but everything else about me, even better than I know myself, fills me with awe. Help me to see and understand all of the ways you show that you care for me. Remind me every day how much your love has done for me and how much I am worth to you.

Personal Reflections

January 10

This is my life work: helping people understand and respond to this Message. It came as a sheer gift to me, a real surprise, God handling all the details. . . God saw to it that I was equipped, but you can be sure that it had nothing to do with my natural abilities.

- Ephesians 3:7-8

This is a great surprise—a sheer gift—God sees every part of our lives, and He cares about every detail. This promise is so full of comfort, it seems almost unbelievable. God loves us so much that He has made Himself involved in every aspect of our lives. He sees you and me, and cares for us every second of every day. I love knowing that He cares so much for me. I know that I can trust Him to handle all the details of my life, to equip me for His service, and to help others understand and respond to His message as I tell everyone of His marvelous grace.

PRAYER: Lord, I am so thankful for the special attention that you give not only to me, but to everyone who will focus on you. Thank you for caring so much about me. My natural abilities— or lack of them—don't seem so important anymore. I have a new sense of trust that you will take of me and guide me. Thank you for equipping me to share your good news with those who don't yet know you.

Personal Reflections

January 11

Saving is all his idea, and all his work. All we do is trust him enough to let him do it. It's God's gift from start to finish! We don't play the major role. If we did, we'd probably go around bragging that we'd done the whole thing.

- Ephesians 2:8-9

I have never been able to trust my own efforts to win me affirmation or honor. Often, my attempts to succeed only make a bigger mess of things. I tell myself, "If only I try harder, I'll finally get it right!" In reality, simply trying harder never really works. God promises that He will do all the work of changing us from the inside out, from start to finish. Even more encouraging, God says He will always love us, flaws and all. All we have to do is surrender to Him, trust him to change us in His own time, and focus on His goodness.

PRAYER: Lord, thank you for your promise that I can depend on you to complete the work you started in me. I know that I don't have to "get it right" to earn your acceptance or love. From now on, I choose to focus on you and give you my whole heart. I love to worship you, because your heart of mercy and goodness and truth is wider than the sea, more immense in grandeur than the heavens.

Personal Reflections

January 12

God can do anything, you know—far more than you could ever imagine or guess or request in your wildest dreams! He does it not by pushing us around but by working within us, his Spirit deeply and gently within us.

- Ephesians 3:20

The nature of God's heart is so loving and caring. Despite my independent, performance-driven nature, God doesn't push me around. The way that He works in my life is far beyond anything I could ever hope for or dare to dream. Just think of that—of being loved more than you ever dreamed possible, of having someone love you who is powerful enough to make your wildest dreams come true, and more! When I remember that God has promised that what He will give us will be far better than we could ever imagine, I am filled with joy and love for Him. His promises are "almost too good to be true," and yet, they are the truest promises there could ever be. His Spirit deep inside us testifies that we can trust every word He says.

PRAYER: Lord, I am so grateful for this promise. On my own, I know that I would self-destruct, like I have in the past. Please remind me of this promise over and over again, and help me to trust your sovereign plans, which are greater than anything I could imagine. Massage your truth into me deeply every day.

Personal Reflections

January 13

Do you think anyone is going to be able to drive a wedge between us and Christ's love for us? There is no way! Not trouble, not hard times, not hatred, not hunger, not homelessness, not bullying threats, not backstabbing... None of this fazes us because Jesus loves us. I'm absolutely convinced that nothing—nothing living or dead, angelic or demonic, today or tomorrow, high or low, thinkable or unthinkable—absolutely nothing can get between us and God's love because of the way that Jesus our Master has embraced us.

- Romans 8:35, 37-39

Many of us have spent years trying so hard to get our spouse, our parents, or our children to love us, but the harder we try, the less we feel loved. Sadly, depending on others to love us unconditionally never works. I'm so glad we don't have to try to make God love us. He loves us unconditionally—just the way we are. And nothing living or dead can ever change that.

PRAYER: Lord, hard times can make anyone feel lonely and unloved. When I am enduring tough times, please show me continual reminders that neither other people, nor any circumstances could separate me from your love. Draw my attention to the unchanging, glorious nature of your love, especially during times I feel unlovable.

Personal Reflections

January 14

You've always given me breathing room, a place to get away from it all,

A lifetime pass to your safe-house, an open invitation as your guest.

- Psalm 61:3-4

I grew up in a rural area where friends would always tell us: "Come visit any time! Our door is always open—you don't even need to knock." This kind of trust between neighbors is often not safe or possible in today's world. Our world is dangerous, and we know that. We feel restless, uneasy, fearful, unable to trust. However, God wants us to come to Him any time, with any problem, and it's always safe to open that door. God gives us a lifetime invitation to get away from the worries and stress of the everyday to come sit in His presence—no conditions, and no exceptions.

PRAYER: Lord, remind me of this promise at all times during each day. So often I feel that I have no one to turn to when I'm struggling, and that I'll have to fend for myself. I feel out of breathe, anxious, fearful, unable to slow down and focus on you. I need the breathing room you offer. I need a place to get away from the pressures and pains of my life, a place where I know I am invited and safe at home. Thank you that your heart is always open. Draw me to yourself whenever I feel weary and worn out. Open the door so I can run into your safe-house, the shelter of your arms.

Personal Reflections

January 15

You've always taken me seriously, God, made me welcome among those who know and love you.

- Psalm 61:5

The Lord has promised that not only can we go to Him at any time for anything that we need, but also that he will show us people who will welcome us with open arms to love and comfort us. We all need a safe person here on earth to share our hearts with, someone who listens to us with compassion and understanding. Professional counseling provides many individuals access to a knowledgeable, caring person who will listen to them and help them sort through struggles and difficult issues. However, this doesn't mean we should discount other mentors or undervalue friendships. God has put friends, mentors, and counselors in our lives to give us strength. In symbiotic friendships the benefits of support and encouragement should be mutual. When we have friends standing beside us who love God and are eager to turn the focus of their lives to Him, we can help each other stay on course. Friendship is important—don't try to "go it alone."

PRAYER: Lord, I love your tender touch, and I long for the friendship of someone here on earth who will care for me like you do. Thank you for promising to bring people into my life whom I can trust and turn to for comfort and counsel.

Personal Reflections

January 16

Be good to me, God—and now!
I've run to you for dear life.
I'm hiding out under your wings
until the hurricane blows over.
I call out to High God,
the God who holds me together.

- Psalm 57:1-2

Most people I know seek out counseling only during a crisis. Likewise, we tend to run to God when we are overwhelmed by the trials we face. When the storms of life come, I am always encouraged by this verse—God's steadfast promise to carry us through any time of trouble or hardship. Running to Him means that you keep going, and it means that you keep your eyes on Him every step of the way. He is the only one who can shelter us from the storm—and we can always hide under His wings during the hurricanes of this life. Even when we feel like we are about to fly apart, His love holds us together.

PRAYER: Lord, so many times I have begged for your help in an emergency. I run to you, knowing that you will care for me. Thank you that you are faithful, especially when I am frightened. I am so small, Lord, and the trials and tempests of this life can be overwhelming and make it hard for me to trust. But when I cry out that I need you, I know that you will answer me. Thank you for holding me together.

Personal Reflections

January 17

. . .your Guardian God won't fall asleep. Not on your life! Israel's Guardian will never doze or sleep. God's your Guardian, right at your side to protect you—Shielding you from sunstroke, sheltering you from moonstroke.

- Psalms 121:4-6

Fear can attack and overcome us any time of day—especially in the dark of night. What a relief to know that God is holding us close every hour of every day! He will never fall asleep on us—He is always on guard, watching over us. The phrase "right at your side" describes God being so close, so personal, with us, protecting us like a bodyguard, or a mother eagle hovering over her young in the nest, talons ready to destroy anyone who tries to harm her babies. That's how much God cares for us!

PRAYER: Jesus, thank you so much that you always are by my side taking care of me. Thank you for never letting go of me, especially when times get tough. Sometimes I feel like you are asleep, or that you have forgotten about me, but this verse reminds me that you can never, never forget about me or fall asleep on guard. Thank you for being my strong, ever-present Guardian, sheltering me from evil and keeping me focused on your glory.

Personal Reflections

January 18

This is what God says, the God who builds a road right through the ocean, who carves a path through pounding waves. . .

- Isaiah 43:16

God does not promise that we won't go through hard times in life, but He does promise to make a way through the very middle of every storm. We trust His good plan, knowing that our only responsibility is to keep our eyes on Him so we don't miss what He is showing us. These verses provide us with a vivid word picture to help our imagination give wings to our faith. Picture God building roads right through the middle of a raging ocean, carving a path through the tossing waves. Now picture Him picking you up, carrying you on the path He has built, right through the center of the storm. This is the kind of power that He possesses, and He chooses to use that power to protect us and keep us safe in His arms as He carries us through all the deep waters we have to face. We can rest assured He will never let us drown.

PRAYER: Lord, it's so easy to get distracted and dismayed by my circumstances during tough times. When I'm afraid or overwhelmed, please draw my attention to the path you are creating through the difficulties of life. Fill me with peace in the midst of the storm.

Personal Reflections

January 19

...he rescues you from hidden traps, shields you from deadly hazards. His huge outstretched arms protect you—under them you're perfectly safe.

- Psalm 91:2-3

We often feel blindsided and shocked by life's crises. The sudden troubles that can befall us often feel like hidden traps, just waiting to trip us up and cause us harm. We can begin to obsess about the deadly hazards that could be right around the corner, hovering over our tomorrows like ugly birds of prey. But an obsessive focus on worrying about all the bad things that can happen only wears us down and makes our lives miserable. Instead, let's focus on this promise: that God sees dangers that we could never anticipate, and He is in the business of protecting those who trust Him. Because He loves us and watches over us, we can rely on Him. Isn't it wonderful to think that under His arms, we are really "perfectly safe"?

PRAYER: Lord, I confess that my natural tendency is to self-protect by trying to anticipate all the bad things that could happen to me and make contingency plans for all of them. I waste so much mental and emotional energy on worry, and I don't want to live like that anymore. Prompt me to quickly run to you when I am afraid and remind me not to get myself in deeper trouble by trying to handle crises myself. Thank you for watching over me.

Personal Reflections

January 20

Are you tired? Worn out? . . . Come to me. . . Walk with me and work with me—watch how I do it. . . Keep company with me and you'll learn to live freely and lightly.

- Matthew 11:28-30

Can you even imagine living freely and lightly when you're feeling so burdened by life's daily struggles? God knows obstacles both great and small will always surround us. But the Lord is greater than any challenging obstacle or any bad day. He promises that if we spend time in His presence and watch Him closely, He will show us how to relax and truly find rest and peace in Him. Are you ready to quit struggling and toiling through each day? Then come to Him. Turn your face to Him, fix your eyes on Him, and just focus on who He is. It's that simple. Living freely and lightly starts now, with this first step. Focus.

PRAYER: Lord, I am worn out. I have been carrying the burden of my obsession with performance and perfection for so long it is hard to know how to lay it down. But Lord, I want the rest and peace that you promise. I know that only you have the wisdom and power to transform my habits of self-rescue. I want you to make this radical change in my life. You are my only hope. Take my hand and help me to walk beside you and give my troubles over to you. Teach me how to keep company with you and live in the freedom of your presence.

Personal Reflections

January 21

Then you called out to God in your desperate condition; he got you out in the nick of time. He spoke the word that healed you, that pulled you back from the brink of death. So thank God for his marvelous love.

- Psalm 107:19-21

Many of us have been unwilling to give up trying to fix things on our own, preferring to struggle on in futility, until we were on the very verge of disaster. Some of us have even wounded ourselves as we frantically tried to escape from the ruins of our tattered lives. Only when we called out to God, calling out for help from the depths of our utter desperation, were we finally able to be rescued. Thankfully, God doesn't punish us for our efforts to help ourselves in our own strength. Instead, He rescues us in His just-right timing, before we can self-destruct. He makes it His specialty to pull us back from the brink of death and heal our shattered hearts with the warmth of His love.

PRAYER: Lord, remind me daily of how desperately I felt my need for you in the midst of my despair. I need this vivid reminder of how lost I was without you, not to shame me or discourage me, but to strengthen my resolve to always depend on you. I know that I need you, and I don't want to be self-reliant anymore. Thank you that I don't have to save myself.

Personal Reflections

January 22

Sheer muscle and will power don't make anything happen. Every word I've spoken to you is a spirit-word, and so it is life-making. . . This is why I told you earlier that no one is capable of coming to me on his own. You only get to me as a gift from the Father.

- John 6:63-65

Sometimes, after a storm, we all too quickly revert to relying on our own efforts to do "life cleanup." This self-focused crisis management can distract our attention from the Lord, so that we forget how He rescued us. In our striving, we forget that the same God who saved us from disaster wants to be involved in our lives every day. Relying on our own strength to get through the daily grind only sets the stage for another disaster, because "sheer muscle and will power don't make anything happen." We need to listen to the spirit-words of Jesus if we are to learn how to draw close to Him.

PRAYER: Lord, thank you that you are so much more than disaster-relief for my soul. Thank you for being a loving friend who wants to be part of my everyday life. Help me to listen to your words, which are full of your Spirit and bring life. Thank you for showing us that the only way to the Father is through you.

Personal Reflections

January 23

The apostles came up and said to the Master, 'Give us more faith.' But the Master said, 'You don't need more faith. There is no "more" or "less" in faith. If you have a bare kernel of faith, say the size of a poppy seed, you could say to the sycamore tree, "Go jump in the lake," and it would do it.'

- Luke 17:5-6

I sometimes fear that my faith is "not enough," and will prohibit me from having a strong relationship with the Lord. This scripture gives my heart great encouragement. My relationship with God does not depend on how great or small my faith may be. God's power and His love for me are much, much bigger than that. He can take a bare kernel of faith, hardly more than a piece of chaff, and build something great in me— a faith in me that can move mountains! Because I know that God is faithful when I am faithless, I know that nothing can separate me from God's love and care for me.

PRAYER: Lord, thank you that my faith rests on your amazing and faithful love. Only you can enable me to trust you, when my heart is weak and my faith flickers. Thank you for being my faith when I have no faith of my own left. Lord, as another man once said, "I believe! But help my unbelief."

Personal Reflections

January 24

It wasn't so long ago that you were mired in that old stagnant life of sin. You let the world, which doesn't know the first thing about living, tell you how to live. You filled your lungs with polluted unbelief, and then exhaled disobedience. We all did it, all of us doing what we felt like doing, when we felt like doing it, all of us in the same boat. It's a wonder God didn't lose his temper and do away with the whole lot of us. Instead, immense in mercy and with an incredible love, he embraced us. He took our sin-dead lives and made us alive in Christ. He did all this on his own, with no help from us! Then he picked us up and set us down in highest heaven in company with Jesus, our Messiah.

- Ephesians 2:1-6

My efforts to "do better" in every area of life—even in my relationship with God—have always worked against me. Trying harder to have more faith or feel closer to God always felt like swimming against the current—destined to failure. But scripture clearly shows us that when we have willing hearts submitted to God, He does the work. Our only responsibility is to choose to focus on God and follow His guidance.

PRAYER: Lord, I am worn out from trying to do better. All my past efforts resulted in failure. Thank you for your promises— I am beginning to feel grateful that you do all the work. I am so relieved to know that you are perfectly capable of handling everything.

Personal Reflections

January 25

God, investigate my life; get all the facts firsthand.
I'm an open book to you;
even from a distance, you know what I'm thinking.
You know when I leave and when I get back;
I'm never out of your sight.
You know everything I'm going to say
before I start the first sentence.
I look behind me and you're there,
then up ahead and you're there, too—
your reassuring presence, coming and going.
This is too much, too wonderful—I can't take it all in!

- Psalm 139:1-4

The Lord made me, understands me, and knows me even better than I know myself. I am an open book to Him. There is nothing about me that He does not know and care about. God is all around me, surrounding me with His loving presence. There is peace in knowing that He is capable of ordering my steps and faithfully ordering my life better than I could on my own. I want Him to think for me, speak for me, and act on my behalf. I want God in full control of me.

PRAYER: Lord, please take over my life. Every moment of every day, go before me in my thoughts, in my words, and in my actions. I believe you are far more capable of guiding my steps and ordering my days than I am of making plans for myself. Thank you that you know me so well and take the time to make good plans for my life.

Personal Reflections

January 26

In the evening his disciples went down to the sea, got in the boat, and headed back across the water to Capernaum. It had grown quite dark and Jesus had not yet returned. A huge wind blew up, churning the sea. They were maybe three or four miles out when they saw Jesus walking on the sea, quite near the boat. They were scared senseless, but he reassured them, 'It's me. It's all right. Don't be afraid.' So they took him on board. In no time they reached land—the exact spot they were headed to.

- John 6:16-21

Giving control of my life to God can be frightening. I am so afraid to let go and relinquish control of things. Self-reliance is in many ways the only life I know. I am an often-fearful follower, and I believe it is for this reason that God highlighted three words in this scripture for me: "near the boat." Over and over, I am seeing the emphasis on the nearness of God to those who choose to trust Him. God comes close to me when I fear. In times when I can't control my fearful tendencies, I can still hang onto the Lord for dear life, and choose to let Him in my boat.

PRAYER: Lord, I am so thankful that hanging onto you and trusting you to save me is a choice—not an effort on my part. When I am afraid, I am not capable of effort. In every moment, I need you close to me so I can cling to you. Thank you for coming near to me.

Personal Reflections

January 27

Your thoughts—how rare, how beautiful!
God, I'll never comprehend them!
I couldn't even begin to count them—any more than I
could count the sand of the sea.
Oh, let me rise in the morning and live always with you!

- Psalm 139:17-18

My own thoughts can often make me feel anxious, angry, or depressed. Many times, I used to wake up in the morning and immediately be plunged into a mess of anxious thoughts about performance and failure, thoughts that swirled in my head like sharks, just waiting for me to wake up and notice them. But the more I read God's word and dwell on His thoughts about me, the more often I wake up with His thoughts on my mind instead of my old anxious ones. Reading the psalms before I drift off to sleep brings me peace in knowing what God thinks of me.

PRAYER: Lord, fill my mind with your thoughts. They clear away my own negative thoughts and draw my attention to you. I want to dwell in your presence and be free of my performance-driven mentality. I'll never be able to comprehend the glory of your thoughts towards me, any more than I could sit down and count them, but I know where I want to be, and what I want to be thinking about every morning when I wake up. Please teach me how I may dwell in your presence, how to focus on you so that I can spend every day listening to your thoughts.

Personal Reflections

January 28

You know me inside and out, you know every bone in my body; you know exactly how I was made, bit by bit, how I was sculpted from nothing into something.

- Psalm 139:15

For a long time, I thought God allowed rough times in my life just to see how much I could handle. In the trials of my life, I often felt like God was bending my fingers backward until I cried "uncle!" Most of the time, though, it is just my bad decisions and other's poor choices that cause me rough times. Now I know that God cries when He sees me hurting. He created me, sculpting my body bit by bit, knitting my life together before I was even born. He knows me inside and out, and doesn't need to test my strength just for the fun of it. Because He loves me and knows me, He longs to be my Rescuer, to step in at the just-right time to save me from myself and remind me that I can always depend on Him in time of need.

PRAYER: Lord, thank you so much for all the times you rescued me when I had reached my breaking point. Bring those times to my mind often so that I may give you all the credit. Thank you that you created me and know me, inside and out, with a deep kind of knowing that makes me confident in your love.

Personal Reflections

January 29

*Celebrate God all day, every day! I mean, revel in him!
. . . Instead of worrying, pray. Let petitions and praises
shape your worries into prayers. . . a sense of God's
wholeness, everything coming together for good, will
come and settle you down. It's wonderful what happens
when Christ displaces worry at the center of your life.*

- Philippians 4:4, 6

Even when I wasn't yet at my breaking point, I used to worry.
I would even worry about worrying so much! I always felt
guilty, and assumed that I had to stop worrying before I was
worthy to pray. As a result, I was perpetually focused on
myself and my worries. This scripture teaches me to praise God
and focus on celebrating Him. As I praise Him, I am finally
able to shape my worries into prayers that I lay at God's feet,
knowing that He will take care of them. I can trust Him to fill
me with peace when I give all my troubles to Him and let Him
replace worry at the center of my life.

*PRAYER: Thank you, Lord, for your promise to settle me down
and bring me peace when I focus on you. Thank you for
displacing the worry that was at the center of my life. Thank
you that I can trust you to take care of me, no matter how
difficult my circumstances.*

Personal Reflections

January 30

'My strength comes into its own in your weakness.'
Once I heard that, I was glad to let it happen. . . Now I
take limitations in stride, and with good cheer. . . I just
let Christ take over!
                                        - 2 Corinthians 12:8-10

In the past, when I caught myself trying too hard in my own strength, I would get so frustrated with myself. Depending on myself and trying too hard was my biggest weakness! Now I understand how my weakness is an opportunity to allow God to take over. I often ask the Lord to show me when I am relying on myself. Even though my tendency will always be to try to take care of things myself, God makes Himself present, and reminds me to let Him care for me. Now I'm able to take my limitations in stride, knowing that it's not up to me to make my life work out in my favor.

PRAYER: Lord, thank you for prompting me to trust you when I am trying too hard without even realizing it. Your reminders make me feel so cared for. I can always rely on you to take control instantly when I refocus on you. I am so glad my life is in your strong, capable hands. Thank you for enabling me to live my life with good cheer, happy to trust in your strength and glory in my weaknesses!

Personal Reflections

January 31

. . . How did your new life begin? Was it by working your heads off to please him? Or was it by responding to God's Message to you? . . . For only crazy people think they could complete by their own efforts what was begun by God.

- Galatians 3:2-3

My instinct is always to try, try, and try again. I don't know any other way to live besides trying. God wants me to give that up and depend on Him completely. It's so simple, yet so profound. Looking back now, I shake my head at how silly I was to think I could please God by working and worrying myself sick, trying to complete the work He began in me, trying to take over His business. What a crazy, crazy idea! While I regret the time I wasted trying to do God's work for Him, I am so grateful that when I realized my mistake, He didn't scold me or punish me, but just welcomed me back. He graciously accepted and forgave me, and picked up right where He'd left off, transforming me from the inside out!

PRAYER: Lord, I choose to focus on you. In the past, I tried to make even this simple choice an effort. Now you are showing me that you don't need effort from me to earn your love and care. You only want me to desire total dependence on you and let you finish the work you began in me.

Personal Reflections

February 1

Christ has set us free to live a free life. So take your stand! Never again let anyone put a harness of slavery on you.

- Galatians 5:1-2

It's tempting for me to blame others for making me feel like I had to be a performance machine in order to please God. Perhaps it is especially easy to blame the church. But in reality, I put the harness of works-based slavery on myself. I chose to live my life trapped in an endless cycle of try-fail-despair-repeat. Perhaps you have chosen this as well. But the good news is that we can also choose to be free from all that. Thanks to God's plan of salvation, we are free in Christ! Now that I've realized this, I no longer let anyone, especially myself, hold my heart captive. I am able to take my stand against the temptation to believe that I have to earn God's approval through my own efforts. Because Jesus did everything for me, I know I never have to go back to that harness of slavery again. I'm free at last! Now that's good news!

PRAYER: Lord, you have given me the gift of freedom. Thank you that I am free of bondage to sin. Thank you that I am free from the condemnation of the law. Thank you for enabling me to take my stand against the voices that tell me I'm not good enough for your love. Teach me to focus on you and not myself or others. Your performance on my behalf is perfect—more than good enough for me!

Personal Reflections

February 2

You're blessed when you stay on course,
    walking steadily on the road revealed by GOD.
You're blessed when you follow his directions,
    doing your best to find him.
That's right—you don't go off on your own;
    you walk straight along the road he set.

- Psalm 119:1-3

Someone recently asked me, "When God is silent, does he want me to figure things out on my own?" We often feel confused about seeking direction from God, and struggle with feeling alone in our dilemma. However, God never leaves you alone, and He doesn't intend for you to be forced to figure things out on your own. In fact, He has already revealed the road that you are to walk. When you ask Him for specific direction and feel that you don't get an answer, be patient. In His silence, He is simply asking you to wait. While you wait, continue to walk on the path He has revealed. Choose daily to keep your focus on Him through praise, reading His Word, and remembering His faithfulness in times past.

PRAYER: Lord, thank you for all the ways you have made for me to stay focused on you while I wait on your guidance. Thank you for fine-tuning my focus while I wait. I love your reminder that I will be blessed when I stay on course, simply focusing on you and your simple instructions for my daily life. The "big, complicated" decisions are not difficult for you. Thank you for your willingness to guide me through every step of the way.

Personal Reflections

February 3

God-friendship is for God-worshipers;
They are the ones he confides in.

If I keep my eyes on GOD,
I won't trip over my feet.

- Psalm 25:14-15

Isn't this incredible? The reward for us if we are God-worshipers is God-friendship—a relationship with God so special that He actually confides in us! Some describe this worship of God as "the fear of the Lord." My fear of God is not that He will hurt me or cause me pain. My only fear comes from knowing that when I take my eyes off of Him, things fall apart. When I am "navel-gazing" instead of focusing on Him, I lose my way and trip over my own feet! This scripture confirms that God has shown me the truth, and as long as my focus is on Him, He will always save me from this danger. He not only offers me protection from my stumblings, but also promises to call me His friend. Now that's a love I never want to live without!

PRAYER: Lord, what a revelation! I fear you because I am afraid to live without you. You are my only hope, and I want to always keep my eyes on you. I am so thankful you do not judge me for the amount of trust or faith I have. All you ask of me is just to keep looking into your eyes of love. Because of your love, I know for sure that you are a trustworthy and faithful God. Thank you for your amazing gift of God-friendship!

Personal Reflections

February 4

You've always been right there for me;
  don't turn your back on me now.
Don't throw me out, don't abandon me;
  you've always kept the door open.
My father and mother walked out and left me,
  but GOD took me in.

Point me down your highway, GOD;
  direct me along a well-lighted street.

- Psalm 27:9-11

In our culture, the way to get it right is through super-human efforts. In God's culture, the only way to get it right is to let Him show us how—never through our own efforts to be perfect. We have only one hope of getting it right, and that is to follow the Lord's direction. Isn't it amazing that we can look back at our lives and say, "God, you've always been there for me?" He has never abandoned us, not once. Even when we felt alone and helpless, all the time He was holding open the door for us to come home, lighting the way for us. That's why we can trust Him to light our paths now, and to point us in the direction He wants us to go. He has always been faithful.

PRAYER: Thank you, Lord, that putting my faith in you and deciding to follow you is a simple choice I make. If I had to rely on my own merit or effort, I would surely fail. Thank you that you've always been there to encourage me and carry me when I was weary and broken. It means so much to me to know that you will always keep the door open for me to come home.

Personal Reflections

February 5

I'm feeling terrible—I couldn't feel worse!
  Get me on my feet again. You promised, remember?. . .
Grace me with your clear revelation. . .
I grasp and cling to whatever you tell me.

- Psalm 119:25,29,31

I frequently focus on and communicate with God through sharing my fear, worries, hurt and even anger with Him. Before I learned to share my heart with God, I used to get stuck in my feelings and turn my focus inward. I would feel alone in these times, trapped in my feelings of fear, worthlessness, or pain. But once I began sharing my feelings with Him, I felt His presence more deeply than ever before, and I realized that I wasn't alone. God has showed me it is always safe to run to Him. Even though waiting is hard for me, and I sometimes get impatient waiting for God to act, I have learned that He is always faithful to get me back on my feet and give me clear vision when I ask.

PRAYER: Lord, I am so grateful that being in your presence is always safe, regardless of how I feel. I could never have imagined that you would accept me even when I'm miserable and needy but now that I know, I am so grateful for your love and care. Thank you that you always answer my cries for help. I choose to focus on your faithfulness and to cling to your promises.

Personal Reflections

February 6

Build me up again by your Word.
Barricade the road that goes Nowhere;
 grace me with your clear revelation. . .
I grasp and cling to whatever you tell me. . .
I'll run the course you lay out for me.

- Psalm 119:28-32

One of the reasons it is critical to stay focused on God while we wait is that He has many ways of showing us what to do. He builds us up through His Word, He barricades the wrong roads, and gives us grace by sending the Holy Spirit to share His thoughts about what to do. When we make decisions, we can know the Lord's will as He confirms it through His Word, the doors that He closes, and the things that He lays upon our hearts. This is why all we need to do is focus on God, clinging to His every word, choosing to run the course He lays out for us.

PRAYER: Lord, thank you for your many ways of telling me what to do. In the past, I used to always worry that I would do the wrong thing. I would worry that I wasn't hearing your answer because I wasn't listening hard enough. I worried that I could stray away from your will by making one tiny wrong decision. All this worry nearly paralyzed me, but you have taught me how to take my focus off myself and look to you alone for the answers.

Personal Reflections

February 7

I look to you, heaven-dwelling God,
 look up to you for help.
Like servants, alert to their master's commands,
 like a maiden attending her lady,
We're watching and waiting, holding our breath.

- Psalm 123:1-3

For many years, my self-focused habits were so ingrained. I was so performance-driven, such a people-pleaser. I was always trying so hard and yet failing, gradually losing hope of ever succeeding. I thought it would be impossible for God to change me. But I learned that it's not up to me to change—the Lord takes a willing heart that chooses Him, and changes even the most stubbornly self-sufficient habits. Now I realize that my only part in this transformation is to continue to look upward to God, waiting with bated breath for His next move. His love never ceases to amaze me.

PRAYER: Lord, a simple choice to focus on you has changed me forever in a profound way. I never imagined I could feel so loved and cared for without a perfect performance on my part. I have gladly given up my endless striving after perfection to earn your love. Thank you that you accept me the way I am, and that you are in the business of making me more like you as I keep my eyes on you. I am changed just by gazing at your glory!

Personal Reflections

February 8

GOD guards you from every evil, he guards your very life. He guards you when you leave and when you return, he guards you now, he guards you always.

- Psalm 121:7-8

Even though I'm prone to fail when I'm in control, it is challenging for me to completely focus on the Lord and yield my control to Him. Thankfully, even when I choose not to focus on Him, God never loses control over my life. He constantly stands guard over me every moment of every day. This verse is so reassuring to me, as I have come to realize that the evils I may face every day are dangers He has already anticipated and that He stands ready to protect me. Knowing that my life is in His hands gives me such peace. When I leave and when I return—no matter where I go—God's presence guards me always.

PRAYER: Lord, I would be afraid to let go of control except that I know you stand guard constantly and protect me day and night. Because you are so good at controlling my life, I can stop straining to control everything in my life. Thank you for your constant presence. I am overwhelmed by the thought that you are always with me, no matter where I am, what I'm doing, or how I've messed up. Your grace is so amazing to me!

Personal Reflections

February 9

GOD, I'm not trying to rule the roost...
I haven't meddled where I have no business...
   I've cultivated a quiet heart.
Like a baby content in its mother's arms,
   my soul is a baby content.

                                  - Psalm 131:1-2

Feeling like I am not in control has always made me uneasy. However, whenever I found myself being controlling to gain some sense of security in a situation, it never turned out well. Especially in relationships, my controlling attitude only caused more harm, creating distance between me and the people I cared about most deeply. Eventually, I realized that my need for security in life and relationships could not be filled by my grasping for control. Instead, God showed me that giving up control to Him is the only answer. It's been a gradual journey, but I really am starting to feel content the more I keep my focus on Him.

PRAYER: Lord, it's one thing for me to yield my control to you, but to find myself actually becoming content and relaxed in your arms was a total surprise to me. I knew this wouldn't be easy, and I am amazed to find myself actually enjoying the feeling of dependence on you. You really are changing me! Thank you for giving me such peace. Thank you for taking control of me. Because of you, I can confidently say, "God is in control, so I can be content!"

Personal Reflections

February 10

I pray to GOD—my life a prayer—
and wait for what he'll say and do.
My life's on the line before God, my Lord,
waiting and watching till morning,
waiting and watching till morning.

- Psalm 130:5-6

Afraid to lose control—yet more afraid of my own failures—I turn to God in constant prayer as I choose to focus on Him. When I am focused on God, my whole life feels like a prayer. I am choosing to just wait on Him and not worry about my circumstances. I watch and wait for Him, instead of taking control of my life into my own hands. Sometimes, I am faced with problems that turn into crises, and it often seems that my life or someone else's life is in some sense "on the line." These crises used to make me turn into a nervous wreck, expending all my energy on damage control. Now that I am choosing to let go of the urge to fix everything and control the outcome of my circumstances, I have a kind of peace I could never have imagined before.

PRAYER: Lord, I know it has taken me over a half a century to finally understand that you are faithful and true to your Word. I am so grateful that you have been patient with me, and that you have never taken away your love for me. Now that I have confidence in your ability to take care of me, I can leave my life in your hands and just rest.

Personal Reflections

February 11

Sing to GOD a brand-new song,
*   praise him in the company of all who love him. . .*
Let them praise his name in dance;
*   strike up the band and make great music!*
And why? Because GOD delights in his people. . .

- Psalm 149:1-4

I sang the song "Jesus loves me" over and over again as a child. Now as an adult, it seems like a brand new song. I have never felt His love like I feel it now—not because He loved me less before, but because I just never realized how much He cared. It was not until I chose to really focus on God, and not on myself or my feelings, that I really knew Jesus loved me. What fills me with awe is the realization that when this psalm says God "delights in His people," that means that He delights in each one of His children . . . including me. The writer of this Psalm goes crazy over this, and we should too! Imagine, the God who created the whole expanse of the universe, finding deep delight in you, His child. That's something to sing and get excited about!

PRAYER: Lord, thank you for the endless ways that you love and care for me. I know you have always loved me in so many ways, but I just didn't notice it. I was laser-focused on my own performance and unsuccessfully trying to please others. Thank you for loving me in spite of that. Now I have a new song in my mouth, because you delight in me!

Personal Reflections

February 12

His love is the wonder of the world. . .
Love GOD, all you saints;
GOD takes care of all who stay close to him

- Psalm 31:21-23

When I was a kid, I learned about the Seven Wonders of the World, great monuments to man's achievements in architecture, mathematics, and artistic genius. But not once in all my growing up years did I ever consider this verse, "His love is the wonder of the world..." That is a mind-blowing thought. Just think about the incredible ways God's love is manifested in the world—in the majesty of mountains and the whimsy of ladybugs, in the warmth of the sun, in the chill beauty of a winter snowfall, in the colors of seasons and sunsets, and in the miracle of new life. The enchantment of tastes, textures, sights, sounds, and smells lies all around us. All we need to do is open our eyes and draw near to the God who created all this, and who promises to take care of all those who choose to stay near Him.

PRAYER: Lord, thank you so much that your love is the greatest wonder of the world. Thank you that you have promised to take care of me, and that through a simple choice to stay close to you, I feel your love more and more every day, without any effort on my part to make you love me.

Personal Reflections

February 13

. . .To live with him in his house my whole life long. I'll contemplate his beauty; I'll study at his feet. That's the only quiet, secure place in a noisy world, The perfect getaway, far from the buzz of traffic.

- Psalm 27:4-5

In the greater Washington, D.C., area, we know a lot about traffic, noise, congestion, busyness, and burn-out. To many in our modern world, true rest seems like an unattainable goal. Caught up in the mind-numbing rat-race of our days, we settle for cheap energy substitutes, living our days powered by caffeine as we slog through papers, meetings, and stop-n-go traffic, in the hopes of catching the latest titillating TV show and snatching a few hours of restless sleep before starting the cycle all over again. The picture of rest and security that this verse presents seems totally foreign to our daily lives. And yet, through a quiet, daily decision to focus on God, I have found a rest and peace that all the bustle and buzz in my world cannot take away. When I focus on Him, His presence overwhelms my problems.

PRAYER: Lord, thank you for showing me how to stay close to you so I can feel your love. When I wonder at your beauty and study at your feet, the noise of the world fades away and I am at peace. No matter how tired or stressed out I may feel, you are my perfect getaway from worry and fear.

Personal Reflections

February 14

He puts a little of heaven in our hearts so that we'll never settle for less. . . Christ's love has moved me to such extremes. His love has the first and last word in everything we do.

- 2 Corinthians 5:5,14

God's love is all about passion—not about effort or performance. We don't "try" to serve Him. His love drives us to desire to serve. We love Him and others out of the overflow of His love for us. His love instills the longing for heaven, for eternity, deep in our hearts, so that we can never settle for the cheap substitutes that try to entrap us. No addictions or indulgence will ever satisfy this deep ache in our hearts for something beyond our experience. Our true home, the place where we really belong, is with God. His love, the wonder of this world, will also be the wonder of the next, when we are able to truly know Him.

PRAYER: Lord, you are the beginning and the end of my passion for living. I live to serve you and only you. Everything I do is not to perform, but to share your love for me. I can hardly wait for the moment when I finally see you face to face. Thank you for putting a longing for that moment in my heart, so that I will never settle for the world's cheap imitations of joy. Until then, I want your love to have the first and last word in everything I do.

Personal Reflections

February 15

Summing it all up, friends, I'd say you'll do best by filling your minds and meditating on things true. . . the best, not the worst; the beautiful, not the ugly; things to praise, not to curse. Put into practice what you have learned from me.

                                                    - Philippians 4:8-9

By reading and writing down these daily scriptures, I am putting into practice what I have learned from Paul. As you join me in reading these devotionals every day, together we retrain our focus on God. Slowly, He has begun to clear my vision and change my focus. I no longer want to focus on my own problems, but instead turn my eyes to Him and focus on His goodness. When we focus on the positive things in life, the good gifts of God, our hearts are filled with praise. Meditating on these things and thanking Him for them becomes a catalyst for deep joy, and we can't help but let those blessings overflow onto those around us.

PRAYER: Lord, I already feel closer to you than the day I began spending time with these Scriptures. I pray that everyone who continues to read will feel more and more loved by you as you change all of our lives. Thank you for your reminders to meditate on the good things you have given us. I am so grateful that you fill my mind with joy. Meditating on your goodness is gradually becoming one of my favorite things to do.

Personal Reflections

February 16

Instead of worrying, pray. Let petitions and praises shape your worries into prayers. . . Before you know it, a sense of God's wholeness. . . will come and settle you down. It's wonderful what happens when Christ displaces worry at the center of your life.

- Philippians 4:6-7

After living as an expert worrier for over 50 years, I am only starting to experience less worry as I focus on Christ. God is drawing my attention to Himself and away from my own worry. I used to try so hard to stop worrying on my own—but my efforts only made me worry more. Now, when I catch myself starting to worry, I reframe whatever I am worrying about into a prayer. I see my worry as an opportunity for God to perform a miracle in my life, bringing me peace even in difficult situations. He has actually replaced my worry with Himself!

PRAYER: Lord, thank you that you made my brain unable to focus on more than one thing at a time! Focus is a choice, not an effort, and I just naturally spend less time in "worry mode" as I choose to constantly refocus back to you. I have felt so much freer since you displaced my worry habit and took your rightful place at the center of my heart. I relish the sense of your wholeness permeating my life, and I enjoy relaxing in your serenity.

Personal Reflections

February 17

God is sheer mercy and grace;
  not easily angered, he's rich in love.
He doesn't endlessly nag and scold . . .
He doesn't treat us as our sins deserve . . .
as far as sunrise is from sunset,
  he has separated us from our sins.

- Psalm 103:8-12

I grew up being taught that I "should" make Christ the center of my life, and that I would find favor with Him by "trying" to serve Him. In other words, I was taught to perform for His love. Realizing that God loves me regardless of my performance has been quite a journey. As I select scriptures to share in these devotionals each day, God has been clearing my vision to see that He loves me, period. No conditions. No expectations. When I focus on Him, I feel the richness of His sheer mercy and grace showering down on me.

PRAYER: Thank you so much that the more I see your face, Lord, the more I desire to focus on you—not out of obligation, but because I really want to know you. Thank you for refusing to nag or scold me for my mistakes. I used to let my bad choices weigh me down with regret and hold me back in despair. But now, I have discovered that in you I can never be defeated by my sins, because you have separated me from them as far as the sunrise is from the sunset!

Personal Reflections

February 18

"If you'll hold on to me for dear life," says GOD,
  "I'll get you out of any trouble.
I'll give you the best of care
  if you'll only get to know and trust me.
Call me and I'll answer, be at your side in bad times;
  I'll rescue you, then throw you a party. . ."

- Psalm 91:14-16

Holding onto God is another powerful way that we can make Him our focus, but we can only come to this focused place once we have truly given up on ourselves. When we finally realize that our only hope is to hold onto Him "for dear life," we can get to know and trust our Rescuer in a whole new way. Isn't it wonderful that God promises to hear us when we call out to Him, and to come and care for us tenderly, intimately? And then, there is the promise of celebration: "I'll rescue you, then throw you a party..." Just imagine what this party might be like, a party thrown by our wild, extravagant God!

PRAYER: Lord, I am so thankful that these scriptures are showing me how to get to know you and trust you. I pray that as I continue to read these scriptures, I will experience your love more and more. Please teach me how to trust you, and help me to let go of my obsession with control and give my life over to you. I want to hold on to you for dear life, and I feel so secure in knowing that you'll never, ever let go of me. Thanks so, so much for your love!

Personal Reflections

February 19

"Because I, your GOD, have a firm grip on you and I'm not letting go. I'm telling you, 'Don't panic. I'm right here to help you.'"

- Isaiah 41:13

One of the most amazing ways I experience God's presence are the moments when He calms my fear or anxiety. I feel like He is actually touching my heart with a firm grip that holds me up. Just listen to these words. Read them over again to yourself, as if He was speaking them to you right now. He has a firm grip on you. He's not going anywhere. He'll never, ever let you go, so there's no need to panic. When you have the Creator of the universe on your side, fear doesn't even make sense anymore!

PRAYER: Lord, as I search your scriptures, I am learning that focus comes through experiencing you with all my senses. Seeing you, hearing you and now being touched by you, I not only know of your love, but I also feel your strong embrace, holding my heart and shielding me from harm. I know that you can be trusted to stay with me and never, ever abandon me. No matter how difficult things get, I can trust you to keep a firm grip on me, and to bring me through hard times to a deeper understanding of you.

Personal Reflections

February 20

If you wake me each morning with the sound of your loving voice,
   I'll go to sleep each night trusting in you.
Point out the road I must travel;
   I'm all ears, all eyes before you.

- Psalm 143:8

As I continue to focus on God with my five human senses, and as I continue to lift up my heart to Him, God touches my life tenderly every day with His loving-kindness. The mornings when I wake up with His words in my ears are the sweetest I can recall. I want to wake up that way every morning, and go to sleep every night with His thoughts in my mind. I want to be obsessed with God, my eyes and ears open, straining for a word, a touch, a glimpse of His majesty. Every day He guides me, and through His loving direction, He tells me what to do. Living in His love has been the most rewarding and life-giving experience I have ever had, and I'm just getting started!

PRAYER: Lord, your words to me are more precious than gold or silver or diamonds, and I want to be aware of your guiding directions throughout every day. I feel like you have literally given me a headset to wear on the playing field. You are like a coach who tells me the right plays to run, and you are like a loving father, who picks me up when I get hurt and cheers me on to victory.

Personal Reflections

February 21

Christ will live in you as you open the door and invite him in. And I ask him that with both feet planted firmly on love, you'll be able to take in with all followers of Jesus the extravagant dimensions of Christ's love. Reach out and experience the breadth! Test its length! Plumb the depths! Rise to the heights! Live full lives, full in the fullness of God.

- Ephesians 3:17-19

Many people I talk to tell me about moments in which they have experienced God's love. They want to hold onto that loving feeling, and they struggle when they think they don't feel God's love anymore. Most people say that the more they try, the harder it gets to recover that emotional high. This scripture reminds us that God's supply of love is beyond comprehension. All that we need to do to experience it is to focus on Him and open the door of our hearts. God will show us the many ways He continuously pours out His love to us.

PRAYER: Lord, thank you so much that you don't expect me or even want me to try to maintain a feeling of your loving-kindness that you give me. You only want me to continue to focus on you, and you will give me ongoing gifts of love in many different packages. Thank you for promising to live in me, and for inviting me to "reach out and experience the breadth" of your fathomless love. I am only beginning to realize the glorious reality of living a full life and experiencing your fullness in me.

Personal Reflections

February 22

If your revelation hadn't delighted me so,
  I would have given up when the hard times came.
But I'll never forget the advice you gave me;
  you saved my life with those wise words.

- Psalm 119:92-93

Nothing makes me feel more special than when God talks to me and reveals His wisdom to me on tough days or during difficult seasons of my life. Remembering His death, His sacrifice for me, I am touched by the power and depth of His love. His love not only saved me from a miserable fate, but in my daily life, He pours out grace on me and fills my heart with delight at His revelations. He guides me with His gentle advice and has saved my life from taking a wrong turn many times. When I remember how faithful and strong He has been for me in the past, I have confidence that He will be there for me in the future and that He is walking with me in the present, even when I don't feel Him. My faith in His love enables me to keep going when I feel like giving up.

PRAYER: Lord, I marvel that you created my brain with two centers—one to reason with and remember important facts; the other to feel and remember special emotions. Thank you that your actions toward me fill my heart with delight and reassure me of how much you care about me. Thank you, Lord, for speaking to both sides of my brain!

Personal Reflections

February 23

His huge outstretched arms protect you—
under them you're perfectly safe;
his arms fend off all harm.
Fear nothing—not wild wolves in the night,
not flying arrows in the day,
Not disease that prowls through the darkness,
not disaster that erupts at high noon.

                                                 - Psalm 91:4-6

When we can't sleep because of troublesome thoughts or feelings that swirl inside our hearts, remembering God's love is the safest, most restful refuge we could ever have. God has set His love so strongly in our hearts and minds that when we reflect on Him, our focus overpowers even our own racing thoughts that worry and distract us. When we are quietly dwelling on the knowledge that God is with us to protect us, and remembering our personal experiences of His love, God tenderly calms our spirit and we fall asleep.

PRAYER: *Lord, I am so thankful for the many nights when remembering your love enables me to drift off to sleep and stay asleep until morning. I am not afraid to go to sleep when I remember that you watch over me all night long. When I am focused on you, I wake up with your tender love still on my mind and a song in my heart.*

Personal Reflections

February 24

If I'm sleepless at midnight,
  I spend the hours in grateful reflection.
Because you've always stood up for me,
  I'm free to run and play.
I hold on to you for dear life,
  and you hold me steady as a post.

- Psalm 63:6-8

The Bible is the best instructional manual on all of life's problems, including sleep disturbance. His Word says to reflect on Him, to relax, to be free and light-hearted, and to "run and play" with Him when we can't sleep. Think about it! We always chide ourselves when we are struggling with insomnia, saying "I have to get some sleep!" Our frustration and anxiety only winds us up tighter, making it completely impossible to sleep. God encourages us to stop trying to fix our own problems, and to focus on His love instead of our sleep-deprived existence. Very often, when we turn our focus to God and away from trying to force ourselves to sleep, our bodies and our spirits relax. As we experience the calm of reflecting on what He has done for us, we are finally able to drift off to sleep in peace.

PRAYER: Lord, your instruction seems so counter-intuitive to me. It goes against all the ways I try to solve my own problems, and yet, it works! Thank you so much for making sure I am finally learning that focus on you is my only part in our relationship.

Personal Reflections

February 25

So here I am in the place of worship, eyes open,
drinking in your strength and glory.
In your generous love I am really living at last!
My lips brim praises like fountains.
I bless you every time I take a breath;
My arms wave like banners of praise to you.

- Psalm 63:2-4

God continually surprises us with His love, even when we feel most week and helpless. Instead of moaning and groaning because he couldn't sleep, David began to worship God. Finding himself in the place of worship, David was overcome with awe and thanksgiving. God made that sleepless night the perfect time to bless David with amazing comfort and the feeling that he was finally, really living every moment in God's love.

PRAYER: Lord, I am so grateful that you turn even my toughest moments into opportunities to experience your love in ways I have never felt before. Certainly, sleepless nights can feel like torture—yet you make a way for me to draw even closer to you. I want to know the closeness and comfort of your presence, even when I feel alone and it seems like all the rest of the world is sleeping peacefully except for me. The next time I feel unable to sleep, please draw near to me and help me to focus on you, so that I find myself worshipping you, my lips brimming with praises.

Personal Reflections

February 26

This is how much God loved the world: He gave his Son, his one and only Son. And this is why: so that no one need be destroyed; by believing in him, anyone can have a whole and lasting life. God didn't go to all the trouble of sending his Son merely to point an accusing finger, telling the world how bad it was. He came to help, to put the world right again. Anyone who trusts him is acquitted.

- John 3:16-18

Many addicts feel that God has given up on them and doubt that God would ever want to help them after they have wrecked their lives. This scripture shows them that no one needs to be destroyed. Anyone who makes a decision to believe in Jesus—including those who have wrecked their lives—can be acquitted and have a whole and lasting life. When we allow ourselves to accept God's love, the Lord establishes our roots of faith deep into the ground. With that grounding, we do not sway in the wind by cares and worries on the surface. These roots are founded in the strength of His love and are deep, wide and long. We are able to grow up to high heights because underneath it all, we know He loves us.

PRAYER: Lord, what an amazing picture of your love! It captures us intellectually and emotionally. There could be no greater example of love in the universe. We want to experience your love in every breath.

Personal Reflections

February 27

Watch what God does, and then you do it, like children who learn proper behavior from their parents. Mostly what God does is love you. Keep company with him and learn a new life of love. Observe how Christ loved us. His love is not cautious but extravagant. He didn't love in order to get something from us but to give everything of himself to us. Love like that.

- Ephesians 5:1-2

Not only do we need to stay focused on God to experience His love, but also so that He can clear our vision and show us how to love by loving us! His love is not mere, tepid tolerance, or cautious, conditional acceptance mixed with concern and disapproval. Instead, His love is wildly extravagant, pouring over us like a waterfall. Knowledge of this love gives us a purpose to live—a purpose that goes beyond self-focus on anger, anxiety, worry, fear and depression. Our passion to love those around us the way He does becomes stronger than any obsession, compulsion, or addiction. We no longer want to love people in order to get something from them, but to help them experience the love He gave us.

PRAYER: *God, I have sought immediate self-gratification from many obsessions, but nothing compares to the long-lasting and fulfilling nature of your love. Focusing on you requires waiting and patience, but the love that I feel from you takes my breath away. You are more than worth the wait!*

Personal Reflections

February 28

If you've gotten anything at all out of following Christ, if his love has made any difference in your life, if being in a community of the Spirit means anything to you, if you have a heart, if you care – then do me a favor: Agree with each other, love each other, be deep-spirited friends. Don't push your way to the front; don't sweet-talk your way to the top. Put yourself aside, and help others get ahead.

- Philippians 2:1-3

God instructs us to focus on Him in order that we may experience how much He loves us—and then share His love with others. For most of my life, I made simple instructions difficult by not reading them carefully or by not really listening to someone else giving me instructions. I made it impossible for God to clear my vision because I made a choice not to focus.

PRAYER: *Lord, thank you so much for your revelation to me in Philippians that you will clear my vision. You have made it clear to me that your instructions are so simple—I can follow them even after a lifetime of making up my own instructions and going my own way. Now, all I want to do is share what you have taught me. My simple prayer is that the time I spend with you will progressively clear my vision so I may know and love you more every day.*

Personal Reflections

March 1

*He comes alongside us when we go through hard times,
and before you know it, he brings us alongside someone
else who is going through hard times so that we can be
there for that person just as God was there for us.*

- 2 Corinthians 1:4

One of the best ways we can keep our attention on God through a tough time is to turn around and help someone else. For one thing, loving and helping those around us keeps our focus off ourselves. But also, serving others makes us turn continually to God for strength and perseverance as we minister to our neighbors. Seeing a desperate need in someone else can remind us that we need to draw on a source of strength much more vast than our own. Through learning to lean on God, we can remain energized and positive as we offer other people encouragement through their own difficulties.

PRAYER: Lord, in a culture where we are taught to look out for ourselves, thank you for teaching me the virtue of caring for others. I never feel abandoned when I focus on other people— in fact, I experience so much love from you when I help others instead of focusing on myself. The rush of your strength flowing through me is such a wonderful feeling.

Personal Reflections

March 2

Remember, our Message is not about ourselves; we're proclaiming Jesus Christ, the Master. All we are is messengers, errand runners from Jesus for you. It started when God said, 'Light up the darkness!' and our lives filled up with the light as we saw and understood God in the face of Christ, all bright and beautiful.

- 2 Corinthians 4:5-6

God taught me to stay focused on Him by showing me I am only a messenger of His Gospel—I'm not required to convince others that God loves them. Simply sharing His message draws the attention of others and keeps me focused on the Lord at the same time. God is the one responsible for lighting up my life and making me into a living lantern to light the way for others. All I understand about God, I have seen in Jesus, who is the light of the world, and whose radiant light reflects on me as on a mirror.

PRAYER: Lord, for years I resisted sharing your message because I was afraid that I would mess up the delivery. But knowing I am just your errand boy takes all the pressure to perform off my shoulders. You do all the work through me when I simply share how your love has changed my own life. All I am is a simple messenger, learning to speak your words.

Personal Reflections

March 3

Now that the worst is over, we're pleased we can report that we've come out of this with conscience and faith intact, and can face the world—and even more importantly, face you with our heads held high. But it wasn't by any fancy footwork on our part. It was God *who kept us focused on him, uncompromised. Don't try to read between the lines or look for hidden meanings in this letter. We're writing plain, unembellished truth, hoping that you'll now see the whole picture as well as you've seen some of the details. We want you to be as proud of us as we are of you when we stand together before our Master Jesus.*

- 2 Corinthians 1:12-14

When I was afraid to mess up, I did not hold my head high. But now I know that God does not expect perfection from us as we serve Him, so there is no more need for shame. I gladly hold my head high, since God has taught me to simply let others see His love in my happy face. Now that I know the plain truth about His grace, I know that I cannot hold myself up, but that His unconditional love keeps me focused on Him and keeps my attention off myself.

PRAYER: Lord, you remind me that you never want me to lower my head in shame. When I mess up, as I constantly do, I am reminded how much I need you. As I look up and see your face, your love shines through any shame I feel.

Personal Reflections

March 4

I quit focusing on the handicap and began appreciating the gift. It was a case of Christ's strength moving in on my weakness. Now I take limitations in stride, and with good cheer, these limitations that cut me down to size... I just let Christ take over! And so the weaker I get, the stronger I become.

- 2 Corinthians 12:9-10

Oh my, I had it backward all my life! I believed I had to fix my weaknesses before I would be able to focus on Him. In this scripture, however, God instructs me to accept my weaknesses as a reminder that I need to focus on Him. That allows His strength to move in on my weakness, and as a result, I become more cheerful, more hopeful, and more focused on the Lord, no matter how many weaknesses I start to see in myself. As I move closer to the Lord, He is changing me to be more like Him, and that is worth everything to me.

PRAYER: Thank you so much that I don't have to fix myself to come to you and enjoy your love. Otherwise, I would continue to dwell on my weakness and never experience your love. My weaknesses really are a gift—they remind me to choose to focus on you.

Personal Reflections

March 5

I have been crucified in relation to the world, set free from the stifling atmosphere of pleasing others and fitting into the little patterns that they dictate. Can't you see the central issue in all this? It is not what you and I do. . . It is what God is doing, and he is creating something totally new, a free life! All who walk by this standard are the true Israel of God—his chosen people. Peace and mercy on them!

- Galatians 6:14-16

My biggest weakness has always been my people-pleasing tendencies. Growing up as the second-oldest in a family of six kids, I constantly sought attention through pleasing others. Of course, the more I tried to please, the more I failed. I have always hated this weakness, but I am so thankful that I can now accept the urge to please others as a reminder to shift my focus to Him. To go from being trapped in the stifling atmosphere of people-pleasing to living in the free air and in the light of His love for me has been an amazing experience. I am beginning to understand what this verse means: the central issue is not what I do, but what God is doing: creating a brand-new life of freedom, focused on His love!

PRAYER: Lord, I confess that my people-pleasing has become a reflexive reaction. I am so thankful that you don't use my people-pleasing weakness to condemn me, but as an opportunity to shift my attention from others and back to you. Thank you for your constant reminders of your unconditional love for me.

Personal Reflections

March 6

Come close, God; get me out of here.
Rescue me from this deathtrap.

You know how they kick me around—
Pin on me the donkey's ears, the dunce's cap.

I'm broken by their taunts,
Flat on my face, reduced to a nothing.

I looked in vain for one friendly face. Not one.
I couldn't find one shoulder to cry on.

- Psalm 69:18-20

Fear of failure is a direct result of holding onto a people-pleasing attitude. The more we attempt to please others, the more fear of failure becomes the center of our attention. Living in constant fear of letting others down leads to an unbearable sense of rejection. In our desperation, we beg God to rescue us. We break our self-focus when we finally turn to the Lord. As soon as we turn to God, He saves us from our feelings of failure.

PRAYER: Lord, thank you for rescuing me over and over again as soon as I cry out to you and take my focus off my own feelings of failure. Just getting to know you is taking away my natural focus on myself, which has always led to self-loathing. I know you see me as so much more valuable than I can understand, and that you have greater things in mind for me than I could imagine. Thank you for capturing my attention through your faithful love.

Personal Reflections

March 7

Just as each day brims with your beauty,
  my mouth brims with praise.
But don't turn me out to pasture when I'm old
  or put me on the shelf when I can't pull my weight.
My enemies are talking behind my back,
  watching for their chance to knife me.
The gossip is: "God has abandoned him.
  Pounce on him now; no one will help him."

- Psalm 71:8-11

This passage runs deep with intense emotion from David, the psalmist. Despite some very intense rejection and betrayal by evil men, David did not choose to run from God. Instead, David ran towards God, straight into His arms. He praised the Lord even while experiencing feelings of loneliness, paranoia, and betrayal. I am learning that God is my only hope when I feel like David, and that even in lonely weakness I can praise Him.

PRAYER: Lord, you are my only hope. The more I praise you with all my heart, the more you give me immense comfort that overrides even the painful intensity of rejection. Lord, nothing overcomes my feelings of rejection like your unconditional love and your deep, deep compassion for me. Thank you that even when I feel like you have abandoned me, your loving presence is always with me, to comfort and sustain me through hard times.

Personal Reflections

March 8

Quiet down before GOD,
  be prayerful before him.
Don't bother with those who climb the ladder,
  who elbow their way to the top.

Bridle your anger, trash your wrath,
  cool your pipes—it only makes things worse.
Before long the crooks will be bankrupt;
  GOD-investors will soon own the store..

- Psalm 37:7-9

Nothing brings on anger quite like rejection and feeling pushed aside. Often, it's easier said than done to "trash your wrath"! Just seconds of focusing on how we have been wronged and treated unjustly can burn us up inside with a caustic, bitter surge of emotions. Only learning to recognize our anger as a call to run to Him can break that spell. What an intense reminder these verses offer: simply focusing on God can quiet the raging storm inside an angry heart.

PRAYER: Lord, my anger rises so quickly—so automatically— whenever I remember how I have been wronged. But you have showed me that this abrupt heart-change is a perfect opportunity to run to you and beg for your transforming power to take over in my life. You use my weaknesses to make me lean on you and trust your love. This tendency brings many opportunities to focus on you, so I want to thank you now for each and every reminder.

Personal Reflections

March 9

You'll find all your everyday human concerns will be met. Give your entire attention to what God is doing right now, and don't get worked up about what may or may not happen tomorrow. God will help you deal with whatever hard things come up when the times comes.

- Matthew 6:33-34

Anger is not the only feeling that can come with rejection. When a boss or a spouse tosses us aside, it seems impossible to not be completely, incessantly anxious about what is going to happen next. We can feel so panicky inside about the future. How can we possibly shift our focus away from these awful feelings? God promises that when we give our entire attention to Him, He will take care of everything—including our anxiety. He will be there in the future as He has been there in the past, waiting to help us with whatever hard things we are facing.

PRAYER: *Lord, thank you that you can even handle this weakness. I need you especially when I am anxious because I have trouble thinking clearly. I can accept my anxiety as a gift, knowing that when I give you my entire attention, you show me how to stay calm. You give me peace so that you can lead me through finding a new job or dealing with losing a spouse.*

Personal Reflections

March 10

Sometimes I ask God, my rock-solid God,
   "Why did you let me down?
Why am I walking around in tears,
   harassed by enemies?"
They're out for the kill...
Taunting day after day,
   "Where is this God of yours?"

Why are you down in the dumps, dear soul?
   Why are you crying the blues?
Fix my eyes on God—
   soon I'll be praising again...

- Psalm 42:9-11

Every emotional affliction is difficult, and challenging to deal with. For many, fighting depression can be the most painful of all. Not only do we feel rejected by others, but we can begin to feel that even God has abandoned us. Such a time can be the toughest time to focus on God. We feel numb inside – how do we focus when we don't feel like we matter to anyone? This Psalm says keep fixated on Him, despite our emotions, and soon we will be comforted.

PRAYER: Lord, thank you so much for not expecting me to "fix" myself before I can come to you and refocus on your face. You have revealed to me through your Word that keeping my eyes fixed on you is how you lift my depression. What a relief! Trying to lift my own depression by myself just makes me feel worse.

Personal Reflections

March 11

Because of the extravagance of those revelations, and so I wouldn't get a big head, I was given the gift of a handicap to keep me in constant touch with my limitations. Satan's angel did his best to get me down; what he in fact did was push me to my knees. No danger then of walking around high and mighty! At first I didn't think of it as a gift, and begged God to remove it...and then he told me,

My grace is enough; it's all you need.
My strength comes into its own in your weakness.

- 2 Corinthians 12:7-9

Have you ever wondered what Paul's handicap might have been? Some biblical scholars have thought that Paul's limitation could have been a compulsive behavior rather than a physical condition. Whatever it was, it brought him to his knees—in the same way I have seen OCD do to some of my clients. A weakness that is on our mind continuously is agonizing, and can make us feel totally defeated every day. But God's amazing love clears our vision to such a degree that we see even an awful limitation as a gift.

PRAYER: Lord, my mind cannot grasp how amazing your grace is to transform such a difficult weakness into a gift. It seems more miraculous than you just removing the handicap in the first place. It is so amazing to think that you have such deep love for us that you really desire to be in constant communication with us!

Personal Reflections

March 12

My counsel is this: Live freely, animated and motivated by God's Spirit. Then you won't feed the compulsions of selfishness. For there is a root of sinful self-interest in us that is at odds with a free spirit, just as the free spirit is incompatible with selfishness. These two ways of life are antithetical, so that you cannot live at times one way and at times another way according to how you feel on any given day. Why don't you choose to be led by the Spirit and so escape the erratic compulsions of a law-dominated existence?

- Galatians 5:16-18

Addictions are compulsions of selfishness that often develop when times are hard. Rather than dealing with anger, anxiety, and depression by reminding ourselves to focus on God and His love, we escape these feelings through all kinds of addictions and focus on them until we are "hooked." Of course, a love affair with any addiction only gives short-lived comfort, and causes all those bad feelings that we were trying to escape from in the first place to quickly resurface.

PRAYER: Lord, thank you for teaching us that addictions are only weaknesses that should prompt us to run to you. Any fix we contrive is temporary at best. You are so right—addictions are at odds with a free spirit. They enslave us and only a continual choice to focus on you can pull us away from their grip.

Personal Reflections

March 13

Keep company with GOD,
 get in on the best.

Open up before GOD, keep nothing back;
 he'll do whatever needs to be done:
He'll validate your life in the clear light of day
 and stamp you with approval at high noon.

- Psalm 37:4-6

Open up all your feelings, your weaknesses, your limitations before God. Follow the example that David sets throughout the Psalms. Whether he was happy or sad, calm or terrified, David brought every emotion, thought, and desire inside his soul and laid it out before God. He continually vented his anguish to God, but he always concluded his psalms and prayers by praising God. Even in his despair. David shows us how to focus on God.

PRAYER: Lord, thank you for inspiring 150 chapters of prayers in the book of Psalms, to give us a pattern for focusing on you. Whatever our personality, whether bold or quiet, we can focus on you and depend on you to clear our vision on our journey. Thank you for your promise of validation and approval. So often I find myself hungering in vain after the approval of others, but knowing that I have your approval makes all the difference. Help me to keep my heart open to your loving eyes.

Personal Reflections

March 14

David came to Saul and stood before him. Saul liked him immediately and made him his right-hand man.

Saul sent word back to Jesse: "Thank you. David will stay here..."

After that, whenever the bad depression from God tormented Saul, David got out his harp and played. That would calm Saul down...

- 1 Samuel 16:21-23

David learned about praise as a young shepherd boy. He had to quickly learn to depend on God so that he could play before the depressed king. King Saul suffered from bad depression, because his defiance of God had caused God to withdraw His spirit from him. Even though Saul rejected God and refused to follow Him, God reached out to Saul through David. God showed David that praise lifted Saul's depression. David saw that God consistently comes through and solves life's issues without fail.

PRAYER: Lord, thank you for showing me that praising you and focusing on you is your bright pathway for our entire journey through life—from childhood to old age. Thank you again that in David you have given us such a great example of how focusing on you works. In these verses, I see that my focus on you can even benefit those who have rejected you, just as David's love for you calmed down the evil king and brought him peace. Please help me to be a signpost for those around me, pointing to your glory.

Personal Reflections

March 15

David answered, "You come at me with sword and spear and battle-ax. I come at you in the name of GOD-of-the-Angel-Armies. . . This very day GOD is handing you over to me. I'm about to kill you. . . The whole earth will know that there's an extraordinary God in Israel. And everyone gathered here will learn that GOD doesn't save by means of sword or spear."

- 1 Samuel 17:45-47

With everyone in Saul's army terrified of Goliath, only David was focused on the Lord and not the giant obstacle between Israel and victory. How did he find the courage to trust God? David remembered God's faithfulness when he killed the bear and lion while he watched his father's flocks. By remembering God's faithfulness in the past, David showed no fear as he relied on the power of God. He was not swayed by the fear of those around him. Yet again – what a testimony of how faithful God is when we simply focus on Him!

PRAYER: Lord, I have the tendency to focus on the battle and the size of the mountain in front of me when I should be remembering your goodness. Thankfully, you fight the battle for me and remove life's obstacles. You keep me from tripping as I look up to you. The story of David and Goliath reminds me that the greater the mismatch, the more clearly you can show your ability to perform.

Personal Reflections

March 16

One late afternoon, David got up from taking his nap and was strolling on the roof of the palace. From his vantage point on the roof he saw a woman bathing. The woman was stunningly beautiful. David sent to ask about her, and was told, "Isn't this Bathsheba, daughter of Eliam and wife of Uriah the Hittite?" David sent his agents to get her. After she arrived, he went to bed with her.

- 2 Samuel 11:2-4

Unbelievable as it seems, it was not the giant Philistine warrior that distracted David from the Lord. Instead, David chose to let a beautiful woman capture his focus. The outcome was horrible and deadly. David went to bed with her. When he learned that Bathsheba was pregnant, David had her husband intentionally killed in battle. While battling Goliath, David kept his focus on the Lord. The outcome was a miracle. But when he was tempted by Bathsheba, David focused on her instead of the Lord, and the outcome was a disaster.

PRAYER: Lord, thank you for showing us so clearly through these two examples what a difference simply focusing on you can make. Your word is full of stories that reveal to us over and over again the importance of keeping our eyes on you. When we continually make that choice, you fight all the battles on our behalf, but when we take our eyes off you, you sorrowfully let us suffer the consequences.

Personal Reflections

March 17

This is GOD speaking, remember! I'll make trouble for you out of your own family. I'll take your wives from right out in front of you. I'll give them to some neighbor, and he'll go to bed with them openly. You did your deed in secret; I'm doing mine with the whole country watching!"

Then David confessed to Nathan, "I've sinned against GOD."

Nathan pronounced, "Yes, but that's not the last word. GOD forgives your sin. You won't die for it. But because of your blasphemous behavior, the son born to you will die."

- 2 Samuel 12:12-14

Sometimes, it takes the admonition of others to get our focus back on God. Through his confession to Nathan, David chose to refocus on God, even after he had committed a horrible sin. He did not run away and hide or focus on his shame, like many of us try to do. He did not even run away after Nathan announced God's consequences. David stood before the Lord and focused on Him once again.

PRAYER: Lord, thank you for your promise to be there when I choose to refocus on you instead of trying to hide in shame or run from the consequences. Thank you that you use your other followers to speak on your behalf and show me my sin.

Personal Reflections

March 18

After Nathan went home, GOD afflicted the child that Uriah's wife bore to David, and he came down sick. David prayed desperately to God for the little boy. He fasted, wouldn't go out, and slept on the floor. The elders in his family came in and tried to get him off the floor, but he wouldn't budge. Nor could they get him to eat anything. On the seventh day the child died.

- 2 Samuel 12:15-16

Like a small child, David cried out to his heavenly Father to reconsider the consequences that came from his disobedience. David knew God was his only hope. God loved David enough to follow through on the consequences. Though the results of his sin hurt worse than anything he could have imagined, David didn't turn his back on God. He knew he'd done wrong, and he focused on God, even through the devastating consequences.

PRAYER: Lord, may we be like small children who accept that Father knows best. Help me to always run to you even after my own wrong-doing. Sometimes I may beg and pray for you to change your mind and spare me from the consequences of my sin, but even when you follow through and let me suffer, I will focus on your love for me. Remind me that hiding in shame or running from my consequences only keeps me from experiencing your steadfast love and the comfort of your everlasting arms.

Personal Reflections

March 19

David noticed that the servants were whispering behind his back, and realized that the boy must have died.

He asked the servants, "Is the boy dead?"

"Yes," they answered. "He's dead."

David got up from the floor, washed his face and combed his hair, put on a fresh change of clothes, then went into the sanctuary and worshiped.

- 2 Samuel 12:19-20

What a story of steadfast focus on God! One of the toughest times to focus on God is after we are corrected or disciplined. Sometimes it hurts, and sometimes it damages our pride. We want to pout and feel sorry for ourselves—which completely absorbs us in self-pity. Earthly fathers may be angry at us after they correct or discipline us, but God loves us deeply and unconditionally and always welcomes us back into His arms. That's why David could immediately return to the Lord in worship. He knew that God's love and comfort would be there.

PRAYER: Thank you, Lord, that we can run into your arms after we mess up. It's then that, like little children, we especially need a hug and your love. It feels so good to know I can cry in your arms even after I have made some awful mistakes. It is so comforting to know that nothing can separate me from your love.

Personal Reflections

March 20

But me he caught—reached all the way
from sky to sea...
I stood there saved—surprised to be loved!

GOD made my life complete
when I placed all the pieces before him.
...he gave me a fresh start.
Indeed, I've kept alert to GOD'S ways;
I haven't taken God for granted.
Every day I review the ways he works...

- 2 Samuel 22:17,20-23

Even after David had committed adultery and tried to cover up his crime by murdering Bathsheba's husband, God remained faithful to David. He gave King David severe correction, but David, like a child with a strict but loving parent, learned to keep his eyes on God. He stayed alert and constantly reviewed the ways God works. Again, the key word is focus. There is nothing God won't do to take care of us. Our only responsibility is to stay focused on God.

PRAYER: Lord, thank you for showing us that correction is a critical way that you draw our attention to you. There are some stern consequences that come out of taking our focus off you and yielding to sin. But we thank you that you love us enough to do anything it takes to teach us to place our attention back on you.

Personal Reflections

March 21

Suddenly, GOD, your light floods my path, GOD drives out the darkness. I smash the bands of marauders, I vault the high fences. What a God! His road stretches straight and smooth. Every GOD-direction is road-tested. Everyone who runs toward him makes it.

- 2 Samuel 22:29-31

I know my efforts always fail, but I know God created my brain so that I can choose to focus—no matter how major the distraction. God tells us that we can even use the distraction as an opportunity to refocus on Him. Moreover, we only have to ask and He will give us reminders through all our weaknesses to draw our attention to Him. Suddenly, we find new strength of purpose. We feel strong enough to vault high fences, sweep our enemies aside, and run head-long down the path towards our God. Now that's a description of intense focus!

PRAYER: Lord, I know you are progressively clearing my vision as I continue to read your Word. You do fulfill your promise to drive out the darkness! The more I read, the more I want to know of the Scriptures. It really does feel like your light is starting to flood my path. Thank you that every road you make is straight and true. Thank you for new strength to run into your outstretched arms.

Personal Reflections

March 22

When I'm far from anywhere,
  down to my last gasp...
You've always given me breathing room,
  a place to get away from it all,
A lifetime pass to your safe-house,
  an open invitation as your guest.
You've always taken me seriously, God,
  made me welcome among those who know and love
you.

- Psalm 61:2-5

Anyone who struggles with panic attacks knows what it feels like to be unable to catch a breath. Even though we know that God promises to take care of us, life can be very frightening. But God will never abandon us when we get scared. No, He rushes to our rescue and gives us room to breathe. God provides a safe house for our spirits when we focus on Him, a place where there are others who know and love Him and who will welcome us with open arms. That is the way God treats those who put their trust in Him!

PRAYER: Lord, not only do you calm our fears and take us to a safe place in our minds, but you also show us friends who can help support us when times are hard. We all get scared sometimes—but we can encourage each other as we share experiences of your faithfulness when we are afraid. Help me to trust in your love whenever I am afraid and lonely and feel helpless to fix my scary situation. Remind me that rescuing me is what you do—every time.

Personal Reflections

March 23

I'll wait as long as he says.
Everything I hope for comes from him,
   so why not?
He's solid rock under my feet,
   breathing room for my soul,
An impregnable castle:
   I'm set for life.

My help and glory are in God...
   God is a safe place to be.

- Psalm 62:5-8

The goodness of waiting has become a foreign concept in American culture—even in Christian circles. My natural tendency is to take charge and create blessings for myself, instead of waiting in God's safe house for Him to bless me. I would have been saved from a lot of problems if only I had waited and continued to focus on God and let Him take action in His time. Now that I know what a solid rock my God is, I choose to wait for Him, because everything good that I hope for comes from Him anyway, so—why not?

PRAYER: Lord, I have to admit I wish I had learned this lesson a long time ago. But I guess it's better late than never! Now I look forward to spending time with you in your safe house while I wait for your direction. Show me your way, Lord. In the meantime, I am going to enjoy my time with you while I wait. You have blessed me with breathing room for my soul, a safe, impregnable castle in the midst of a siege, a shelter in a dry desert land.

Personal Reflections

March 24

Really! There's no such thing as self-rescue,
  pulling yourself up by your bootstraps.
The cost of rescue is beyond our means,
  and even then it doesn't guarantee
Life forever...

Anyone can see that the brightest and best die,
  wiped out right along with fools and dunces.
They leave all their prowess behind,
  move into their new home, The Coffin...

- Psalm 49:7-10

This verse holds a vivid reminder of what *not* to do while I wait! Obviously, self-rescue is never the answer, and this verse gives a vivid depiction of where it leads. While I wait on God to rescue me, reading scriptures like this one are great encouragement to resist the urge to save myself—reminding me that continuing to focus on God will have the final outcome of true, full life forever. Dwelling on the assurance that I am Heaven-bound is a great way to focus on God while I wait!

PRAYER: Lord, you've made it clear that we will have hardships while we wait on you. But you made my brain with the wonderful ability to imagine life with you in heaven. You have even given scriptures that help my imagination. During tough times, you give me amazing mental images of life with you in Heaven, which help me to resist any desire on my part to attempt self-rescue.

Personal Reflections

March 25

We aren't immortal. We don't last long.
  Like our dogs, we age and weaken. And die.

This is what happens to those who live for the moment,
  who only look out for themselves:
Death herds them like sheep straight to hell;
  they disappear down the gullet of the grave;
They waste away to nothing—
  nothing left but a marker in a cemetery.

- Psalm 49:12-15

Another vivid word picture of what not to do while waiting! Living for the moment and looking out for ourselves is a natural tendency, but it is a road that leads only to hell. Far from being a scare tactic, this verse on hell is an urgent warning to stay away from self-focused agendas and from depending on our own abilities to give us happiness. The only life worth living is one that takes account of eternity, and this verse is a powerful motivator to stay focused on my heavenly Father.

PRAYER: Lord, we often use the scriptures on Heaven and Hell to try harder to somehow earn our way into your presence. Thank you for your clear message that we don't earn our way into Heaven—we never could. Eternal life in Heaven is your precious gift to us. This gift is more than worth waiting for while we focus on you and how much you love us.

Personal Reflections

March 26

So don't be impressed with those who get rich
  and pile up fame and fortune.
They can't take it with them;
  fame and fortune all get left behind.
Just when they think they've arrived
  and folks praise them because they've made good,
They enter the family burial plot
  where they'll never see sunshine again.

- Psalm 49:16-19

Here's a third vivid reminder of what not to focus on while we wait! The love of money is an American tradition that seems to come naturally in our culture. God allows some people who focus on Him to be monetarily successful because He knows they will use it unselfishly for His glory. The temptation is to fall in love with the money God gave us. Love of money definitely can take our focus off Him. Eternal life is the only treasure worth waiting for. You can't take money with you!

PRAYER: Lord, I am so thankful for your reminder that fame and fortune get left behind when we die. I don't want my life to be left behind. I want to spend eternity with you. I would rather focus on your riches in glory than focus on money here on earth. Please help me to use the money you give me here on earth wisely, to help others and to share your love with those who don't yet know you.

Personal Reflections

March 27

Generous in love—God, give grace!
  Huge in mercy—wipe out my bad record.
Scrub away my guilt,
  soak out my sins in your laundry.
I know how bad I've been;
  my sins are staring me down.

You're the One I've violated, and you've seen
  it all, seen the full extent of my evil.
You have all the facts before you;
  whatever you decide about me is fair.

                                        - Psalm 51:1-4

It was God who made our brains with the ability to remember feelings in vivid, living color. That ability helps us remember how bad we felt in our sin as a strong reminder that we totally depend on Him to keep us on the right path. When we mess up, our memory flashes back to previous sins, and helps us stay focused on our God who rescued us then and still rescues us from ourselves. God wants us to stay in touch with our sin—not so we dwell in shame, but to remind us when we take our eyes off Him, our old selves haven't changed a bit.

PRAYER: Lord, although we hate a lot of our feeling memories and wish we could forget the negative ones, I'm glad you remind us through these memories how bad we felt living in sin and trying to live under our own willpower. These bad memories are strong motivators to stay focused on you and wait for you to perform in me.

Personal Reflections

March 28

Enter me, then; conceive a new, true life.

Soak me in your laundry and I'll come out clean,
scrub me and I'll have a snow-white life.
Tune me in to foot-tapping songs,
set these once-broken bones to dancing.
Don't look too close for blemishes,
give me a clean bill of health.
God, make a fresh start in me...

- Psalm 51:6-10

God not only made our brains to be able to record vivid memories of bad feelings, but He created our minds to remember intense and amazing feelings as well. When we focus on Him, God is faithful to remind us how wonderful we felt the first time He cleaned us up, and how loved and accepted we feel every time we confess our sin and let Him clean us up again. When God makes a fresh start in us, He scrubs us and soaks us and gently wipes off the stains of our old life, clothing us in His bright-white righteousness!

PRAYER: Lord, I am starting to see that your scriptures show us countless ways to focus on you. No wonder you are able to clear my vision! You draw my attention to you continually every day. I want to shout and dance and sing about how you cleansed my heart and gave me a brand-new fresh start, washed clean from blemishes, whole and healthy before you. Thank you for setting me free!

Personal Reflections

March 29

I'll sing anthems to your life-giving ways.
Unbutton my lips, dear God;
  I'll let loose with your praise.

Going through the motions doesn't please you...
I learned God-worship
  when my pride was shattered.
Heart-shattered lives ready for love
  don't for a moment escape God's notice.

- Psalm 51:15-17

These verses are loaded with instructions on how to remain focused on God while we let Him perform in us. First, let loose with your voice, even if it's only in the shower or in the car where no one can hear you. Second, open your lips with heartfelt worship as you remember how you felt His love at your loneliest point. Your heart-felt praise never escapes His notice! Third, remain focused on Him. To those who are ready for love, God pours out His heart-store in a wild, beautiful, extravagant way.

PRAYER: Lord, I am so thankful you made our brains with memories that recall how you rescued us at our lowest point. Those feeling memories are just as strong today as they were the day you saved us, even if that was many years ago. The day my pride was shattered and I realized how much I need you is still the best day of my life. Please never let me forget how much you care for me.

Personal Reflections

March 30

Silence is praise to you,
  Zion-dwelling God,
And also obedience.
  You hear the prayer in it all.

We all arrive at your doorstep sooner
  or later, loaded with guilt,
Our sins too much for us—
  but you get rid of them once and for all.

- Psalm 65:1-3

Praise does not mean only singing songs to the Lord. Praise also includes silent obedience when our souls are quiet and humble, following God's will in us. In these moments, we only want to see the Lord get the glory. We are so grateful He took away our awful feelings of guilt that we couldn't get rid of on our own. We remember His love, and He takes away the deep shame that kept us in hiding from Him.

PRAYER: By focusing on you, Lord, we can finally clearly see that you really have washed away all our sin and guilt. We hated how awful we felt when we were stuck in the swamp of our sin and shame. Now we want to obey what you show us, and we want to praise you in gratitude, with song and with silence, with love and with joy. We know you performed a miracle in our brokenness, and we can't take our eyes off you!

Personal Reflections

March 31

Say of God, "We've never seen anything like him!"
  When your enemies see you in action,
  they slink off like scolded dogs.
The whole earth falls to its knees—
  it worships you...

 Take a good look at God's wonders—
  they'll take your breath away.
He converted sea to dry land;
  travelers crossed the river on foot.

- Psalm 66:3-6

A great way to focus on God is to read and remember His wonders and miracles from the past. When we really dwell on these memories, they take our breath away and bring us to our knees. We can take the time to give our full attention to reflecting on Him as we allow God to perform in us rather than devoting all our efforts to making it on our own. Just as He did for the Israelites escaping from Egypt, He can part the waters that lie in front of us, giving us a solid place to stand.

PRAYER: Thank you, Lord, for the insight that my obsessive efforts to perform only interfere with my focus on you. I don't want to waste any more time on my own futile attempt to earn your love and care. I'd rather focus on you and have you take my breath away as I thank you for the wonders you perform in my life. I want to fall to my knees and worship you, my lips breathing your praise every morning and evening.

Personal Reflections

April 1

Sing hymns to God;
all heaven, sing out...
Enjoy GOD,
cheer when you see him!

Father of orphans,
champion of widows,
is God in his holy house.
God makes homes for the homeless,
leads prisoners to freedom...

- Psalm 68:4-6

When we focus on God with our five senses, we can really enjoy our relationship with Him. Watch the smiles on the faces of widows when you help them with household chores. Hear the gratitude in the voices of the homeless when they thank you for feeding them. Feel the hugs of the orphans when you play ball with them. God is the champion of widows and orphans, a shelter for the homeless, an open door for those who are trapped. When we imitate our Father and devote time to helping the helpless, we enjoy Him in a unique way.

PRAYER: Lord, remembering the times when we gave of our time and attention to the needy without wanting anything in return brings us happy memories. Seeing the smiles on their faces gives us a greater desire to give more of our time to helping others. This focus takes our attention off our own struggles and reminds us how well you have taken care of us.

Personal Reflections

April 2

No doubt about it! God is good—
  good to good people, good to the good-hearted.
But I nearly missed it,
  missed seeing his goodness.
I was looking the other way,
  looking up to the people
At the top,
  envying the wicked who have it made,
Who have nothing to worry about,
  not a care in the whole wide world.

- Psalm 73:1-5

It's possible to spend a lifetime focused on what other people have, but as long as we continue in envy, we will miss God's goodness in our own lives! Many people have found success by the world's standards, but they have no desire to depend on God. From the outside, it may look like they have it made, that they don't have a care in the whole wide world. However, they are missing out on the presence of God in their empty lives. When we look at them and envy them simply for their success, we forget that knowing God is what really counts. We forget that we see God most clearly in the lives of those who are broken and desperate for help.

PRAYER: Lord, even if we have material wealth, we will always be poor in spirit without you. Money and fortune don't bring us joy—only your love makes us truly happy. I want to keep my eyes on you alone, and not the rich and famous, for they have nothing to offer if they are not centering their lives on you.

Personal Reflections

April 3

You're all I want in heaven!
  You're all I want on earth!
When my skin sags and my bones get brittle,
  GOD is rock-firm and faithful.
Look! Those who left you are falling apart!
...But I'm in the very presence of GOD —
  oh, how refreshing it is!
I've made Lord GOD my home.
  GOD, I'm telling the world what you do!

- Psalm 73:25-28

When we stay focused on God and enjoy being in His presence, He becomes our dwelling place. We feel at home with the Lord, safe and sound. He becomes all we want and desire both now and for eternity. Even as we get old, His presence is refreshing to our body and our spirit. As we grow in knowledge and understanding of God's love for us, we want to stay connected to Him forever.

PRAYER: Lord, I am grateful that I can call you my home for now and forever. You are my greatest hope and desire in my life. How good it feels to desire you more than anything else. Every other desire fades in comparison to you! I feel so full of joy in your presence. Even when people betray and abandon me, I know I am safe in your love. Focusing on your presence, I can weather any storm. I know you are on my side to strengthen me, even when I get tired and my body starts to fail me. I am at home in you, and I want to let the world know how amazing you are!

Personal Reflections

April 4

And I'll take up the lute and thank you
  to the tune of your faithfulness, God.
I'll make music for you on a harp,
  Holy One of Israel.
When I open up in song to you,
  I let out lungsful of praise,
  my rescued life a song.
All day long I'm chanting
  about you and your righteous ways...

  - Psalm 71:22-24

In more than half a century of living, I have never felt this way before—I have never felt anything even close! As I read these scriptures, God has drawn my attention to Him in a focused way that I never could have imagined. I have felt His love so strongly, and I long for Him more every day. He has shown me a whole new sort of life in Him, a life of music and thanksgiving. My heart wants to overflow into singing! Even if I feel self-conscious about my ability to make music, turning my focus to Him enables me to open up and praise Him without thinking about how I sound to others. My whole life is becoming a song of joyful thanks to God.

PRAYER: Lord, my fervent prayer is that every person who reads these scriptures every day will, in their own unique way, experience the same love that you are showing me. You are all I want to dwell on. All my life I was told I "should" witness to others. Now, I want to tell others what you have shown me!

Personal Reflections

April 5

We thank you, God, we thank you—
your Name is our favorite word;
your mighty works are all we talk about.

You say, "I'm calling this meeting to order,
I'm ready to set things right.
When the earth goes topsy-turvy
And nobody knows which end is up,
I nail it all down,
I put everything in place again..."

- Psalm 75:1-4

It sure seems like few people know which end is up in our world today. I want to shout from the rooftops that focus on Jesus is the only answer! People say that it is so hard to focus on God with all the worldly distractions around us. While I agree that many distractions bid for our attention, I am reminded that seeking God through prayer and scripture reading is just a simple choice that must be made daily. Make the choice—don't turn it into an effort.

PRAYER: Lord, thank you that by simply reading your word for a few minutes each day, we can focus on you and wait for you to begin a new work in us. You are performing in us while we simply watch you work. Each day, a little more of you grows inside us. Your name becomes our favorite word, your work in our lives our favorite thing to talk about. Before we know it, we can't contain your love and we can't help sharing with others how you made us new.

Personal Reflections

April 6

Listen, dear friends, to God's truth,
bend your ears to what I tell you.
I'm chewing on the morsel of a proverb;
I'll let you in on the sweet old truths,
Stories we heard from our fathers,
counsel we learned at our mother's knee.
We're not keeping this to ourselves,
we're passing it along to the next generation—
GOD'S fame and fortune,
the marvelous things he has done.

- Psalm 78:1-4

As much as I enjoy sharing these scriptures with my own generation, I find that I enjoy sharing it with the next two generations even more, because their young age will allow them to have so much more time to experience God's love. It seems that young adults in our American culture are especially receptive to His love. Young pastors and young people of the next generation are pouring into churches all over our country eager to receive the gospel message.

PRAYER: Lord, I pray that both young and old will flock to you like never before. We all desperately need you to show us new signs and wonders of your power and love. May people be touched by you in small and large congregations, led by pastors who focus only on you and share your message to the masses of broken people in our world.

Personal Reflections

April 7

Will the Lord walk off and leave us for good?
  Will he never smile again?
Is his love worn threadbare?
  Has his salvation promise burned out?
Has God forgotten his manners?
  Has he angrily stalked off and left us?
"Just my luck," I said. "The High God goes out of business
  just the moment I need him."

- Psalm 77:7-10

It's possible to feel abandoned by friends and by God, even when you're trying to focus on Him. For King David of the Old Testament, this feeling was a frequent experience, as it can be for us, as well. We can feel so good in His presence, enjoying the good times—and then some kind of trouble catches us by surprise. Our automatic feeling is fear that He has abandoned us, just like friends and family can desert us when catastrophe strikes. The only thing to do is to stay focused on Him and honestly share with God exactly how we feel.

PRAYER: Thank you, Lord, for being the one person in my life with whom I can share exactly how I'm feeling. I can share with you my fears of being alone or abandoned by those I love. I can tell you when I am afraid that you are not really there. Sharing my heart keeps me focused on you so you can show me what to do next.

Personal Reflections

April 8

Once again I'll go over what GOD has done,
lay out on the table the ancient wonders;
I'll ponder all the things you've accomplished,
and give a long, loving look at your acts.

O God! Your way is holy!
No god is great like God!
You're the God who makes things happen;
you showed everyone what you can do—
You pulled your people out of the worst kind of trouble...

- Psalm 77:11-15

Even after we share our feelings with God, we tend to take our focus off Him and revert to worrying over our troubles and trying to fix them on our own, which only makes things worse. We can take a cue from David to avoid this unfortunate cycle. Immediately after David shared his fear that God had left him alone, he shifted his focus to reviewing the wonders God performed in the past. He took a long look at God's accomplishments— which lead him to praise God's greatness.

PRAYER: Lord, you carefully teach us step-by-step how to stay focused on you even when we are in big trouble and are afraid you have abandoned us. You never require us to overcome our fears before we can receive your help. The only thing we have to do is to stay focused on you in the midst of our fear. You transform our fear into praise when we dwell on your faithfulness.

Personal Reflections

April 9

One day spent in your house, this beautiful place of worship,
  beats thousands spent on Greek island beaches.
I'd rather scrub floors in the house of my God
  than be honored as a guest in the palace of sin.
All sunshine and sovereign is GOD,
  generous in gifts and glory.
He doesn't scrimp with his traveling companions.
  It's smooth sailing all the way with GOD-of-the-Angel-Armies.

- Psalm 84:10-12

Sustained focus on God can be described as "dwelling in His house"—a beautiful place of worship. We will feel more joy scrubbing floors in His house than we ever could while relaxing on Greek island beaches. What an amazing word picture of what focus on Him feels like! God says one single day in His house praising Him is better than a thousand days relaxing on the beach or basking in the splendorous halls of powerful men.

PRAYER: Lord, reading all these scriptures is giving me such a clear picture of how wonderful life in your presence really is! We can be happy in any position in life as long as we remain close to you. Even better, when I am excited about my relationship with you, I want others to also experience this same joy and peace. Sharing your love no longer feels like a task I am supposed to do as a Christian. Instead, I find that I can't wait to talk about you! You make me want to stay focused on you.

Personal Reflections

April 10

What a beautiful thing, GOD, to give thanks,
to sing an anthem to you, the High God!
To announce your love each daybreak,
sing your faithful presence all through the night,
Accompanied by dulcimer and harp,
the full-bodied music of strings.

You made me so happy, GOD
I saw your work and I shouted for joy.
How magnificent your work, GOD!

- Psalm 92:1-5

Here is another clear word picture that describes how happy we can be when we keep our focus on God. He promises to be right at our side in bad times and to get us out of any trouble. He really does provide a safe-house to dwell in, morning, noon and night. He never leaves us. As if we need a bonus, He shares His profound thoughts with us as He keeps us safe. He gives us such a wonderful feeling of being special to Him. No wonder we sometimes feel like shouting for joy!

PRAYER: Lord, as I continue my focus on you, it seems like you share more and more thoughts with me. I know these thoughts come from you because they are new and fresh. They are such good thoughts and I feel like your only child—that's how special you make me feel. You are so incredible that I know you can make all your children feel special, like an only child.

Personal Reflections

April 11

Sing to GOD a brand-new song.
He's made a world of wonders!

He rolled up his sleeves,
He set things right.

GOD made history with salvation,
He showed the world what he could do.

He remembered to love us, a bonus
To his dear family, Israel—indefatigable love.

The whole earth comes to attention.
Look—God's work of salvation!

- Psalm 98:1-3

So often when we work long hours all week, we grow very tired and resentful of all the hard work we do. We may put in the hours, but we are miserable the whole time. God's strength, however, is unending. He never gets tired working on our behalf 24/7. Plus, He loves us—that's why He loves the work He does for us. He never grows tired or weary of loving us, and He remembers His love for us for all eternity, and we can never escape His love. It doesn't get any better than that!

PRAYER: Lord, thank you for this new thought from your Word—that you never get tired of me. I can be so needy and high-maintenance. You are always there for me emotionally, to comfort me when I'm down, and to love me when I feel unlovable. Thank you for rolling up your sleeves and setting things right in my messed-up life, and never making me feel like a waste of your time.

Personal Reflections

April 12

GOD made the heavens—
Royal splendor radiates from him,
A powerful beauty sets him apart...

Let's hear it from Sky,
With Earth joining in,
And a huge round of applause from Sea.

Let Wilderness turn cartwheels,
Animals, come dance,
Put every tree of the forest in the choir—

An extravaganza before God as he come...

- Psalm 96:5-6, 11-13

Enjoying God's creation can be an amazing part of our focus on Him. Breathtaking scenery can bring us to tears of joy as we dwell on His beauty. When we are feeling down and stuck in thinking too much about our problems, an escape to nature can draw our attention away from our misery as God shows us how much He cares through the sights, sounds, smells, taste and touch of His handiwork. God made the world special to show us how much He loves us. Our enjoying of it is one of the ways we thank Him!

PRAYER: Lord, your love is everywhere around me, the sky, the trees, the water, and all the other sights, sounds and smells of nature. You made my brain, not only to think, but to feel your love through my five senses. Thank you for designing me so that I can enjoy your beauty through everything you have made.

Personal Reflections

April 13

O my soul, bless GOD.
  From head to toe, I'll bless his holy name!
O my soul, bless GOD,
  don't forget a single blessing!

He forgives your sins—every one.
  He heals your diseases—every one.
  He redeems you from hell—saves your life!
  He crowns you with love and mercy—a paradise crown.
  He wraps you in goodness—beauty eternal.
  He renews your youth—you're always young in his presence.

- Psalm 103:1-5

I remember the old hymn we sang when I was young: "count your many blessings, name them one by one." As a child, I wasn't worried about staying young, but nowadays so many in our culture obsess over products to keep looking young, even though we know every day brings us closer to death. Here's a new thought: focus on the Lord and His blessings keeps us young on the inside.

PRAYER: Thank you, Lord, for the many benefits of staying focused on you. Even as my body grows old, I can stay young on the inside until I meet you in heaven. Lord, I pray that young and old will be drawn to your word and discover the awesome feeling of your love. Please continue to give me new thoughts about how amazing you are, and keep reminding me of your goodness. I never want to forget a single one of the many blessings you have given me.

Personal Reflections

April 14

Some of you wandered for years in the desert,
  looking but not finding a good place to live,
Half-starved and parched with thirst,
  staggering and stumbling, on the brink of exhaustion.
Then, in your desperate condition, you called out to GOD...

He put your feet on a wonderful road
  that took you straight to a good place to live.
So thank GOD for his marvelous love...
He poured great draughts of water down parched throats;
  the starved and hungry got plenty to eat.

- Psalm 107:4-9

"Wandering for years in the desert" is such an accurate description of trying to perform in life on our own. We are looking for answers in all the wrong places. No wonder life gets worse when we try to succeed on our own! No wonder we are starving and thirsting to death. Yet, as soon as we look to God and away from the desert, he takes us straight to our home in Him and gives us the nourishment we so desperately need.

PRAYER: Thank you, Lord, for not holding out on us, even when we have resisted looking to you for help for so long. When we cry out to you, you immediately come to our rescue with your amazing love. Many of us wandered in an emotional desert for years, starving for love. We never found what we were looking for until we called your name. As we focus on you, we receive your emotional nourishment every day, far beyond what we ever imagined.

Personal Reflections

April 15

I'll never forget the trouble, the utter lostness,
the taste of ashes, the poison I've swallowed.
I remember it all—oh, how well I remember—
the feeling of hitting the bottom.
But there's one other thing I remember,
and remembering, I keep a grip on hope...

- Lamentations 3:19-21

When we remember our wandering in the desert for years, we re-experience the pain of hitting bottom. God made our minds to be able to store vivid memories of our failures, intense memories that drive us into His arms. We want to stay focused on Him so that we never end up back where we came from, in the desert of self-dependence and desperation. Remembering our dark times can bring us hope when we remember how our God rescued us. He has sworn never to leave us or forsake us!

PRAYER: Lord, I marvel at how you made my brain to remember experiences with my five senses, even down to the taste in my mouth. The ability to remember things in full sensation goes beyond the bad memories to the memory of how you saved me, giving me powerful, almost physical reminders that my hope is in you, and not in my own performance.

Personal Reflections

April 16

GOD'S loyal love couldn't have run out,
his merciful love couldn't have dried up.
They're created new every morning.
How great your faithfulness!
I'm sticking with GOD (I say it over and over).
He's all I've got left.

- Lamentations 3:22-24

When we are in those dark places that remind us of the dark time before we knew God's love, this is what we must focus on. The writer says he is convinced that "God's loyal love couldn't have run out!" Are you convinced of that truth? God showers us every morning with His love. Like rain to water the plants, His love waters our need to feel loved. In the desert, our own efforts to perform yielded only dust. Everything dried up. We had nothing left. He became our only hope. Now, even when times are hard, we can confidently say, "I'm sticking with God!" and trust that He will come through for us.

PRAYER: Lord, thank you for your morning showers of love that remind me of your faithfulness. I am grateful that your love never dries up. I will keep reminding myself of this over and over again to keep me focused on you. I may not be able to perform correctly, but I can easily repeat many times that I am sticking with you. I know that even when I find it hard to stick with you, you never give up on me.

Personal Reflections

April 17

*God proves to be good to the man who passionately
waits,*
   to the woman who diligently seeks.
It's a good thing to quietly hope,
   quietly hope for help from GOD. . .

When life is heavy and hard to take,
   go off by yourself. Enter the silence.
Bow in prayer. Don't ask questions:
   Wait for hope to appear.

- Lamentations 3:25-29

Sometimes we need this reminder badly. When things aren't going well for us, the last thing we want to do is wait. We hate being passive; we want to be out and doing something! Yet in this passage, waiting is described not as passive, but as "passionate." For the one who knows God, waiting on Him can be a way of diligently seeking His face. These instructions on how to wait for God to come through are very specific and clear. One: get off by yourself away from distractions. Two: focus on the silence. Three: bow your head in prayer. Four: resist breaking the silence by asking questions. Five: don't try to build your own hope. Allow God to show you hope, while you maintain your quiet focus on Him.

PRAYER: Lord, once again, this scripture reminds me that your Word is the best "how to" textbook ever written. Thank you for being so specific and clear on how to stay focused by quietly waiting on you. Your instructions are so critical in today's world of information overload and constant distractions.

Personal Reflections

April 18

Some of you were locked in a dark cell...
Punished for defying God's Word,
   for turning your back on the High God's counsel—
A hard sentence, and your hearts so heavy,
   and not a soul in sight to help.
Then you called out to GOD in your desperate condition...
He led you out of your dark, dark cell,
   broke open the jail and led you out...
   he snapped the prison bars like matchsticks!

                            - Psalm 107:10-14, 16

In the desert of our own performance-based living, we turn our back on God and do not listen to His instructions. As a result of looking away from Him, we become locked in our own mental and emotional prison. The harder we try to fight our way out on our own efforts, the more we feel locked in. Only then do we turn our focus back to Him and cry out for help

PRAYER: Lord, I have no faith left in my own efforts to perform. They only lead me to a dark place in my heart and mind. Thank you that I only have to cry out and refocus on you, and you take care of all the rest. With your power and love, you destroy all the wasted years I spent working to imprison myself in the dungeon of shame and despair. You shatter the heavy doors I built and snap like matchsticks the prison bars I made. You lead me out of my own mental and emotional misery and bring me home.

Personal Reflections

April 19

I love GOD because he listened to me,
  listened as I begged for mercy.

Death stared me in the face,
  hell was hard on my heels.
Up against it, I didn't know which way to turn;
  then I called out to GOD for help...
GOD is gracious—it is he who makes things right,
  our most compassionate God.
GOD takes the side of the helpless;
  when I was at the end of my rope, he saved me.

- Psalm 116:1, 3-6

I love God because turning my focus to Him is the only thing in my life that has ever worked. My own repeated efforts to perform kept me stuck in the desert. I was a slave to my own efforts. They never worked. I didn't know which way to turn. I had tried every other turn. When I finally chose to turn to Him and cried out for Him to rescue me, He listened and did all the work to rescue me. I just hung onto Him for dear life.

PRAYER: Lord, I will thank you over and over again for listening and saving me from myself. It feels so good to finally quit on myself and follow you. I am so glad you have promised to give me fresh reminders every day to continue to draw my attention to you. I am grateful my only part is the constant choice to keep looking your way. Finally, the pressure is off to keep up my futile efforts to perform.

Personal Reflections

April 20

Oh, GOD, here I am, your servant,
your faithful servant: set me free for your service!
I'm ready to offer the thanksgiving sacrifice
and pray in the name of GOD.
I'll complete what I promised God I'd do,
and I'll do it in company with his people. . .

Praise GOD, everybody!
Applaud GOD, all people!
His love has taken over our lives;
GOD'S faithful ways are eternal.

- Psalm 116:16-18; 117:1-2

When God rescued me from my emotional prison, He set me free for his service, to spread His word to the world! His love took over my life, and now I love reading and writing down these scriptures, because it brings me closer to Him. I want to stay focused on Him, because I know if I go back to focusing on myself, I will end up back in that prison cell where I was for almost sixty years, enslaved by my own efforts to perform. I am so glad that God's love has taken over my life!

PRAYER: Lord, I will continually thank you for setting me free to serve you. As hard as I tried for years and years, I was never able to set myself free from my guilty bondage to performance. The more I tried, the more defeated I felt. I was such a slave to my negative emotions that I was never focused on spreading your word. Again and again I will say it: thank you for setting me free for your service!

Personal Reflections

April 21

How can a young person live a clean life?
   By carefully reading the map of your Word.
I'm single-minded in pursuit of you;
   don't let me miss the road signs you've posted.
I've banked your promises in the vault of my heart
   so I won't sin myself bankrupt.
Be blessed, GOD;
   train me in your ways of wise living.
I'll transfer to my lips
   all the counsel that comes from your mouth.

- Psalm 119:9-13

Many people practice double-mindedness, focusing on their party life Friday and Saturday nights and dragging themselves to church on Sunday morning. These verses give us step-by-step instructions on how to be single-minded in our focus on God. 1) Read and use His Word as our road-map to life. 2) Pray that God won't let us miss His road signs. 3) Reflect and stay focused on His promises so they are locked in our heart. 4) Repeat His counsel aloud and share it with others.

PRAYER: Lord, although I have always hated road-maps and written instructions, I am grateful that your instructions are so clear that I can follow them. I want to keep learning because every day I read more of your Word, you increase my desire for you and other passions become less inviting. The joy you give me far surpasses anything I have ever felt or experienced in my life.

Personal Reflections

April 22

I delight far more in what you tell me about living
  than in gathering a pile of riches.
I ponder every morsel of wisdom from you,
  I attentively watch how you've done it.
I relish everything you've told me of life,
  I won't forget a word of it..

- Psalm 119:14-16

God's Word gives clear instruction on how not to forget His teachings on how to live. First, we are to read His instructions on how to live rather than focus on how to get rich. Second, we are to dwell on (not just skim the surface of) each and every word of God's wise teaching. Third, we are to intently watch how Jesus lived His life. Fourth, we are to savor the richness of His parables on living. If we do this, we won't find it easy to forget what He says to us through His word, His life, and His Spirit. Along the way, we will experience the delight that comes from listening to Him and meditating on His wisdom.

PRAYER: Lord, thank you again that your instructions (on how to focus on your words so I don't forget) are so clear and not at all confusing to me. Even better, by following your instructions I have started an exciting new journey on how to live that gives me way more joy than money or influence or cleverness ever did. Thank you that your wisdom far surpasses my own efforts to figure out life!

Personal Reflections

April 23

GOD, teach me lessons for living
  so I can stay the course.
Give me insight so I can do what you tell me—
  my whole life one long, obedient response.
Guide me down the road of your commandments;
  I love traveling this freeway!
Give me a bent for your words of wisdom,
  and not for piling up loot.

- Psalm 119:33-36

I always thought that understanding God's wisdom was dependent on my intelligence and hard work, like doing well in school. This scripture basically says if I stay on His highway and keep fully focused on Him, He will do the rest. He will give me lessons to keep me on course. He will give me insight and provide constant tutoring so I stay on course. He even gives me the desire to seek Him and His wisdom instead of amassing money.

PRAYER: Lord, I am so thankful that, as long as I am single-minded in my focus on you, I can totally depend on you for wisdom and desire. That's wonderful because trying to be smart or trying to be inspired only distracts me from you. It never has worked to try to get excited about reading your scriptures before I start. Now, I just start reading and you provide the excitement. Thank you for revealing your love and your wisdom to me as I choose to spend my time focusing on you.

Personal Reflections

April 24

Divert my eyes from toys and trinkets,
*   invigorate me on the pilgrim way.*
Affirm your promises to me—
*   promises made to all who fear you.*
Deflect the harsh words of my critics—
*   but what you say is always so good.*
See how hungry I am for your counsel;
*   preserve my life through your righteous ways!.*

- Psalm 119:37-40

I am hungry not because I worked up an appetite, but because what God tells me is so amazing! In His wisdom, He reminds me to keep my eyes and thoughts off alluring toys and trinkets because they will distract me from Him. Not only are His loving promises so irresistible, but also He deflects the words of others who try to bring me down by filling me with a deep sense that He loves me no matter what. He knows if I get distracted by criticism, I will get discouraged and take my focus off Him, so He protects me by reminding me to keep my focus on Him and what He thinks of me.

PRAYER: Lord, I am grateful for your constant reminders to divert my eyes and deflect my thoughts from either harsh words or alluring pleasures. All of us are so easily distracted that, even when we look or think about these diversions for a second or two, we start driving down the wrong highway.

Personal Reflections

April 25

Remember what you said to me, your servant—
I hang on to these words for dear life!
These words hold me up in bad times;
yes, your promises rejuvenate me.
The insolent ridicule me without mercy,
but I don't budge from your revelation.
I watch for your ancient landmark words,
and know I'm on the right track..

- Psalm 119:49-52

Because He cares for us, God consistently reminds us that there will be tough times ahead in this life. He knows that people make bad choices and cause trouble in our lives. He knows how much the harsh words of others can hurt us. However, He is clear that the wisdom He taught us and the promises He gave us will sustain us through the hard times. He promises to rejuvenate us through His faithfulness, even when the opposition is relentless. Because of this, we can remain focused on the ancient landmarks and keep our eyes on His revelation of love.

PRAYER: Lord, I could never sustain my focus on you, especially in tough times, without the constant ways you love me and care for me. I feel like you always have a headset on me, giving me non-stop wisdom and encouragement. I don't have to fear that you will take me out of the game and sit me on the bench.

Personal Reflections

April 26

But when I see the wicked ignore your directions,
I'm beside myself with anger.
I set your instructions to music
and sing them as I walk this pilgrim way.
I meditate on your name all night, GOD,
treasuring your revelation, O GOD.

- Psalm 119:53-55

Nothing can mess with our ability to focus quite like anger. When we are angry, we can't seem to think straight. We are overwhelmed by our feelings, we "see red," and we act like a totally different person than we do when we are calm. Have you noticed that when we try to "think our way through anger," we usually just end up intensifying our feelings? Rather than trying to think his way out of anger, David switched his focus to God, intensifying his focus the angrier he got. He set scriptures to music, meditating on God's name all night long. As the night went on, David's anger finally gave way to a feeling of gratefulness as he treasured God's revelation to him.

PRAYER: Lord, many books have been written on methods for anger management, but no method comes close to these instructions in your Word. When we follow your directions and focus on you through praise and meditation, our anger fades and we end up feeling closer to you as we treasure the revelation of your amazing love for us.

Personal Reflections

April 27

Because you have satisfied me, GOD, I promise
to do everything you say.
I beg you from the bottom of my heart: smile,
be gracious to me just as you promised.
When I took a long, careful look at your ways,
I got my feet back on the trail you blazed.
I was up at once, didn't drag my feet,
was quick to follow your orders.

- Psalm 119:57-60

David gave God the credit for lifting his anger, saying that God satisfied him with His revelation (verse 55). I am so relieved to learn that I can depend on God to lift my anger, because I certainly never experienced any success trying to overcome anger on my own. David reported that, after he took a long look at God's ways, he was up at once and back on his feet, eager to follow God. Overwhelmed with gratitude for God's gracious favor, he got back on the trail God had blazed for him, leaving all his anger at others behind him.

PRAYER: Once again, Lord, I am filled with praise and thanksgiving at your clear, step-by-step instructions on how to deal with the problem of anger. We know that anger is a normal feeling we experience in everyday life. Denial of our anger is not a healthy option. Thank you that focusing on you is the secret to overcoming this feeling and not being thrown off course by our anger.

Personal Reflections

April 28

I'm homesick—longing for your salvation;
   I'm waiting for your word of hope.
My eyes grow heavy watching for some sign of your promise;
    how long must I wait for your comfort?
There's smoke in my eyes—they burn and water,
    but I keep a steady gaze on the instructions you post.

- Psalm 119:81-83

Homesickness is a normal feeling, one we often experience when we miss someone with whom we have a close friendship. David felt very close to God, and he was very vocal in his complaint about having to wait for God to give him some sign of His promises. However, even though his tears and lack of sleep interfered with his vision, David was determined to keep waiting and watching with a steady gaze for God, his closest companion. He was convinced that God would show up, even though in the meantime he felt all the anguish of homesickness and longing.

PRAYER: Lord, I am so glad you love me no matter what. By far, you are the safest relationship I will ever have, because I am secure in knowing that your love for me will never change. Thank you that you can handle any feeling or any complaining on my part. I often get frustrated and miss you when I have to wait on you to come through for me, but you are always well worth the wait.

Personal Reflections

April 29

I watch my step, avoiding the ditches and ruts of evil
so I can spend all my time keeping your Word.
I never make detours from the route you laid out;
you gave me such good directions.
Your words are so choice, so tasty;
I prefer them to the best home cooking.
With your instruction, I understand life...

- Psalm 119:101-104

We often see our evil desires as very appealing compared to focusing on God. We know we should focus on Him, but really, we would rather be spending our time on earthly attractions. However, David's focus on God yielded such appealing results that he didn't want to waste his time on detours, ditches, or ruts of evil. In fact, when he tasted the fruit of following God's directions, David described them as better than any home cooking.

PRAYER: Thank you, Lord, that you want to give us the same amazing feelings of your love that you gave David. Plus, you give us a clear, simple recipe of how to taste your goodness like David did. You direct us to give you our undivided attention and watch you perform your will in us far beyond what we can ever imagine. Knowing that my only part is to focus on you and you will do the rest—now that's a recipe that even I can follow.

Personal Reflections

April 30

Every word you give me is a miracle word—
how could I help but obey?
Break open your words, let the light shine out,
let ordinary people see the meaning.
Mouth open and panting,
I wanted your commands more than anything.

- Psalm 119:129-131

When David continued focusing on the Lord, he was blessed with an unmatched desire to obey God's commands. He longed for more instructions from God, and for more of God's wonderful, miraculous love. No earthly attraction or any addiction could compete with his intense desire for God. When we focus on God, He creates a desire in us for Him, a desire for the light of His word that surpasses our desire for anything else in the whole world. We are hanging on every word He speaks!

PRAYER: Lord, I have worked in the profession of addiction treatment for over thirty years and nothing in my education or professional training comes close to your expert teaching on how to overcome addictions. You have shown me that addictions are problems of misplaced focus. Only you have the power and love to draw our attention to you and give us the choice to turn our backs on the many addictions of this world.

Personal Reflections

May 1

I call out at the top of my lungs,
"GOD! Answer! I'll do whatever you say."
I called to you, "Save me
so I can carry out all your instructions."
I was up before sunrise,
crying for help, hoping for a word from you.
I stayed awake all night,
prayerfully pondering your promise.

- Psalm 119:145-148

Over the years of working with addictions, I have heard many stories of addicts being up all night using drugs or getting up before sunrise to go searching for a chemical to make them feel better. They were totally focused on their addiction. This scripture describes how David cried out to God to show him what to do. He would be awake all night pondering or focusing on the promises in God's word. He woke early in the morning, declaring his dependence on God for guidance and rescue. The depth of David's focus is inspiring! Today, take a minute to ponder this thought: every moment we crave our addiction can be a reminder to call out to God instead and focus on His promises.

PRAYER: Lord, thank you for showing me that what we focus on becomes our desire. Focusing on our addictions fuels our desire to get high. When we focus on you, you create a new desire in us for more of you. The more I ponder on these scriptures I am reading, the more desire I feel for you.

Personal Reflections

May 2

Put your hand out and steady me
since I've chosen to live by your counsel.
I'm homesick, GOD, for your salvation;
I love it when you show yourself!
Invigorate my soul so I can praise you well,
use your decrees to put iron in my soul.
And should I wander off like a lost sheep—seek me!
I'll recognize the sound of your voice.

- Psalm 119:173-176

When we are focused on our addictions, we miss them, want more of them, and they call out to us. When addicts can't find drugs, they go into withdrawal. They find a way to get high to steady themselves. They are temporarily invigorated until they crash again. When we focus on God, we want more of Him. Our desire for Him becomes like an addiction, without the negative consequences. Our hunger for His presence drives us to seek Him more and more every day. When He calls out to us, we recognize His voice because we have been spending time with Him. Our relationship grows stronger, and His strength puts iron in our souls, so that we do not waver in our faith when tough times come.

PRAYER: Lord, thank you that you love to call out to me and invigorate me with your love. And there is no crash afterward! I am so grateful your love is permanent and you are always there to steady me when I simply stay focused on you and wait for your comfort.

Personal Reflections

May 3

Those who think they can do it on their own end up obsessed with measuring their own moral muscle but never get around to exercising it in real life. Those who trust God's action in them find that God's Spirit is in them—living and breathing God! Obsession with self in these matters is a dead end; attention to God leads us out into the open, into a spacious, free life. Focusing on the self is the opposite of focusing on God. Anyone completely absorbed in self ignores God, ends up thinking more about self than God.

- Romans 8:5-7

While we may not have issues with addictions to alcohol or drugs, we are all very susceptible to becoming hyper-focused on the instant gratification that addictions offer. Addictions require that we be completely absorbed in self, an obsession that results in totally ignoring God and what God is doing. Performance addiction offers a particularly potent poison; a person who is enslaved to a lifestyle of perfectionism has to be completely self-focused in order to keep up with the incessant demands of the compulsion. Shifting our focus to Jesus is the only way to break the chains. Keeping our attention on God allows Him to create a new desire in us—a desire for Him.

PRAYER: Lord, our only hope is to focus on you and depend on you to create a desire in us that is stronger than the attraction of addictions. Thankfully, this is a promise that you fulfill in anyone who finally gives up on their own willpower and allows you to lead them into a life of freedom from obsession.

Personal Reflections

May 4

When God lives and breathes in you (and he does, as surely as he did in Jesus), you are delivered from that dead life. With his Spirit living in you, your body will be as alive as Christ's!

So don't you see that we don't owe this old do-it-yourself life one red cent. There's nothing in it for us, nothing at all. The best thing to do is give it a decent burial and get on with your new life. God's Spirit beckons. There are things to do and places to go!

- Romans 8:11-14

In all the years of treating addictions, I have heard clients say over and over again that they feel dead inside. Their hyper-focus on self, and their obsession with getting high in order to feel good, yielded nothing but emptiness inside. All their futile efforts gave them no fulfillment whatsoever, and they certainly don't owe their old life one more ounce of effort. Thankfully, if we choose to focus on God, He has a whole new life awaiting His seekers.

PRAYER: Lord, I am so thankful that you live and breathe life into us, just as you did in Christ. To experience your love inside us, showing us a new life, after we have been dead inside for years—this feeling is miraculous. Addicts try to con themselves and others, claiming they have things to do and places to go, when they are only going to get high. Your love allows me to see right through my old addictions. My life was empty then, but now I am giving up my addictions to follow you, and it is amazing!

Personal Reflections

May 5

Anyone, of course, who has not welcomed this invisible but clearly present God, the Spirit of Christ, won't know what we're talking about. But for you who welcome him, in whom he dwells—even though you still experience all the limitations of sin—you yourself experience life on God's terms. It stands to reason, doesn't it, that if the alive-and-present God who raised Jesus from the dead moves into your life, he'll do the same thing in you that he did in Jesus, bringing you alive to himself?

- Romans 8:9-10

How incredible that our limitations don't interfere with being delivered from our dead life. The only thing that would keep us from experiencing this new life is not to welcome Him in. All we need to do is invite God to rescue us from our dead life, and He will bring us to a new life just like He brought Jesus back to life. We will know life on God's terms—ever-abundant, over-flowing—because the Spirit of God Himself is coming to dwell within us.

PRAYER: Thank you so much, Lord, that in spite of all my sin, you love me anyway. No one else is remotely capable of a love like yours. I am not even capable of loving myself in this condition, but I am so happy that you love me just the way I am and have promised to show me a new way to live. Every day, I become a little more alive and a little more aware of your presence. Thank you for making me new.

Personal Reflections

May 6

...God's Spirit is right alongside helping us along. If we don't know how or what to pray, it doesn't matter. He does our praying in and for us, making prayer out of our wordless sighs, our aching groans. He knows us far better than we know ourselves, knows our pregnant condition, and keeps us present before God. That's why we can be so sure that every detail in our lives of love for God is worked into something good.

- Romans 8:26-28

I was taught that how and what I prayed for was critical to my prayers being answered. Of course, I made my prayers performance-based, so I thought when my prayers went unanswered that this was my fault. God is showing me that the quality of my prayer doesn't even matter to him. He only wants me to focus on Him and let Him do all the work, even in my prayer life.

PRAYER: Lord, I am so relieved that my prayers are always answered based on your faithfulness and knowing what's best for me, rather than my efforts. Finally, after so many years, I feel the pressure to perform being lifted off my shoulders. You continue to clear my vision about so many things in life. Thank you again for showing me and instructing me as I continue to read these scriptures.

Personal Reflections

May 7

God knew what he was doing from the very beginning. He decided from the outset to shape the lives of those who love him along the same lines as the life of his Son... After God made that decision of what his children should be like, he followed it up by calling people by name. After he called them by name, he set them on a solid basis with himself. And then, after getting them established, he stayed with them to the end, gloriously completing what he had begun.

- Romans 8:29-30

What commitment God has to each of us who invite Him to run our lives everyday! He never lets us out there on our own. He calls us each by name. We are all special to Him in our own way. He fills our basic needs to feel loved and cared for throughout every day in spite of any circumstance. He talks to us all day long and watches over us at night. He gives us all that and more, as a result of a simple choice on our part to welcome Him into our lives and focus on Him.

PRAYER: Lord, I am amazed more every day how all these scriptures describe in such detail how much you love and care for us and show us how to live. For so many years I read so little of your Word and missed out on so much you wanted to show me. Your Word is becoming more irresistible every day.

Personal Reflections

May 8

When everything was hopeless, Abraham believed anyway, deciding to live not on the basis of what he saw he couldn't *do but on what God said he* would *do...*

Abraham didn't focus on his own impotence and say, "It's hopeless. This hundred-year-old body could never father a child." Nor did he survey Sarah's decades of infertility and give up. He didn't tiptoe around God's promise asking cautiously skeptical questions. He plunged into the promise and came up strong, ready for God...

- Romans 4:18-20

What a relief that I don't have to make myself believe in something I know I can't do. Rather than focus on my impotence, I simply make a choice to shift my focus to what God promises He will do. Through writing down these scriptures, I am making a simple choice to focus on what God says He will do in His Word. You can make the same choice by simply choosing to continue to read these scriptures every day. Go ahead— plunge into the promises!

PRAYER: Lord, with every scripture I have studied so far, you make it so clear that you carry the total burden of working in my life for my good as I simply choose to stay focused on you. You do all the heavy lifting. Thank you, because I have become so worn out from the pressure to perform life on my own. I am so glad you have clearly shown me that it's a good thing to give up on myself and let you carry me.

Personal Reflections

May 9

If you're a hard worker and do a good job, you deserve your pay; we don't call your wages a gift. But if you see that the job is too big for you, that it's something only God can do, and you trust him to do it—you could never do it for yourself no matter how hard and long you worked—well, that trusting-him-to-do-it is what gets you set right with God, by God. Sheer gift.

David confirms this way of looking at it, saying that the one who trusts God to do the putting-everything-right without insisting on having a say in it is one fortunate man...

- Romans 4:4-6

Growing up on a large dairy farm, I learned at a young age how to work hard. I also learned that my work gave me the right to have a say in what I was doing. To admit that the job of life is too big for me, to give up having a say, has taken me a lifetime. Now that this burden has been lifted, I don't even want a say anymore. When I exert effort to control my life, I just mess up His plan for me. Now I just want to praise Him more and more for this precious gift of His willingness to run my life.

PRAYER: Lord, I thank you over and over again for showing me what you could do in me before I ran my life completely into the ground. You are my only hope. I am starting to feel a great sense of anticipation when I think about what you want to do in and through me. What a relief that I am only the vessel and you do all the hard work from beginning to end.

Personal Reflections

May 10

A sight to take your breath away!
Grand processions of people
 telling all the good things of God!

But not everybody is ready for this, ready to see and hear and act. Isaiah asked what we all ask at one time or another: "Does anyone care, God? Is anyone listening and believing a word of it?" The point is: Before you trust, you have to listen. But unless Christ's Word is preached, there's nothing to listen to.

- Romans 10:15-17

My purpose for writing these devotionals is to give everyone something to listen to—something brief and concise so that focus is possible. I know from studying the brain that we only listen when we focus. Every day, I hear over and over again, "does anyone care?" This is my way of caring: giving people scriptures so they have something to listen to, and teaching them how to focus so listening is possible. Keep reading every day and trust will come as God shows you how trustworthy He really is.

PRAYER: Lord, thank you for showing me the steps I need to take to trust in you. I always thought that trust was something I had to try to achieve on my own before I could listen. You have clearly shown me through these scriptures that trust can only come from you as a result of listening to you as I focus on your word. I pray that you show everyone who reads these scriptures this same simple truth.

Personal Reflections

May 11

Say the welcoming word to God—"Jesus is my Master"—embracing, body and soul, God's work of doing in us what he did in raising Jesus from the dead. That's it. You're not "doing" anything; you're simply calling out to God, trusting him to do it for you. That's salvation. With your whole being you embrace God...

- Romans 10:7-10

In our American culture, even in our churches, we are fixers. We pride ourselves in performing well, especially in our Christian walk. But by trying to fix everything in my life, I only broke everything. In the act of receiving salvation, "not doing anything" is only possible through giving up any say-so in life, and calling out to God to do a work in us. And what an amazing work He is willing to do in us! No less than the work He did when he raised Jesus from the dead. What a relief!

PRAYER: Thank you, Father, for your willingness to heal my brokenness and raise me from emotional death. I am so thankful you showed me that I don't need to be doing anything, and gave me permission to stop trying to fix my life. I am so glad my only "job" is to call out your name, ask for your help, and choose to focus on you for my strength every day. Retiring from my performance-based living is such a relief!

Personal Reflections

May 12

As you learn more and more how God works, you will learn how to do your work. We pray that you'll have the strength to stick it out over the long haul—not the grim strength of gritting your teeth but the glory-strength God gives. It is strength that endures the unendurable and spills over into joy, thanking the Father who makes us strong enough to take part in everything bright and beautiful that he has for us.

- Colossians 1:11-12

What a new definition for the concept of work! Here is a definition that's not based on our effort or grit, but on our simple choice to depend on God. When we choose to depend on Him, we invite Him to make us emotionally strong, with a "glory-strength" that far surpasses anything we could achieve on our own. By choosing to thank Him and give Him credit when we could never endure on our own, He gives us the joy to want to fix our eyes on Him through the unendurable.

PRAYER: Lord, I never imagined anyone could give me positive emotional strength to carry me through hard times. I thought I had to work hard to feel good through rough periods in my life. Any effort I put into feeling good only reminded me of how bad I felt. Only you have been able and willing to freely give me the gift of emotional wellbeing in any circumstances. Thank goodness my only part is to depend on you to take care of me.

Personal Reflections

May 13

"Don't weep and carry on." They said this because all the people were weeping as they heard the words of The Revelation.

He continued, "Go home and prepare a feast, holiday food and drink; and share it with those who don't have anything: This day is holy to GOD. Don't feel bad. The joy of GOD is your strength!"

So the people went off to feast, eating and drinking and including the poor in a great celebration. Now they got it...

- Nehemiah 8:9-10,12

Now, I finally understand what the children's song meant by saying: "The joy of the Lord is my strength." Instead of focusing and dwelling on my own misery, I go and share my abundance with the poor, thanking God for how He has taken care of me and enabled me to help others. When I start thanking Him, He brings me His joy, which is my fuel—His strength, energizing me. God even created me with a brain that releases a pleasure chemical through my body when I give Him thanks. Who says God doesn't want us to feel good?

PRAYER: Thank you that you created us with the ability to feel pleasure, and that you want us to feel your joy, which feels better than any natural or chemical high. No matter what we have relied on over the years, your joy is so much more powerful and life-sustaining. You've clearly shown me that, especially during difficult times, I can always count on your joy as fuel to keep me going.

Personal Reflections

May 14

Dear friend, listen well to my words;
   tune your ears to my voice.
Keep my message in plain view at all times.
   Concentrate! Learn it by heart!
Those who discover these words live, really live;
   body and soul, they're bursting with health.
Keep vigilant watch over your heart;
   that's *where life starts.*

- Proverbs 4:20-23

This scripture instructs us to pay very close attention to who our heart says, is if different from what many churches teach when they say that we should never rely on our feelings to make decisions about life. Brain scientists now know that every experience we have in life travels through the feeling center of our brain before it reaches the thinking side. God created our brains to function like this so we have sensory signals to warn us of danger or alert us to pleasure. When these sensory signals are filtered through God's voice and His Word, we discover how to really live.

PRAYER: Lord, thank you for showing me how to ignore all of my thinking and sideshow negativity about life by tuning my ears to your voice and listening closely to learn everything you have to say to me. Also, thank you for your clear recipe in this Proverb for how to combine my sensory signals with your voice so that the road before me is smooth.

Personal Reflections

May 15

Summing it all up, friends, I'd say you'll do best by filling your minds and meditating on things true, noble, reputable, authentic, compelling, gracious—the best, not the worst; the beautiful, not the ugly; things to praise, not things to curse. Put into practice what you learned from me, what you heard and saw and realized. Do that, and God, who makes everything work together, will work you into his most excellent harmonies.

- Philippians 4:8-9

The more I keep God's message in plain view at all times, the more clearly I realize how different His thoughts about my life are from my own running personal commentary in my head, which always seemed to be how terrible things are. These sideshow distractions gripped my thinking, even when life was not terrible. Conditioned to think negatively about my life, I woke up every morning to these thoughts—before I had any clue whether it would be a good day or a bad day. Now I let God's Word and His voice do my thinking for me. What a relief, His words are pure and lovely! Now I wake up sometimes with His thoughts already in place in my mind.

PRAYER: Lord, thank you that my negative self-talk is just a reminder to shift my focus to your thoughts. I am no longer held captive in my own mental prison, dwelling on my negativity. You show me how to keep your message in view. My negative thoughts are still there, but only to remind me to focus on your words.

Personal Reflections

May 16

Be cheerful no matter what; pray all the time; thank God no matter what happens. This is the way God wants you who belong to Christ Jesus to live.

- 1 Thessalonians 5:16-18

God has shown me through writing these devotionals that giving thanks is the catalyst for joy which is the fuel God uses to energize us. This formula to have God's energy in us is so simple, yet so profound—human effort is not part of the equation. In fact, human effort gets in the way and sabotages God performing in us. Our effort only works against what God wants to do in us and through us. God doesn't even want our study of His word to be an effort. He promises to give us a desire (an acquired taste) for His Word when we continually give Him thanks all day long.

PRAYER: Lord, I am so glad your formula to produce your energy in me is so simple. Despite its simplicity, I have spent years trying to improve on your formula. After years of failure, I finally quit trying to have a say-so, and simply want to follow what you say. I feel like I am blindfolded, holding onto your hand for dear life. It's a safe feeling to have my eyes closed as I sense your strong grip on my hand and my sideshow distractions fade away.

Personal Reflections

May 17

Don't be naive. There are difficult times ahead. As the end approaches, people are going to be self-absorbed, money-hungry, self-promoting, stuck-up, profane, contemptuous of parents, crude, coarse, dog-eat-dog, unbending, slanderers, impulsively wild, savage, cynical, treacherous, ruthless, bloated windbags, addicted to lust, and allergic to God. They'll make a show of religion, but behind the scenes they're animals. Stay clear of these people.

- 2 Timothy 3:1-5

We are surrounded by self-focused people, even in the church. I admit I have been a "bloated windbag" my whole life, telling my opinions to everyone who would listen. We can be so full of ourselves and our own thinking. I am sick of my own thinking; it doesn't help me or anyone else. Now I only want to think His thoughts and share what He has to say. God has given me clear instructions to take my focus off myself and all those other self-focused people and only look into His eyes.

PRAYER: Lord, what a relief to be free of all the confusion of self-focused people, especially myself. Now I only want to please you. Living in a world full of puffed-up people, it is easy to follow in the footsteps of those who focus on their own needs, lusts, and opinions, and it is difficult to keep my mind clear to hear your voice. Thank you for clearing my vision for me as I choose to focus on you.

Personal Reflections

May 18

Don't hit back; discover beauty in everyone. If you've got it in you, get along with everybody. Don't insist on getting even; that's not for you to do. "I'll do the judging," says God. "I'll take care of it." Our Scriptures tell us that if you see your enemy hungry, go buy that person lunch, or if he's thirsty, get him a drink. Your generosity will surprise him with goodness. Don't let evil get the best of you; get the best of evil by doing good.

- Romans 12:17-21

Giving thanks every day is the catalyst for receiving the joy of the Lord! This joy becomes strength, penetrating deep into our heart, enabling us to see the beauty in everyone. We don't want to be judgmental anymore, once we experience the freedom to love and be loved. When someone messes up, we feel compassion rather than anger. We want to bless them rather than point out their faults. Be patient, because God's word says experiencing this joy is an acquired taste.

PRAYER: Lord, I pray that everyone who reads these devotionals will acquire a taste for the joy of the Lord. I have never experienced such joy before, or such deep emotional satisfaction. Keep reminding me that giving you thanks is the catalyst that starts this gift of joy. Thank you that I don't have to earn this gift or even feel thankful. Help me to thank give regardless of how I feel and depend on you to provide fuel for my emotional well-being.

Personal Reflections

May 19

So, friends, take a firm stand, feet on the ground and head high. Keep a tight grip on what you were taught, whether in personal conversation or by our letter. May Jesus himself and God our Father, who reached out in love and surprised you with gifts of unending help and confidence, put a fresh heart in you, invigorate your work, enliven your speech.

- 2 Thessalonians 2:15-17

The instructions "take a firm stand" and "keep a tight grip" are not intended for us to try to be strong in our own strength. These instructions simply mean to stay focused on Him by communing with followers of God. When we busy ourselves with thanking God, there is no time for our side-show distractions. As we stay focused, we see how God repeatedly reaches out in love and surprises us with gifts, progressively building our confidence in Him. His unending help puts a fresh heart in us through repeated infusions of hope.

PRAYER: Lord, I am so thankful that building hope is not my job but a gift from you. I repeatedly let myself down, but you repeatedly lift me up, giving me strength to keep my focus on you every day. These daily devotionals have shown me a creative way to stay busy focused on you and to stay out of my own head and my side-show distractions. Thank you for promising to put a fresh heart into me!

Personal Reflections

May 20

But don't let it faze you. Stick with what you learned and believed, sure of the integrity of your teachers—why, you took in the sacred Scriptures with your mother's milk! There's nothing like the written Word of God for showing you the way to salvation through faith in Christ Jesus. Every part of Scripture is God-breathed and useful one way or another—showing us truth, exposing our rebellion, correcting our mistakes, training us to live God's way. Through the Word we are put together and shaped up for the tasks God has for us.

- 2 Timothy 3:14-17

I know that "waiting" has been a key component of embracing that the Lord will clear my vision and that my own efforts to see clearly have been frustrating and futile. However, since I chose to focus on the Lord, I have stopped "waffling" over who runs my life every moment of each day—me or God. Now, I am totally amazed that God talks to me non-stop, continually adjusting and clearing my vision. Though it took me 60 years to learn to listen to His voice, I don't let this faze me. I am so thankful that His message is available to everyone, young and old, who desire to be in an intimate relationship with Him.

PRAYER: Lord, thank you for showing me that your message to focus on you is simple and clear and written for all ages. Thank you for the opportunity to share this message with young and old. Regardless of my age, I am so grateful I finally stopped waffling and yielded my life completely to you.

Personal Reflections

May 21

I remembered the old days,
  went over all you've done, pondered the ways you've
worked,
Stretched out my hands to you,
  as thirsty for you as a desert thirsty for rain.

- Psalm 143:5

These daily devotionals are becoming like a journal of praise and thanks to my heavenly Father. I never in my wildest dreams imagined God would give me such joy from reading and writing the Scriptures. The more God shares with me the closer and closer I feel to Him, and I pray that each of you experience those feelings of closeness with Him as well. The Lord has single-handedly met my need to feel loved and cared for. I "know that I know that I know" that His love and not the law has rescued me in the nick of time. With all my people-pleasing and pressure-to-perform habits I was focused on myself and not Him.

PRAYER: What a relief, Lord, that you have rescued me from myself. I am finding such freedom in wanting you to perform in me. I no longer want any say-so in how to live my life. My natural tendency is still to do things myself and to let my thoughts fill with anxiety, but I am learning that these tendencies are only reminders to shift my focus to you. Lord, please continually remind me of my tendencies to do my daily life without you. I am grateful for your many reminders to shift my focus to you so I can hear your voice.

Personal Reflections

May 22

Forget about self-confidence; it's useless. Cultivate God-confidence. No test or temptation that comes your way is beyond the course of what others have had to face. All you need to remember is that God will never let you down; he'll never let you be pushed past your limit; he'll always be there to help you come through it. So, my very dear friends, when you see people reducing God to something they can use or control, get out of their company as fast as you can.

- 1 Corinthians 10:12-14

acting medications. Despite God's promise that He will never allow us to go through more than we can handle, many of us believe that God does not provide the immediate relief drugs do. We may avoid prayer, reading His word, or going to church, all because we are upset at God for our troubles. Although we often complain that God waits until the last minute to rescue us, typically the problem is that we wait until the last minute before we cry out to Him. God is never slow to action; His timing is perfect. He does answer us in the nick of time, once we give up on our own efforts and call out to Him.

PRAYER: Lord, even though some of my struggles seem to last forever, thank you for providing ongoing, fast-acting relief that brings me joy and pulls me through crises and long ordeals. I am so grateful that you don't expect me to be thankful for the ordeal itself, but that you are 100% reliable to carry me through it.

Personal Reflections

May 23

...If we give up on him, he does not give up—
for there's no way he can be false to himself.

- 2 Timothy 2:13

One of my biggest challenges as a Christian counselor is to answer questions about trust and faith. Almost everyone I work with has serious doubts about their level of trust and faith in God. Most condemn themselves for their lack of trust and faith, and sincerely believe the false-teaching of many churches that lack of trust and faith causes Christians to fail. God says in His Word that measuring our trust and faith has no place in our relationship with Him. He is a trustworthy and faithful God. When He says that if you have the faith of a mustard seed, He will move mountains, God means that if we simply make the choice to put out trust and faith in Him, He will do the rest.

PRAYER: Thank you, Lord, that trust and faith are choices, not feelings or effort-based. Thank you also that when I do choose to put my trust and faith in you every day, that you are faithful to sustain me and fill me with joy in your presence. My experience has shown me that you are completely reliable and trustworthy and have never let me down. While faith is not a feeling, choosing to trust you results in lots of joyful feelings in me when I contemplate your faithfulness.

Personal Reflections

May 24

Be cheerful no matter what; pray all the time; thank God no matter what happens. This is the way God wants you who belong to Christ Jesus to live.

- 1 Thessalonians 5:16-18

People who struggle to believe that focus is a choice, not an effort, often admit that their problem is trying to stop bad habits or behavior. In their attempt to stop, they maintain focus on their problem. It seems to be a universal law that once I hear a noise, I can't stop hearing that noise. Despite my best effort, the noise seems to get louder. I can only stop hearing that noise if a more prominent sound draws my attention somewhere else. Studies show that it takes three seconds for a more pronounced sound, sight, smell, taste, or touch to steal our attention. Our senses make a simple choice to focus on what is more prominent. No effort is required. Likewise, the practice of giving thanks makes God preeminent in our lives. As He becomes our central focus, He provides an endless supply of reminders to draw our attention to Him.

PRAYER: Lord, thank you so much that you will not allow any circumstance to be more prominent than you as long as I choose to give thanks in all things. Your supply of gifts is endless. How you love and care for me draws me closer to you every day. My heart overflows with thanksgiving; you make me feel so special. All you ask is that you have your way in my life as I continually thank you.

Personal Reflections

May 25

He was there before any of it came into existence and holds it all together right up to this moment. And when it comes to the church, he organizes and holds it together, like a head does a body. He was supreme in the beginning and—leading the resurrection parade— he is supreme in the end. From beginning to end he's there, towering far above everything, everyone.

- Colossians 1:16-18

A client recently shared with me that their spouse would "drain the joy out of a rainbow." Many of us struggle with negative thoughts that rob us of joy and emotional energy. I used to teach clients techniques to counter their negative thinking with positive thoughts about themselves, but this was ineffective, both in my practice and in my own life. No matter how hard I tried, I could not overcome my negative self-talk with positivity. Through His Word, God has shown me a whole new therapeutic approach for my clients and myself, which lines up with how He created our brains. When we choose to dwell on God's faithfulness and thank Him for who He is, this draws our attention to Him and away from our negativity.

PRAYER: Lord, the longer I make the simple choice to focus on you, the more I see how impossible it is to miss your captivating presence. Thank you for how prominent your presence is everywhere. You are drawing me closer to you every day. I want to talk to you; I want to read your word. I desire you so much, no effort is required.

Personal Reflections

May 26

*...then he told me, My grace is enough; it's all you need.
My strength comes into its own in your weakness. Once
I heard that, I was glad to let it happen. I quit focusing
on the handicap and began appreciating the gift. It was
a case of Christ's strength moving in on my weakness.
Now I take limitations in stride, and with good cheer,
these limitations that cut me down to size—abuse,
accidents, opposition, bad breaks. I just let Christ take
over! And so the weaker I get, the stronger I become.*

- 2 Corinthians 12:9-10

Over and over again clients tell me that they are trying their best to be strong. They struggle to be strong in their faith, hope, trust, and love. My attempts to be strong have always failed and God is showing me why. He says that He doesn't expect that or even want that from us. He wants us to completely depend on Him for His strength. When we struggle to be strong we are in a battle for control, and we are working against or interfering with His strength. We can only give our focus or individual attention to one person: ourselves or God. He certainly instructs us to focus on Him through thanksgiving.

*PRAYER: Lord, thank you that thanksgiving can focus my heart
on how you love and care for me even during unendurable
times. My natural tendency is to get mad at you for not stopping
my pain, but you have clearly shown me that people's choices,
including my own, cause my pain, while you have always been
faithful to heal my wounded heart.*

Personal Reflections

May 27

Like a woman having a baby,
*   writhing in distress, screaming her pain...*
We writhed in labor but bore no baby...
Nothing came of our labor.
*   We produced nothing living.*
*   We couldn't save the world.*

- Isaiah 26:17-18

We have tried and tried and tried to do things on our own, striving, struggling, pushing, even writhing and screaming, but we got no results except more trouble. This verse paints a vivid picture of our useless struggle. Like a woman exhausted by the agony of labor, unable to bring forth her child, we also are unable to produce life for ourselves. My autopilot is still to push myself and not focus on experiencing God with my five senses. Yet, my only hope is in Him for His endless patience as He teaches me utter dependence on Him.

PRAYER: Lord, remind me to depend upon you and not my own striving. May my struggling be a vivid reminder of vain effort and my need to focus on you. You have created me magnificently, able to see your beauty in the sunrise, hear you in children's laughter, smell you in a fresh cut field, taste you in my favorite meal, feel you against my palm as I hold someone's hand. May I savor each moment as I praise you.

Personal Reflections

May 28

Help, God—the bottom has fallen out of my life!
  Master, hear my cry for help!
Listen hard! Open your ears!
  Listen to my cries for mercy.
I pray to God—my life a prayer—
  and wait for what he'll say and do.
My life's on the line before God, my Lord,
  waiting and watching till morning,
  waiting and watching till morning.

- Psalm 130:1-2,5-6

I can't tell you how many times I have lost hope to the point of hopelessness. Despair hurts so bad that I determine to rebuild my hope, typically by working hard or surrounding myself with new people upon whom to rely. Trying to rely more on myself has resulted in utter failure my entire life, because God simply wants to show me that my hope can only be sustained through Him.

PRAYER: Lord, your teaching about hope is so clear and simple, yet I have missed the point all these years. Culture and church alike have helped me miss the point! Well-meaning Christians place total emphasis on my faith, my hope, my trust. This emphasis derails me from total dependence on you, as I measure my growth in terms of my faithfulness, my hopefulness, and my trustworthiness, instead of yours. Hope, faith, trust, even love—this all belongs to you, and we receive these free gifts with outstretched arms.

Personal Reflections

May 29

Sometimes I ask God, my rock-solid God, "Why did you let me down? Why am I walking around in tears, harassed by enemies?" They're out for the kill, these Tormentors...Taunting day after day, "Where is this God of yours?" Why are you down in the dumps, dear soul? Why are you crying the blues? Fix my eyes on God—soon I'll be praising again. He puts a smile on my face. He's my God.

- Psalm 42:9-11

For years I was taught to thank God for the hurt in my life, because pain would make me stronger. The more I study, the more I learn that man's sin, not God, causes hurt and pain. In His love, God shows me ways to experience His joy in a hurtful situation. My strength doesn't come from my pain, but from the joy of the Lord! So even though I hate to feel pain, I am thankful that God always brings me through seemingly unendurable times. I no longer try to embrace the pain, but rather allow God to embrace me and carry me through the pain.

PRAYER: Lord, as I read more of your message, my appetite for your words only grows stronger. I ask that others who read these devotionals will acquire the same taste for your words you have given me. Now that I have tasted your goodness, I can't imagine how awful I would feel without your Word in my heart each moment of every day. You are my only hope!

Personal Reflections

May 30

I waited and waited and waited for GOD.
At last he looked; finally he listened.
He lifted me out of the ditch,
pulled me from deep mud.
He stood me up on a solid rock
to make sure I wouldn't slip.
He taught me how to sing the latest God-song,
a praise-song to our God.
More and more people are seeing this:
they enter the mystery,
abandoning themselves to GOD.

- Psalm 40:1-3

Growing up on a farm, digging ditches was a chore that never seemed to end. Looking back, my entire life seems like one never-ending chore of digging myself into a huge ditch. The harder I tried to dig myself out, the deeper I got into trouble. My efforts to achieve success in life only resulted in covering myself in dirt. Then, when I finally dug so deep that I couldn't see any light, I called out to the Lord in desperation, and He rescued me!

PRAYER: Thank you, Jesus. I finally quit trying to dig my way through life and you have so lovingly rescued me and pulled me out of the deep mud I was stuck in. I feel you holding onto me when I slip, ensuring that I don't fall back into the ditch of my old ways. I am so thankful that many others are also surrendering their lives to your grace and love!

Personal Reflections

May 31

Open your eyes and there it is! By taking a long and thoughtful look at what God has created, people have always been able to see what their eyes as such can't see: eternal power, for instance, and the mystery of his divine being.

- Romans 1:20

As a child of the 1960s I remember the song so well, "Love is all around me. It is everywhere I go." I enjoy changing the words of the 1960s love song to "God is all around me. He is everywhere I go." Someone recently asked me, "God speaks to everyone in different way, so how do I know what He is saying to me?" I replied that God wants to speak to all of us, all the time, in every way, and if we are listening, we can't miss what He says. God supplies me with a huge library of His words in every venue imaginable. In nature, I am surrounded by a symphony of sights and sounds. He literally invades my thoughts and feelings on a continual basis. I experience Him everywhere.

PRAYER: Lord, thank you for showing me more and more creative ways to focus on you every day. Thank you for drowning out my own negative thoughts and feelings with your thoughts and feelings about me. Although experiencing your continual presence did not seem natural at first, I have acquired a taste for your love, and now I know that I never want to live without you again. You are amazing!

Personal Reflections

June 1

Skilled living gets its start in the Fear-of-GOD, insight into life from knowing a Holy God.

- Proverbs 9:10

For all my clients and readers who are engineers, God is the master engineer who so clearly spells out exact formulas and equations for daily living. God clearly tells us that these formulas and equations are very different from our natural tendencies. He says that following His methods is an acquired taste, but promises that if we listen closely, His instruction will keep us out of trouble, will make our road smooth and will result in us bursting with health. God wants us to be fully aware of our own emotional triggers and side show thought patterns because they are so distinctly different from the thoughts and feelings He gives us when we keep His teaching in plain view.

PRAYER: Lord, for so many years I have complicated my life with my own formulas and equations for living. I have even allowed well-meaning Christian teachers and writers to influence me with their equations and formulas for successful living. Finally, I am paying close attention to your simple, clear-cut instructions. As I acquire more and more of a taste for the simplicity of following you, I marvel at your wisdom and your unconditional love.

Personal Reflections

June 2

It only takes a spark, remember, to set off a forest fire. A careless or wrongly placed word out of your mouth can do that. By our speech we can ruin the world, turn harmony to chaos, throw mud on a reputation, send the whole world up in smoke and go up in smoke with it, smoke right from the pit of hell.

- James 3:5-6

Over and over again I wish I could take back words I say, especially when my words are nasty. Anger or rejection triggers always precede my nasty words and I have never been able to overcome those feelings. What a relief that God doesn't want me to overcome my feelings on my own, but to let them remind me I need Him to rescue me. Thankfully, God always rescues me when I keep His message in plain view and closely listen to His thoughts. He not only gives me His new thoughts and ideas to replace my sideshow distractions, He also attaches new feelings to His instructions that wash away my anger and hurt.

PRAYER: Lord, I never imagined that you would not only think for me but that you would also feel on my behalf. The joy I feel when I follow your instruction is indescribable, and it melts away my ugly feelings that enslaved me for so many years.

Personal Reflections

June 3

GOD'S name is a place of protection—good people can run there and be safe.

- Proverbs 18:10

Some of us acquire a taste for keeping a vigilant watch over our heart and paying close attention to our feelings, and stop our focus at that point by staying stuck on how we feel. God intends for those emotional triggers to remind us to run to Him and what He says. When we stay focused on Him, He gives us new thoughts to dwell on which create new feelings to embrace. We acquire a taste for God when we accept His leading not only at an intellectual level, but start to feel confident in Him at an emotional level. We begin to trust Him to build feelings of desire and drive in Him that we never experienced before.

PRAYER: Lord, not having any say-so in my life is true freedom in you. I have become so weary of my natural tendencies to follow my own direction, and I feel so relieved that you want to run my life. I am grateful you are giving me clear instructions on how to closely follow you. I never imagined the joy that springs out of my thankfulness for how you meet my needs to feel loved and cared for—every moment of every day, in spite of any circumstance, good or bad. Thank you for increasing my confidence in you!

Personal Reflections

June 4

I give you all the credit, GOD—
  you got me out of that mess,
  you didn't let my foes gloat.
GOD, my God, I yelled for help
  and you put me together.
GOD, you pulled me out of the grave,
  gave me another chance at life
  when I was down-and-out.

- Psalm 30:1-3

As a counselor, I often talk to people who have a defeatist attitude about themselves and spend a lot of time in a rut feeling so low. I used to push clients to try to feel better about themselves and improve their attitude. So often, the harder we try the worse we feel. As we focus on our feelings we stay stuck in our own sideshow distractions of how much of a downer we are. Although God instructs us to pay close attention to how we feel, our feelings or emotional triggers are only a reminder of how much we need Him to give us new thoughts and feelings about ourselves. No medication or positive self-talk can yield the powerful results of God's loving care of us, lifting us up and giving us joy as we cling to Him with a thankful heart in all circumstances.

PRAYER: Lord, I pray that these truths would sink into me deeply, and that everyone who reads these devotionals would acquire a taste for how your instructions work. With depression and anxiety reaching epidemic proportions, you are the only answer to our life problems.

Personal Reflections

June 5

What I'm getting at, friends, is that you should simply keep on doing what you've done from the beginning. When I was living among you, you lived in responsive obedience. Now that I'm separated from you, keep it up. Better yet, redouble your efforts. Be energetic in your life of salvation, reverent and sensitive before God. That energy is God's energy, an energy deep within you, God himself willing and working at what will give him the most pleasure.

- Philippians 2:12-13

When I initially read the phrase "redouble your efforts," I cringed, because my efforts have always yielded negative results. The harder I try, the more I fail. God has showed me that "redouble" simply means to spend more and more time in His presence, thank Him continually for everything big and small in my life. My thankfulness is the catalyst for God to release His joy deep within me. This joy is His energy and fuel for my soul that drives my passion for serving Him. Every day I feel more and more spiritually alive as the day progresses even when I grow physically tired toward evening.

PRAYER: Thank you, Lord, that you give me energy to live full of your love, passionate to serve you. You have doubled my desire to give you my full attention. I used to feel guilty for not spending time with you, but now I know that "responsive obedience" means following you out of desire, not out of guilt or obligation.

Personal Reflections

June 6

Keep your eyes straight ahead; ignore all sideshow distractions. Watch your step, and the road will stretch out smooth before you. Look neither right nor left; leave evil in the dust. Dear friend, pay close attention to this, my wisdom; listen very closely to the way I see it. Then you'll acquire a taste for good sense; what I tell you will keep you out of trouble.

- Proverbs 4:25-5:2

The instructions to keep our eyes straight ahead clearly indicates that focus is more intent than just looking. Many of us struggle with being distracted by mental sideshows or background static, similar to radio noise. I have spent most of my life distracted, instead of giving the present moment my full attention. Through uniting these scriptures, God has shown me that He created me with the five senses of touch, taste, smell, sound, and sight to keep my focus straight ahead and not be distracted by my own mental static. Allowing God to use all five of my senses draws my attention away from the right or left, and stretches the road smoothly in front of me.

PRAYER: Thank you, Lord, that after years of only half-listening to you, you have cleared my vision so that I can see what undivided attention to you looks like. You have shown me clearly how to use my sensory focus to follow you. You have also shown me that this full focus is an acquired taste that you are always fine-tuning on my behalf through your creative genius in activating my senses.

Personal Reflections

June 7

Fix this picture firmly in your mind: Jesus, descended from the line of David, raised from the dead. It's what you've heard from me all along. It's what I'm sitting in jail for right now—but God's Word isn't in jail! That's why I stick it out here—so that everyone God calls will get in on the salvation of Christ in all its glory. This is a sure thing:
If we die with him, we'll live with him;
If we stick it out with him, we'll rule with him...

- 2 Timothy 2:8-12

How do we fix a picture firmly in our mind? Certainly not by effort or struggle to remember with the logical side of our mind. We fix a picture firmly in our mind through the sensory side of our brain: sight, sound, smell, touch, and taste. I still vividly recall, without any effort in trying to remember, a graphic Easter sermon from over 20 years ago, by a pastor who described the gruesome death of Christ on the cross. Whenever I need to feel loved and cared for, this sensory memory gives me so much gratitude that my Savior will never forsake me or give up on me.

PRAYER: Lord, I have a lot of powerful memories that have lasted for a lifetime. Thank you for the amazing mind you have created for each of us. I will never forget and always want to fix my mind on your incredible love for me. I cannot contain this feel and am thrilled that you give me so many opportunities to share your love with others.

Personal Reflections

June 8

Repeat these basic essentials over and over to God's people. Warn them before God against pious nitpicking, which chips away at the faith. It just wears everyone out. Concentrate on doing your best for God, work you won't be ashamed of, laying out the truth plain and simple. Stay clear of pious talk that is only talk. Words are not mere words, you know. If they're not backed by a godly life, they accumulate as poison in the soul.

- 2 Timothy 2:14-17

I am living proof that repeating the basic essentials over and over finally brought me to a consistent focus on following Christ, rather than waffling over and over in my own efforts. My own efforts brought me so much anxiety that I was guilty of pious nitpicking that chipped away at my focus and faith in Him. This pious nitpicking wore me out and I finally gave up on myself. Now I only want to experience God in every way possible. I can't stand religious rhetoric anymore. I hate the "should's" and "ought-to's." I want to serve Him and share His love with others simply because He loves me so much.

PRAYER: Lord, I am thankful Your message has all of life's answers and simple how-to instructions to follow on a daily basis. Your instructions are so clear that all I need to do is follow. No questions are needed for further clarification—no nitpicking on what You mean in Your instructions. Your recipes for daily living have very few ingredients and include simple instruction that we can't mess up if we simply focus and follow.

Personal Reflections

June 9

You're going to find that there will be times when people will have no stomach for solid teaching, but will fill up on spiritual junk food—catchy opinions that tickle their fancy. They'll turn their backs on truth and chase mirages. But you—keep your eye on what you're doing; accept the hard times along with the good; keep the Message alive; do a thorough job as God's servant.

- 2 Timothy 4:3-5

My only goal in writing these daily devotionals is to keep His message alive by doing a thorough job of focusing on Him and watching Him clear our vision. My prayer is that by daily focus on the simple and plain truths in His word that those who read these scriptures will not turn to spiritual junk food or catchy opinions that tickle their fancy. I chased mirages for years. I listened to eloquent speakers who were impressed by their own words and not by God's simple plain truth. In our churches, we have tried to be so creative in our efforts to be seeker-sensitive that we have turned our backs on the simple Gospel message.

PRAYER: Lord, thank you so much that your simple message is more seeker-sensitive than any church could ever try to be. Simply by reading your word over and over again and listening to you relate to me, I have discovered how irresistible you are. You have been an acquired taste that has captured my full attention. Thank you that my fancy is now only tickled by you and not by spiritual junk food and catchy opinions.

Personal Reflections

June 10

The first thing I want you to do is pray. Pray every way you know how, for everyone you know. Pray especially for rulers and their governments to rule well so we can be quietly about our business of living simply, in humble contemplation. This is the way our Savior God wants us to live...Eventually the news is going to get out. This and this only has been my appointed work: getting this news to those who have never heard of God, and explaining how it works by simple faith and plain truth.

- 1 Timothy 2:1-7

This scripture offers instructions on how to focus on God. Regardless of whether I am a counselor or a car salesman, my business is to live in humble reflection and share with others what God shares with me. These daily devotionals are simply one of my ways of sharing with others. Eventually, the word will get out that focus on Him is the simple, good way to live. Enjoy the journey and enjoy sharing these devotionals with others.

PRAYER: Lord, I never imagined that you would give me the joy of sharing your word with others. I always thought telling others about you was important but too hard. Of course, I also thought reading your word was too hard. Thank you for showing me the joy of reading your word and sharing it with others. I will never forget the day when you showed me that you will clear my vision and my pressure to clear my own vision was gone.

Personal Reflections

June 11

Gently encourage the stragglers, and reach out for the exhausted, pulling them to their feet. Be patient with each person, attentive to individual needs. And be careful that when you get on each other's nerves you don't snap at each other. Look for the best in each other, and always do your best to bring it out. Be cheerful no matter what; pray all the time; thank God no matter what happens. This is the way God wants you who belong to Christ Jesus to live.

- 1 Thessalonians 5:14-16

I was a straggler until September 6, 2011, and remembering how God lifted me up helps me to be gentle with others. I love the word picture of "pulling them to their feet." People simply need me to help them stand up so they can focus on Him. My part is easy. Through writing these scriptures every day I am just repeating over and over again God's instructions on how to focus: "Pray all the time; thank God no matter what happens." Our continual thanks is the catalyst for His joy that keeps us cheerful even when we are going through unendurable times.

PRAYER: Lord, thank you for lifting me to my feet every morning and holding me throughout the day. I often have thoughts that are negative about myself and my life. Thank you for teaching me to prevent these thoughts from distracting me from you. Thank you for teaching me that they are simply reminders of how much I need you and want you to lift me up throughout each day.

Personal Reflections

June 12

But friends, you're not in the dark, so how could you be taken off guard by any of this? You're sons of Light, daughters of Day. We live under wide open skies and know where we stand. So let's not sleepwalk through life like those others. Let's keep our eyes open and be smart. People sleep at night and get drunk at night. But not us! Since we're creatures of Day, let's act like it. Walk out into the daylight sober, dressed up in faith, love, and the hope of salvation.

- 1 Thessalonians 5:4-8

What an amazing scripture, so loaded with truth! Paul is telling us as believers that our eyes have been permanently opened— so why would we walk around with our eyes closed? He says that the only thing we need to be wise is to keep our eyes opened and focused on God, who continually shows us how to live. When we keep our eyes fixed on Him, we are able to walk around in daylight staying out of trouble because He has dressed us in the outfits of faith, hope, and love.

PRAYER: Lord, thank you so much for keeping life so simple. I only have to open my eyes, and you surround me with constant direction on how to follow you and live life without getting into trouble. The only times I stumble and fall are when I close my eyes and sleepwalk, as if I can't count on you. When I keep my eyes open, you pass on your divine wisdom to me that keeps me focused and positive during the day.

Personal Reflections

June 13

Regarding life together and getting along with each other, you don't need me to tell you what to do. You're God-taught in these matters. Just love one another! You're already good at it; your friends all over the province of Macedonia are the evidence. Keep it up; get better and better at it. Stay calm; mind your own business; do your own job.

- 1 Thessalonians 4:9-11

Focus does not determine our salvation. Jesus' death on the cross and His resurrection from the dead saved us. Our simple acceptance of His death to pay for our sins and our trust in Him to make us holy guarantees our eternal life with Him. We are alive with Him, regardless of whether we keep our eyes open to focus on Him, or keep our eyes closed and sleepwalk through life. Our focus on God is for our benefit, not to impress Him. By reminding each other to focus on Him, and cheering each other on to stay awake and not sleep, we also benefit others, because God doesn't want anyone to be left behind.

PRAYER: Thank you, Lord, that you do not want anyone to perish but for all to have eternal life. Your love alone encourages me to keep my eyes open and see your amazing grace in our lives. The more I focus on you, the more thankful I feel as I watch you in action all day long in the lives of your children. I find myself with the freedom to relax and stay calm in my daily tasks, knowing you are taking care of me.

Personal Reflections

June 14

You paid careful attention to the way we lived among you, and determined to live that way yourselves. In imitating us, you imitated the Master. Although great trouble accompanied the Word, you were able to take great joy from the Holy Spirit!—taking the trouble with the joy, the joy with the trouble.

- 1 Thessalonians 1:5-6

This scripture provides a great description of how focus on God operates at its best. Focus is a simple process of imitating God and others who also imitate Him. In our culture, imitation is devalued. "Original" and "creative" are words that are highly valued. However, trying to be original or innovative in how we run our lives requires a focus and confidence in self, not God. We elevate ourselves and ignore how clearly God shows us how to live. Let me be clear—those who simply want to follow and imitate Christ may experience great trouble. However, we also experience the pure joy He gives us as we closely observe and stick with God.

PRAYER: Lord, your joy in my life has been indescribable since the day when I first began to simply focus on you and your Word. Despite lots of trouble in my life, I feel completely loved and cared for by you every day. The way you always walk and talk with me simply amazes me. You are incredibly creative and always fresh in your love languages toward me. All I want to say is simply thanks.

Personal Reflections

June 15

Because of the Master, *we have great confidence in* you. *We know you're doing everything we told you and will continue doing it. May the Master take you by the hand and lead you along the path of God's love and Christ's endurance.*

- 2 Thessalonians 3:4-5

As a Christian counselor, I have great confidence in my clients to experience success in focus therapy, because I have great confidence in God, the Master. I want to show my clients how to focus on God and let Him take them by the hand. I have no doubts that as long as they let Him keep a firm grip on their hand, the Lord will show them His love and lead them out of pain into healing. No matter who you are, you, too, can pass along these simple but powerful guides to life. When we share these truths with those around us, our own focus on God is sharpened and we see Him even more clearly.

PRAYER: Lord, I am so thankful that you have made my role in the lives of others so clear and simple. I just pass on the detailed, step by step instructions you teach in your word on how to live life each moment of every day. What a privilege to pass on your instructions over and over again to so many people. I am so thankful that what you show me to pass on to others also keeps your teaching fresh in my life every day.

Personal Reflections

June 16

Simon said, "Master, we've been fishing hard all night and haven't caught even a minnow. But if you say so, I'll let out the nets." It was no sooner said than done— a huge haul of fish, straining the nets past capacity... Simon Peter, when he saw it, fell to his knees before Jesus. "Master, leave. I'm a sinner and can't handle this holiness. Leave me to myself." ...Jesus said to Simon, "There is nothing to fear. From now on you'll be fishing for men and women." They pulled their boats up on the beach, left them, nets and all, and followed him.

- Luke 5:5-11

I have been working so hard my entire life and have never felt I could catch a break. Simon experienced the same frustration fishing all night and not getting any results. Yet, the minute he followed the Lord's instructions, he got a huge haul of fish. Since the day I followed the Lord's instructions and began sharing these scriptures, there has been a huge response. God has transformed my life as well as the lives of others, as He shows me that there is nothing to fear.

PRAYER: Lord, with the fear gone, I've discovered the pure joy of fishing for men and women and sharing with them your clear instructions on how to live each day, focused on you. I will continually thank you for clearing my vision and showing me how to live and giving me your words of instructions to teach others.

Personal Reflections

June 17

"No one lights a lamp and then covers it with a washtub or shoves it under the bed. No, you set it up on a lamp stand so those who enter the room can see their way. We're not keeping secrets; we're telling them. We're not hiding things; we're bringing everything out into the open. So be careful that you don't become misers of what you hear. Generosity begets generosity. Stinginess impoverishes."

- Luke 8:16-18

There have been many times where I have been hesitant to share the how-to-live instructions that God is showing me in His word. Even within Christian circles, God's simple instructions to simply focus on Him and not try to perform are not well received. We live in a culture that demands achievement and success, and we attend churches that feature similar standards of performance and self-improvement, coated with spiritual-sounding talk. Yet despite the risk of unpopular teaching, I am not keeping a secret of what God says in His word. I want to bring everything I read out into the open. I want to share what He says with anyone who will listen.

PRAYER: Lord, I am grateful for the desire you have instilled in me to share what you teach in your Word. Your message contains all the answers to life's struggles. Help me not to be a miser with what I hear, but to lavishly pour it out on the people I meet. Help me to be generous with your incredible good news!

Personal Reflections

June 18

"Don't bargain with God. Be direct. Ask for what you need. This is not a cat-and-mouse, hide-and-seek game we're in. If your little boy asks for a serving of fish, do you scare him with a live snake on his plate? If your little girl asks for an egg, do you trick her with a spider? As bad as you are, you wouldn't think of such a thing— you're at least decent to your own children. And don't you think the Father who conceived you in love will give the Holy Spirit when you ask him?"

- Luke 11:10-13

What a promise: that the Lord will give the Holy Spirit when we ask Him! As a child of the King, I know the Holy Spirit resides in me, so why not ask the Holy Spirit to run every second of my life? With my total attention on God, I am discovering that He gives me instructions down to the very last detail of life. He has procured amazing results, despite the fact that I have nothing to give Him. The difference in my life with Him running the show is so dramatic that I gladly give him the credit. My perfectionism has lifted. I feel total freedom in Him.

PRAYER: Lord, even when I mess up, my failures are simply a reminder to turn my focus back to you. No more beating myself up. I am humbly grateful that I can totally rely on you. Lord, keep reminding me that everything in my life, big and small, good or bad, is just an opportunity to thank you for your care.

Personal Reflections

June 19

"I tell you, love your enemies. Help and give without expecting a return. You'll never—I promise—regret it. Live out this God-created identity the way our Father lives toward us, generously and graciously, even when we're at our worst. Our Father is kind; you be kind. Don't pick on people, jump on their failures, criticize their faults—unless, of course, you want the same treatment. Don't condemn those who are down; that hardness can boomerang. Be easy on people; you'll find life a lot easier. Give away your life; you'll find life given back, but not merely given back—given back with bonus and blessing. Giving, not getting, is the way. Generosity begets generosity.".

- Luke 6:35-38

God promises that in Him we can be kind even when we are at our worst. When we experience negative emotions, God instructs us to use those feelings as a reminder to ask Him to give us His joy in the midst of our sour mood. Instead of dwelling on negative thoughts, God instructs us to thank Him, so that we can have His joy to supersede our feelings. That is the only way to be kind to those who treat us unkindly.

PRAYER: Thank you, Lord, that you show us how to be generous and gracious, especially when we don't feel like it. We cannot show others your love on our own, but when we experience your joy, we receive the strength to imitate your love as we focus on you.

Personal Reflections

June 20

Whenever, though, they turn to face God as Moses did, God removes the veil and there they are—face-to-face! They suddenly recognize that God is a living, personal presence, not a piece of chiseled stone. And when God is personally present, a living Spirit, that old, constricting legislation is recognized as obsolete. We're free of it! All of us! Nothing between us and God, our faces shining with the brightness of his face. And so we are transfigured much like the Messiah, our lives gradually becoming brighter and more beautiful as God enters our lives and we become like him.

- 2 Corinthians 3:16-18

Over and over again, scriptures in God's word repeat the basic essential instruction how to live a Christian life: focus on God. Whenever, we turn to face God, He removes the veil and see Him face to face. We see a living, personal presence and feel a living Spirit inside us. Nothing stands between us and God and we are free. We take our focus off our problems by turning to face Him. As we keep our eyes on Him we are transfigured into gradually becoming like Him.

PRAYER: Lord, thank you for this amazing promise that you will transform us into the likeness of Jesus as we follow you. I am so grateful that our only part is to fix our eyes on you. We all have plenty of experience with focus—it's just that we continually focus on the wrongs things. I choose to shift my focus to you.

Personal Reflections

June 21

We couldn't be more sure of ourselves in this—that you, written by Christ himself for God, are our letter of recommendation. We wouldn't think of writing this kind of letter about ourselves. Only God can write such a letter. His letter authorizes us to help carry out this new plan of action. The plan wasn't written out with ink on paper, with pages and pages of legal footnotes, killing your spirit. It's written with Spirit on spirit, his life on our lives!

- 2 Corinthians 3:4-6

When we are face to face with God and He lifts the veil, we couldn't be more sure of what God says to us and shows us what to do. What God says is so different than our self-talk that only God could be saying it. His words are alive—they are written with His spirit, His life on our life. We are covered by Him, so others see Him—not us. What we say we get straight from Him, and we long to share His words with others.

PRAYER: Lord, I have never in my entire life been bold about sharing you until now. This scripture tells me why. I was never sure if it was you or I talking. Staying face-to-face in your presence makes it impossible for me to have a case of mistaken identity. I know you are covering me. What you say to me is so clear and different from what I would say. That certainty makes me want to shout your message from the rooftops. I am so glad you are clearing my vision!

Personal Reflections

June 22

So if you're serious about living this new resurrection life with Christ, act *like it. Pursue the things over which Christ presides. Don't shuffle along, eyes to the ground, absorbed with the things right in front of you. Look up, and be alert to what is going on around Christ—that's where the action is. See things from* his *perspective.*

- Colossians 3:1-2

How do we avoid being distracted by the things right in front of us? It seems so unnatural, especially after many years of not being focused on God. Proverbs says it is an acquired taste to focus on Him. But how? We focus on God through our five senses. We see Him through nature. We experience the sound of His music in our ears. We read and listen to His words over and over again. We feel His special touch in the routine logistics of life, like keeping the red light green when we are running late. We spend time reflecting on how amazing He is through sharing with other followers of Jesus.

PRAYER: Thank you, Lord, for the countless creative ways that you draw our attention to you and distract us from being absorbed with the things right in front of us. Thank you that focus on you solves our obsessing over our current situation. When we take our eyes of our problems and fix them to you, you kindly give us directions to show us what to do and say to take care of everything we have to deal with in life.

Personal Reflections

June 23

Your old life is dead. Your new life, which is your real *life—even though invisible to spectators—is with Christ in God.* He *is your life. When Christ (your real life, remember) shows up again on this earth, you'll show up, too—the real you, the glorious you. Meanwhile, be content with obscurity, like Christ.*

- Colossians 3:3-4

In our old life, we would distract ourselves from all of the things right in front of us through various addictions like food, porn, alcohol and drugs, gambling, shopping, and video games. These were intense, sensory escapes that captured our full attention, but ended up bringing us to the end of our rope. We begged for those escapes to die, but they remained, tugging at our hearts, never bringing us the satisfaction we craved. Slowly we came to realize that these escapes were not real. Our sensory experiences with God are the real thing. He becomes our life—the one we live for every day.

PRAYER: Lord Jesus, thank you that you are our permanent escape from our addictive escapes. Only you can captivate our senses and draw our attention away from these powerful distractions which provide immediate, but only temporary, relief. As we give you our total attention, you freely give us relief.

Personal Reflections

June 24

Let the peace of Christ keep you in tune with each other, in step with each other. None of this going off and doing your own thing. And cultivate thankfulness. Let the Word of Christ—the Message—have the run of the house. Give it plenty of room in your lives. Instruct and direct one another using good common sense. And sing, sing your hearts out to God! Let every detail in your lives—words, actions, whatever—be done in the name of the Master, Jesus, thanking God the Father every step of the way.

- Colossians 3:15-17

How do we give God our full attention? As we give Him our total focus, every detail of our lives—words, actions, thoughts—are done in the name of the Master, Jesus, glorifying Him every step of the way. Rather than going off and doing our own thing, we sing our hearts out to God. Those are real, clear instructions for how to practice sensory focus. We used to give this undivided attention to our addictions. God says that when we give Him that kind of intense focus, He will give us new life.

PRAYER: Lord, now that I am finally giving your Word room in my life and appreciating that you are in charge of everything, I am fascinated how clear your instructions are on how to relate to you. Thank you for these daily opportunities to share your teaching with so many people. Let the peace of God keep us in tune with each other and in step with you. We never want to wander off again and just do our own thing.

Personal Reflections

June 25

Don't tolerate people who try to run your life, ordering you to bow and scrape, insisting that you join their obsession with angels and that you seek out visions. They're a lot of hot air, that's all they are. They're completely out of touch with the source of life, Christ, who puts us together in one piece, whose very breath and blood flow through us. He is the Head and we are the body. We can grow up healthy in God only as he nourishes us.

- Colossians 2:18-19

With God's clear instructions on how to give Him our total, undivided attention, we are no longer slaves to people who try to run our lives, ordering us to bow and scrape and perform to please them. We are free of our people pleasing that was our total focus in our old life. We need only Him to nourish us. Those who needed to try to run our lives were just full of hot air, anyway. Now that Christ, the source of life, has put us together in one piece and has His very breath and blood flowing through us, we can grow up healthy in God.

PRAYER: Thank you for giving us permission not to tolerate anyone breathing down our necks trying to get us to perform better for them. Thanks for showing us that they are completely out of touch with your word and you, the source of life. They are never worth our attention. They just give the illusion of being pious and humble and ascetic. They are just showing off themselves. We want to show off who you are.

Personal Reflections

June 26

"Are you tired? Worn out? Burned out on religion? Come to me. Get away with me and you'll recover your life. I'll show you how to take a real rest. Walk with me and work with me—watch how I do it. Learn the unforced rhythms of grace. I won't lay anything heavy or ill-fitting on you. Keep company with me and you'll learn to live freely and lightly.".

- Matthew 11:28-30

Throughout all my years of employment, I remember when I got a new job how much I liked the initial two weeks of job preparation of just watching. Then I became anxious when I had to start performing on the job every day, and my boss evaluated me. This scripture shows us that our entire work for the Lord is walking with him while we watch Him do all the performing in our lives and others. No wonder He says you can live freely and lightly. No wonder He says that when you get tired and worn out from performance based religion that we can get away with Him and rest.

PRAYER: Lord, I am so thankful you teach us the unforced rhythms of grace as we walk with you and watch your handiwork. I am grateful that I no longer feel like I have to keep forcing myself to try harder at life every day. No wonder I was so worn out and tired. I can finally recover my life knowing that you promise not to lay anything heavy or ill-fitting on me.

Personal Reflections

June 27

Watch out for people who try to dazzle you with big words and intellectual double-talk. They want to drag you off into endless arguments that never amount to anything. They spread their ideas through the empty traditions of human beings and the empty superstitions of spirit beings. But that's not the way of Christ. Everything of God gets expressed in him, so you can see and hear him clearly. You don't need a telescope, a microscope, or a horoscope to realize the fullness of Christ, and the emptiness of the universe without him. When you come to him, that fullness comes together for you, too. His power extends over everything.

- Colossians 2:8-10

How simple our work is in our relationship with God. When we keep our watch steadfastly on Him, there is nothing to figure out or achieve. We don't need to buy special tools to try to see Him better. By continually watching Him with all five of our senses we can see and hear Him clearly. At the same time, by giving Him our undivided attention, we are able to avoid people who try to dazzle us with big words and intellectual double-talk.

PRAYER: Lord, once again your scripture repeats the same instructions. I am grateful they are so simple and clear. I am grateful that my only job is to watch. I had become so tired and worn out trying to figure out and achieve in life. You have given me such clear permission to simply watch and rest in you.

Personal Reflections

June 28

Every time you cross my mind, I break out in exclamations of thanks to God. Each exclamation is a trigger to prayer. I find myself praying for you with a glad heart. I am so pleased that you have continued on in this with us, believing and proclaiming God's Message, from the day you heard it right up to the present. There has never been the slightest doubt in my mind that the God who started this great work in you would keep at it and bring it to a flourishing finish on the very day Christ Jesus appears.

- Philippians 1:3-6

In yesterday's scripture, we found out that when we keep company with God we learn to live freely and lightly. In our culture, we are taught that living freely and lightly is what we do only on vacations. In today's scripture, Paul says that as we walk with God and watch him perform in our lives we can depend on Him to keep at this great work He began in us until He brings us to a flourishing finish when Christ appears.

PRAYER: Thank you, Lord, for your promise that I can rest in you every day, not just relax when I am on vacation. Your commitment to keep at your work in me until the day Christ appears is a dedication and commitment that I never imagined was possible in my life. Your promise to give me a great finish inspires me to walk with you and watch you more closely than ever before.

Personal Reflections

June 29

Pray diligently. Stay alert, with your eyes wide open in gratitude. Don't forget to pray for us, that God will open doors for telling the mystery of Christ, even while I'm locked up in this jail. Pray that every time I open my mouth I'll be able to make Christ plain as day to them. Use your heads as you live and work among outsiders. Don't miss a trick. Make the most of every opportunity. Be gracious in your speech. The goal is to bring out the best in others in a conversation, not put them down, not cut them out.

- Colossians 4:2-6

I continue to be amazed that so many scriptures repeat the same basic instructions on how to live. Stay alert with your eyes wide open is simply another instruction about focus with all of our five senses. When we focus intently on Him, we are filled with gratitude. When we feel so thankful to God we can't help but being gracious in our speech and bringing out the best in others, not putting them down or cutting them out.

PRAYER: Lord, thank you for showing us your life secrets. Because of our insecurities, many of us are naturally impatient in our relationships with others. We don't make the most of every opportunity to make you known to others. I have learned through writing these devotionals that it takes no effort to share your love. I long to share your love with others because I am so grateful for how you are changing me.

Personal Reflections

June 30

Don't lie to one another. You're done with that old life. It's like a filthy set of ill-fitting clothes you've stripped off and put in the fire. Now you're dressed in a new wardrobe. Every item of your new way of life is custom-made by the Creator, with his label on it. All the old fashions are now obsolete. Words like Jewish and non-Jewish, religious and irreligious, insider and outsider, uncivilized and uncouth, slave and free, mean nothing. From now on everyone is defined by Christ, everyone is included in Christ.

- Colossians 3:9-11

When we give God all of our attention, He strips off our old clothes, burns them, and dresses us in a whole new wardrobe—uniquely designed just for us, and stamped with His label, letting others know this is God, not us. To feel that I am totally defined by Him is much more than just a boost in confidence—even more than a total makeover. I feel like I have a whole new life ahead of me, without the pressure of how to live that life, because God is running my life now. I am going along for the ride, abiding in Him for this new life of love.

PRAYER: Lord, I feel like a stranger to my old self, and I am thankful, because I never liked my old self very much. I really like the brand new wardrobe you've given me: compassion, kindness, strength. I know these qualities are your gifts to me, because I have never been able to achieve those characteristics on my own.

Personal Reflections

July 1

May God our Father himself and our Master Jesus clear the road to you! And may the Master pour on the love so it fills your lives and splashes over on everyone around you, just as it does from us to you. May you be infused with strength and purity, filled with confidence in the presence of God our Father when our Master Jesus arrives with all his followers.

- 1 Thessalonians 3:11-13

God's love fills my life with confidence, as long as I maintain a steadfast focus on Him. For all the many years I ran my own life, my confidence level was high after I performed well and low after I performed poorly. I was like a yo-yo. Now that I totally depend on God to run my life, I am confident in Him never to fail me. I have discovered that He is always dependable and never lets me down. My only down moments occur when I take my eyes off Him. I quickly get nervous and uncomfortable. However, my moments of worry are now a reminder to put my focus back on Him. I no longer get mad at myself when I have moments of insecurity.

PRAYER: Lord, thank you for showing me that my worries and insecurities are opportunities to run to you, not invitations to feel sorry for myself. I feel completely confident in your ability to run my life every single moment of the day. I have acquired a strong taste and desire to depend on you. I no longer want to run my life like I used to before you cleared my vision.

Personal Reflections

July 2

One final word, friends. We ask you—urge is more like it—that you keep on doing what we told you to do to please God, not in a dogged religious plod, but in a living, spirited dance. You know the guidelines we laid out for you from the Master Jesus.

- 1 Thessalonians 4:1-3

Most of my Christian life, since I was saved at age 13, has been spent trying to please God in a dogged religious plod. I was taught by my religious leaders that pleasing God was based on my performance. Despite my best efforts, for many years I have felt like a failure. Since last fall, when God inspired me to begin writing these daily scriptures, I have discovered that God's Word says something very different than what I was taught for many years. I was in fact taught the opposite of what His Word says. I was wrongly taught that His love is not about our feelings but about what we know. Yet, His word plainly emphasizes over and over again that we experience His love through our five senses.

PRAYER: Thank you, Lord, for clearing my vision and showing me that you intend for us to please you through a living, spirited dance. Since I was never taught how to dance, I am so relieved that my heart-dance can be just as pleasing to you as physical dancing. I will dance through my life with joyful abandon in honor of you!

Personal Reflections

July 3

Meanwhile, we've got our hands full continually thanking God for you, our good friends—so loved by God! God picked you out as his from the very start. Think of it: included in God's original plan of salvation by the bond of faith in the living truth. This is the life of the Spirit he invited you to through the Message we delivered, in which you get in on the glory of our Master, Jesus Christ.

- 2 Thessalonians 2:13-14

I have been thanking God more in the past six months than I did throughout my first 60 years, even though during the past six months I have encountered some of the most difficult circumstances in my life. While I don't thank God for my circumstances, I continually thank Him for getting me through these difficulties. I give God all the credit for my thankful heart because He has cleared my vision and showed me what it means to totally focus on Him with my five senses. I see a strong correlation between my focus on Him and my new, thankful heart.

PRAYER: Lord, I am so thankful when I feel your loving hand leading me through turbulent waters. Even when I close my eyes, afraid to look at my circumstances, I know you won't lose your firm grip on my hand. This dependence on you refreshes my heart to understand the truth of your Word, which declares that I am loved by you, picked out for your own from the start. Thank you for the life I have by your Spirit.

Personal Reflections

July 4

So, friends, take a firm stand, feet on the ground and head high. Keep a tight grip on what you were taught, whether in personal conversation or by our letter. May Jesus himself and God our Father, who reached out in love and surprised you with gifts of unending help and confidence, put a fresh heart in you, invigorate your work, enliven your speech.

- 2 Thessalonians 2:15-17

These verses certainly confirm that God is our energy source. When we focus on Him and keep a tight grip on what He says to us in conversation and through His word, we see how He reaches out to us in love and surprises us with unending help and confidence. He even puts a fresh heart in us, which invigorates our work and enlivens our speech. God gives us daily, fresh passion to live our day. In medication terms, what an amazing antidepressant! He brings to life my sense of sight, sound, smell, taste, and touch. I feel His presence with all of my senses as He manifests His love everywhere.

PRAYER: Lord, without you I would feel cold and lifeless. I have never been able to feel positive about my life, no matter how hard I tried. I am so thankful I don't have to try anymore. You give me a fresh start every day, and you build my energy throughout the day so that I feel more alive in my heart at the end of the day, even though I am physically tired.

Personal Reflections

July 5

Tell those rich in this world's wealth to quit being so full of themselves and so obsessed with money, which is here today and gone tomorrow. Tell them to go after God, who piles on all the riches we could ever manage—to do good, to be rich in helping others, to be extravagantly generous. If they do that, they'll build a treasury that will last, gaining life that is truly life.

- 1 Timothy 6:17-19

For most of my life, I tried really hard to do good, help others, and be generous. But my obsessive focus on making money in order to be generous was really a product of my self-focus and desire to prove success to others. Because my focus was on myself, and because I was trying to please myself by pleasing others, my plan backfired. I wasn't pleased with myself, and neither were the people around me. Now, I see that when I go after God, He accomplishes good through me, doing all the work of helping others and being generous. He has given me freedom from my pressure to perform and please others.

PRAYER: Lord, thank you for keeping your instructions on how to live so simple. Thank you for reminding us that we can never please others on our own strength. Letting go of control and just being a vessel so you can do your work through me is such a relief from the bondage of people-pleasing. Thank you for releasing me from having to prove myself.

Personal Reflections

July 6

And so this is still a live promise. It wasn't canceled at the time of Joshua; otherwise, God wouldn't keep renewing the appointment for "today." The promise of "arrival" and "rest" is still there for God's people. God himself is at rest. And at the end of the journey we'll surely rest with God. So let's keep at it and eventually arrive at the place of rest, not drop out through some sort of disobedience.

- Hebrews 4:8-11

Our modern-day culture emphasizes life-goals of performance and achievement and lots of hard work. Maybe we want to relax after years of hard work and making lots of money . . . but rest? What does that word mean? Our culture even says to play hard, to compete and to win. God gives us a very unique goal in our relationship with Him. He wants us to keep at our focus on Him until He leads us to the place of rest. He challenges us not to drop out through some sort of disobedience. In other words, don't disobey Him through taking our eyes off Him and focusing on something else.

PRAYER: Lord, thanks for making it clear that our disobedience is taking our eyes off you. When we focus on anything other than you, that is what gets us into trouble. The list of distractions is endless—even "good" things can be our idols. Thank you for making your instructions so simple. If we closely focus and follow you, you will never lead us into trouble.

Personal Reflections

July 7

My dear friends, if you know people who have wandered off from God's truth, don't write them off. Go after them. Get them back and you will have rescued precious lives from destruction and prevented an epidemic of wandering away from God.

- James 5:19-20

My deep desire is that precious lives will be rescued through these daily scriptures. This is the way God has shown me to go after those who have wandered off and lost their way. This is also a major way that God keeps me focused on Him. The way God rescued me and did not write me off gives me compassion and patience for others who have lost focus. To read that the numbers of people losing focus and wandering away from God has reached epidemic proportions inspires me even more to follow Christ's plan for me to treat this epidemic.

PRAYER: Lord, show me what I can do as part of your master plan to deal with this epidemic of people losing focus on you. Lord, I thank you every day for making me one of your servants to reach others who have lost sight of you. I pray that those who read these scriptures will be inspired to share your plan of rescuing all those who have wandered away from you. Their lives are so precious in your sight, and I know you do not desire even a single one of us to be lost. Thank you for your grace and mercy!

Personal Reflections

July 8

We who have run for our very lives to God have every reason to grab the promised hope with both hands and never let go. It's an unbreakable spiritual lifeline, reaching past all appearances right to the very presence of God where Jesus, running on ahead of us, has taken up his permanent post as high priest for us, in the order of Melchizedek.

- Hebrews 6:18-20

Wow! What a guarantee . . . unbreakable! When we focus on God and run for our very lives to Him, there is no reason not to grab the promised hope with both hands and never let go. This running to Him is not an exercise in physical speed but a desperate emotional need that says, "I cannot go on for another second in life without clinging to my Lord and Savior." Many of us have experienced moments of hanging onto God for dear life. Only when we cling onto Him all the time is the promise fulfilled that God is an unbreakable spiritual lifeline.

PRAYER: Thank you, Lord for clearing my vision that clinging to you is not an act of my will or strength but an experience of emotional longing and neediness. I need you so badly that I don't want to live another minute without you. I don't hold onto you because I am supposed to, I hold onto you because I can't go on another day without a constant heartfelt connection with you. That is the definition of a spiritual lifeline and I am so grateful that you made it unbreakable.

Personal Reflections

July 9

God's Word is better than a diamond,
*　better than a diamond set between emeralds.*
You'll like it better than strawberries in spring,
*　better than red, ripe strawberries.*
There's more: God's Word warns us of danger
*　and directs us to hidden treasure.*
Keep me from stupid sins,
*　from thinking I can take over your work;*
Then I can start this day sun-washed,
*　scrubbed clean of the grime of sin.*

- Psalm 19:10-13

Many of us have wandered away from His word, and the psalmist says there is no possibility of finding our way without reading God's road map. I am not suggesting that we read His word out of obligation, but so we can reap the benefits. Through His word, God will warn us of danger, direct us to hidden treasures, and keep us from stupid sins of arrogance. We can start every day scrubbed free of the nasty dirt of sin; we can enjoy smells and tastes that are even better than red, ripe strawberries; we can see clearer than cut diamonds; we can end up feeling more precious than an emerald ourselves!

PRAYER: Lord, thank you that when I read your word, you show me how focusing on you through reading your word brings my five senses alive. I know that trying to read your word just because I think I should never works, because I focus on my own performance rather than enjoying how you perform in me. Please continue to show me the beauty of your word, more precious than diamonds!

Personal Reflections

July 10

Are you hurting? Pray. Do you feel great? Sing. Are you sick? Call the church leaders together to pray and anoint you with oil in the name of the Master. Believing-prayer will heal you, and Jesus will put you on your feet. And if you've sinned, you'll be forgiven—healed inside and out.

- James 5:13-15

What clear, concise instructions God gives us to rescue those who have wandered off. Pray, sing, and allow others to minister in Jesus' name. No expectations to perform or achieve. Just be ready to receive, and Jesus will deliver. He will do the performing in those who have wandered of as we share with them. We are the messengers who bring the instructions for how to focus on Him and trust Him to save us. Fortunately, as we read God's word, He gives the same instructions over and over again to keep our part clear and simple to follow. Isn't it amazing that when we trust in God, that simple trust has the power to deeply heal us and those around us?

PRAYER: Lord, thank you for these instructions that remind us that we don't need a Ph.D. to share you with others. Even the verse that says "a believing prayer will heal you" doesn't mean we have to have supernatural faith to be healed of our shame or depression, or to help others with their own heart sicknesses. Too often, we feel pressure to think of something wise to share to make others believe, but all we have to do is focus on you and let you perform through us.

Personal Reflections

July 11

God makes a huge dome
  for the sun—a superdome!
The morning sun's a new husband
  leaping from his honeymoon bed,
The daybreaking sun an athlete
  racing to the tape.
That's how God's Word vaults across the skies
  from sunrise to sunset,
Melting ice, scorching deserts,
  warming hearts to faith.

- Psalm 19:4-6

The psalmist uses sensory words here to remind us again to enjoy God's Word, not struggle or labor as we read. God is too magnificent to ignore. As long as I focus on Him, God is too vast to miss as His words vault across the skies. His words are so hot that they melt ice and scorch the desert. His words are so alive they bring our dead hearts to life and faith in Him.

PRAYER: Lord, thank you that your love shines through your word more brightly than the morning sun. You even warm us to faith, letting us know that you alone (not our efforts to be positive) are the author of faith. Sometimes, even in the darkest nights, our faith in you shines the brightest because you are our only hope, our only joy, our only friend. Thank you, Jesus.

Personal Reflections

July 12

God's glory is on tour in the skies,
God-craft on exhibit across the horizon.
Madame Day holds classes every morning,
Professor Night lectures each evening.
Their words aren't heard,
their voices aren't recorded,
But their silence fills the earth:
unspoken truth is spoken everywhere.

- Psalm 19:1-4

Reading these verses heightens our sensory awareness and focus on God through the silence of nature, which can speak louder than sound. The light and dark in the skies instruct us day and night on how to feel God's presence without even speaking. God created His creation to be this amazing so that He could speak to us through sights, smells, taste and touch. Not hearing any noise brings our other four senses alive. How brilliant is God's formation of our senses! Because He made us this way, we can experience Him now in an intense way and not be inclined to wander away from Him anymore.

PRAYER: Lord, these verses can teach us how reading your word can be so powerful in drawing us to you. The magnetic force of your word overcomes our natural tendency to wander off. We simply are given the freedom of choice to read your word or join the epidemic of wanderers who stray as they skip your word. May all of us who desire your word more and more every day testify to those who still wander.

Personal Reflections

July 13

The revelation of GOD is whole
and pulls our lives together.
The signposts of GOD are clear
and point out the right road.
The life-maps of GOD are right,
showing the way to joy.
The directions of GOD are plain
and easy on the eyes.
GOD'S reputation is twenty-four-carat gold,
with a lifetime guarantee.
The decisions of GOD are accurate
down to the nth degree.

- Psalm 19:7-9

God's instructions through His word are not only plain and clear; they come with a lifetime warranty. In our world where change is constant, God's word remains the same. His revelation through scripture is whole and complete and does not ever need a single alteration. They are tried and true to the nth degree. Thank God for instructions easy on our eyes and plain to see. In a complex, confusing world, God's word provides a life-map that points out the right road.

PRAYER: Lord, thank you for your promise that I won't mess up as long as I maintain my focus on you. Now that I've tried and failed so many times, I am grateful that I don't have to figure anything out. Continue to clear my vision as I focus on you.

Personal Reflections

July 14

A hostile world! I call to GOD,
 I cry to God to help me.
From his palace he hears my call;
 my cry brings me right into his presence—
 a private audience!

- Psalm 18:6

This one verse is worth an entire book of words. To be able to feel and experience a private audience with God in a hostile world is life-changing. Once we experience what it feels like to cry out to Him and sense His immediate presence, we are never the same. It's not that we become self-confident. We simply feel secure in His loving embrace. We want to rest in His arms. We want to stay in His presence. Then He really takes our relationship to a new level when He shows us we can feel His touch even when we have to concentrate at work or focus on meeting the needs of others. He talks to us the whole time. He never lets go. Even for those of us who can't multi-task, God handles the task of letting us know we can stick close to Him while we go about our daily business.

PRAYER: Lord, thank you for giving me a private audience and your undivided attention. You make me feel special in a way that is not humanly possible. Hold me tight, never let me go. I depend on you now for even silly little things. I love how you remind me in those small details how important I am to you.

Personal Reflections

July 15

What a God! His road
  stretches straight and smooth.
Every GOD-direction is road-tested.
  Everyone who runs toward him
Makes it.

- Psalm 18:30

One simple verse, with such a clear, powerful guarantee. Are you tired of not making it? Have the day-to-day hardships of life worn you out? God knows we have no self-sustaining energy left. He knows we are dead on our feet. He urges us to run to Him, not with our own energy (we have none left), but in desperation as we quit on ourselves. When we give up and quit trying to make it on our own, that's when He can step in and save us. He wants us to surrender so we will want to run to Him and let Him carry us. The road back to Him stretches straight and smooth before you and me and every weary traveler. And the road is paved with this promise: that everyone who runs to Him will make it. Everyone who runs to Him will up end in His arms.

PRAYER: Lord, even though it seems so wrong to give up, I am so grateful that quitting on myself is a necessary beginning to a whole new life, completely dependent on you for everything. What I say, what I do, even how I feel. I am so tired of me. I welcome you with open arms to be my dwelling place and live my live for me. I choose to focus on you. I simply want to abide in you and thank you as you run my life with your joy and strength in me.

Personal Reflections

July 16

From the four corners of the earth
   people are coming to their senses,
   are running back to God.
Long-lost families
   are falling on their faces before him.
God has taken charge;
   from now on he has the last word.

                           - Psalm 22:27-28

These verses are such an inspiration for me to keep writing devotionals about focusing on God. When we focus on Him, we want Him to have the last word. For years I waffled on my focus because I wanted the final word. But when I grew tired of wandering and insisting on my own way, I welcomed God taking over. Now, I just want to share with others what He has shown me. People are so hungry for God, and most of them don't even know that it is Him they want so desperately. There was a time when I had no idea what would fill the gaping hole inside of me, but then I came to my senses and ran to God. It is so encouraging to know that people all over the world can run back to Him simply by focusing on Him.

PRAYER: Lord, the world provides so many appealing distractions to entice us to wander away from you. However, our wandering always results in self-destruction, so we can count on people from all over the world wanting to run back to you. Help us to spread the word about your grace far and wide to the four corners of the earth, as we read and share these scriptures on focus. Spread these scriptures on focus far and wide to the four corners of the earth.

Personal Reflections

July 17

Your beauty and love chase after me
every day of my life.
I'm back home in the house of God
for the rest of my life.

- Psalm 23:6

It is so reassuring that as we run back to God, He runs toward us and chases us with His beauty and love. What is most amazing is that God can chase us from every direction because His beauty and love are everywhere. However, we only notice Him chasing us when we focus on Him. How simple, yet how rewarding! The best news of all is that He chases us every day, pursuing our hearts no matter what we are doing or thinking or saying, whether we are having a good day or a bad one. When we falter and lose focus, we can simply turn back to Him and He is all around us everywhere, inviting us back into His arms.

PRAYER: Lord, thank you for another powerful stand-alone verse in your scriptures. I am especially thankful that you chase after everyone, not just a few of us. Thank you that you are not willing that any of us should perish. You desire that everyone run to you. Not only that, but we have the promise that when we die, you will welcome us into our safe house in you for all eternity. With such great news at our fingertips, you make the job of sharing your love with others simple and easy. Everyone needs to read these scriptures and hear what you have to say!

Personal Reflections

July 18

From now on every road you travel
Will take you to God.
Follow the Covenant signs;
Read the charted directions.

- Psalm 25:10

This verse is another stand-alone message that says it all. Since God chases us from all directions, every road will take us to Him as long as we follow His written word (charted directions). In His word, He clearly tells us how to get to Him. All of His road signs gives us the same, simple instructions on how to focus on Him. He never makes us take a detour because of reconstruction, and His simple, clear signs, never fade, never wear out, and never even need a little bit of touch-up paint. He is directing each of us individually, guiding us in our own personal lives. Through His word, we can teach others to follow the signs, the maps, and the charts, and to listen to His personal directions, so that we can all travel towards God together.

PRAYER: Lord, we are so grateful that your directions never, ever change. We are glad that wherever we lost our way, all roads lead back to you when we choose to follow the same simple instructions all around us. You make it so simple to focus on you once we make that choice. No mystery, no secret shortcuts, you give all of us the same exact road-map making it so simple to share your way with each other.

Personal Reflections

July 19

My question: What are God-worshipers like?
Your answer: Arrows aimed at God's bull's-eye.

They settle down in a promising place;
Their kids inherit a prosperous farm.

God-friendship is for God-worshipers;
They are the ones he confides in.

If I keep my eyes on GOD,
I won't trip over my own feet.

- Psalm 25:12-15

We only worship what we focus on with our undivided attention. Many of us worship the countless addictions. This scripture gives us a creative view of how to focus so intently that we are worshiping. Anyone who has mastered target shooting with the bow and arrow knows the importance of a single line to view the bull's eye without any other sensory distractions like noise or sudden movements. When we have our arrow aimed at God, who wants to be our bull's eye, we become the ones He confides in and shares His instructions on how to live.

PRAYER: Lord, what a promise that you won't let us trip over our own feet as long as we keep our eyes on you. Some of us have tripped over our own feet our entire lives before we became desperate for you and chose to follow the instructions in your word. Now we can settle down in your house of rest and look forward to our rich inheritance in heaven with you.

Personal Reflections

July 20

Keep watch over me and keep me out of trouble;
Don't let me down when I run to you.

Use all your skill to put me together;
I wait to see your finished product.

- Psalm 25:20-21

This scripture provides instructions that seem totally counter-intuitive in our culture today. We never wait for anything, and we are constantly striving to stay out of trouble by our own efforts. In God's eyes, there is a guaranteed outcome to refusing to wait on Him and taking things into our own hands. God knows that trouble is guaranteed whenever we try to run our own lives. Our only hope for staying out of trouble is to run to Him. We are scared. That is why we beg God to watch over us and to use all His skill to put us together. Rather than take over ourselves when we feel inpatient, we stay focused as we keep depending on Him and waiting for His finished product. We know that He will never let us down.

PRAYER: Lord, it has taken many years for me to learn to stop trying to take over whenever I became impatient, even though I got in trouble every time. Thank you for showing me that the secret to trust is to keep reading your word, because your scriptures are loaded with reminders that the key is to stay focused on you, believing your promises. Thank you for these many reminders.

Personal Reflections

July 21

Blessed be GOD—
he heard me praying.
He proved he's on my side;
I've thrown my lot in with him.
Now I'm jumping for joy,
and shouting and singing my thanks to him.
GOD is all strength for his people,
ample refuge for his chosen leader;
Save your people
and bless your heritage.
Care for them;
carry them like a good shepherd.

- Psalm 28:6-9

I overheard a customer in a store tell the clerk that God must have been on her side today. This scripture reassures us that he is on our side every day and carries us like a good shepherd. God doesn't just help us to walk—God literally carries us. He becomes our refuge. When we experience that kind of strength from God, we are filled with so much of His joy that we shout and sing our thanks to Him. In scripture after scripture, we see these three words tied together: thanks, joy and strength.

PRAYER: Lord, I am so thankful you keep repeating the same simple instructions over and over throughout the Bible. Your repetition is an amazing key to staying focused on you. I love the simplicity of your instructions. A big part of falling in love with reading your word is seeing how clear you make everything. Thank you for hearing my prayers and giving me the gift of joy and strength in you.

Personal Reflections

July 22

I bless GOD every chance I get;
my lungs expand with his praise.

I live and breathe GOD;
if things aren't going well, hear this and be happy:

Join me in spreading the news;
together let's get the word out.

- Psalm 34:1-3

These instructions on how to be happy are as clear and simple as anyone could ever ask for. They tell us how to be happy even when things aren't going well. Instructions:

1. Bless God every chance you get,
2. Bombard God with praise,
3. Live and breathe God, and
4. Join together with other God-praisers in spreading the news of His love and faithfulness.

These simple things can make even a bad day better, and shine the light of hope on even the darkest shadows. When we bless God every chance we get, our very being expands to be able to live and breathe God.

PRAYER: Lord, now I know the secret to the happiness that you give! When I thank you and praise you all the time even for small details, when I have been spreading the news and getting the word out about your great goodness, that is when I am truly happy. I now know that I have come to the point where can I live and breathe you even in the midst of trouble.

Personal Reflections

July 23

Look at him; give him your warmest smile.
Never hide your feelings from him.

When I was desperate, I called out,
and GOD got me out of a tight spot.

GOD'S angel sets up a circle
of protection around us while we pray.

Open your mouth and taste, open your eyes and see—
how good GOD is.
Blessed are you who run to him.

Worship GOD if you want the best;
worship opens doors to all his goodness.

- Psalm 34:5-9

Somewhere along the way, traditional Christian teaching gave the opposite of these instructions in Psalm 34. We have been incorrectly taught to control our feelings in our relationship with God as if feelings are inherently evil and would get us in trouble. God created our feelings for the purpose of worshiping Him. He created our feelings so we could see and taste His love, not just know of His love intellectually. A close, intimate relationship with God opens a door to experiencing all His goodness!

PRAYER: Thank you, Lord, for revealing in this passage how to feel close to you and experience your goodness. This closeness frees us from our anxious fears and allows us to cling to your unconditional love. We can only feel completely safe with our eyes fixed on you as we continually run to you.

Personal Reflections

July 24

This is the core of our preaching. Say the welcoming word to God—"Jesus is my Master"—embracing, body and soul, God's work of doing in us what he did in raising Jesus from the dead. That's it. You're not "doing" anything; you're simply calling out to God, trusting him to do it for you. That's salvation. With your whole being you embrace God setting things right, and then you say it, right out loud: "God has set everything right between him and me!"

- Romans 10:7-10

It makes me happy just to know that I am not doing anything—and that I don't need to do anything! My part is simply focusing on Him by continually calling out to Him and asking Him to do everything. That's salvation. By depending completely on Him, He saves me from my own self-destruction. I depend on Him with my whole being—meaning all of my thoughts and my five senses focus on Him.

PRAYER: Thank you so much, Lord, that you don't expect me to try to think my way into trusting you. You simply ask me to cry out to you with all of my thoughts and all of my feelings and you do all of the work of setting things right between you and me. That's why I am happy. You have made me happy. You have done for me what I could never do for myself.

Personal Reflections

July 25

Scripture reassures us, "No one who trusts God like this—heart and soul—will ever regret it." It's exactly the same no matter what a person's religious background may be: the same God for all of us, acting the same incredibly generous way to everyone who calls out for help. "Everyone who calls, 'Help, God!' gets help." But how can people call for help if they don't know who to trust? And how can they know who to trust if they haven't heard of the One who can be trusted? And how can they hear if nobody tells them?

- Romans 10:11-15

This scripture makes us want to shout from the rooftops to everyone within hearing distance. No one who focuses on God and calls out to Him with heart and soul will ever regret it. God will work the same transformation for everyone who comes to Him, regardless of their former religious background. He will be incredibly generous and make us happy as we depend on Him.

PRAYER: Thank you, Lord, for how you inspire us to share your amazing words over and over again. You are the greatest motivational teacher ever, and all your instructions are so simple and clear! Our cultural icons—even our church leaders—have given so many complicated instructions that we have totally missed your simple message. Not anymore! I pray that you will inspire everyone who reads these devotionals to share your plain teaching.

Personal Reflections

July 26

How can we sum this up? All those people who didn't seem interested in what God was doing actually embraced what God was doing as he straightened out their lives. And Israel, who seemed so interested in reading and talking about what God was doing, missed it. How could they miss it? Because instead of trusting God, they took over. They were absorbed in what they themselves were doing. They were so absorbed in their "God projects" that they didn't notice God right in front of them, like a huge rock in the middle of the road.

- Romans 9:30-32

How is it possible for people who don't seem interested in what God is doing end up actually embracing Him? How is it that those who seem so interested end up missing God? When we get too involved in our "God projects," we tend to ignore God. We are so pleased with ourselves for doing His work that it becomes about us and not Him. Those who aren't interested in God focus on the world and all its pleasures, yet they end up empty. People who recognize their own emptiness are primed and ready to embrace God out of their own sheer misery.

PRAYER: Lord, send these devotionals to those primed to seek you, and also to those so self-absorbed in God projects that they are growing weary of their own efforts. We are all in desperate need of a Savior. I pray that these scriptures will draw the attention of many to notice you right in front of them.

Personal Reflections

July 27

Believe me, friends, all I want for Israel is what's best for Israel: salvation, nothing less. I want it with all my heart and pray to God for it all the time. I readily admit that the Jews are impressively energetic regarding God—but they are doing everything exactly backward. They don't seem to realize that this comprehensive setting-things-right that is salvation is God's business, and a most flourishing business it is. Right across the street they set up their own salvation shops and noisily hawk their wares. After all these years of refusing to really deal with God on his terms, insisting instead on making their own deals, they have nothing to show for it.

- Romans 10:1-3

How easy it is for us to set up our own "salvation shops," insisting on making our own deals, noisily hawking our wares. No wonder we have nothing to show for it! We have claimed God's business, as if we deserve to take all the credit for saving ourselves. Unfortunately, many churches have become their own businesses. They have forgotten their only purpose is to spread God's word. God does all the rest—He saves, He teaches, and He loves us unconditionally—our only part is to encourage each other as we share what Jesus has taught us.

PRAYER: Lord, thank you for showing me that my ministry to others has only one purpose: to share what you have taught me about focusing on you. Sharing your instructions teaches me twice: once as I read your Word, and twice as I share it with those around me. Deepen my understanding of your salvation plan.

Personal Reflections

July 28

Moses wrote that anyone who insists on using the law code to live right before God soon discovers it's not so easy—every detail of life regulated by fine print! But trusting God to shape the right living in us is a different story—no precarious climb up to heaven to recruit the Messiah, no dangerous descent into hell to rescue the Messiah. So what exactly was Moses saying?

> *The word that saves is right here,*
> *as near as the tongue in your mouth,*
> *as close as the heart in your chest.*

- Romans 10:5-8

What a powerful teaching about our frustrating inability to save ourselves and God's amazing ability to revive us simply through His Word. Anyone who tries living by the law and his own effort will soon discover that every detail of his life becomes bondage. But when we trust God to shape us, everything changes. What a motivator to share His word every chance we get!

PRAYER: Lord, I am so grateful that your word is right here— as near as the tongue in my mouth and as close as the heart in my chest. Your word is rapidly becoming so dear to me because it keeps me focused on you. You are clearing my vision and giving me a new perspective on just how wonderful you are. As you teach us how to live, the simplicity of your loving instructions continues to stand out to me, over and over again.

Personal Reflections

July 29

I can anticipate the response that is coming: "I know that all God's commands are spiritual, but I'm not. Isn't this also your experience?" Yes. I'm full of myself—after all, I've spent a long time in sin's prison. What I don't understand about myself is that I decide one way, but then I act another, doing things I absolutely despise. So if I can't be trusted to figure out what is best for myself and then do it, it becomes obvious that God's command is necessary.

- Romans 7:14-16

The theme that stands out in these verses is our inability to understand or figure out our failures. We fail in figuring out what is best for us. Finally, at the age of 60, I stopped trying to manage and control my own life and accepted that only God can keep me from doing things I absolutely despise. Only God can show me the right way to live, and help me to live the right way. My part is to live and breathe God, focusing on Him with all my senses, thanking Him and praising Him every day.

PRAYER: Lord, finally after so many years in sin's prison, you have rescued me from my own obsession with understanding myself and figuring out my own life. What a relief from the mental and emotional torture of trying to fix my own problems, trying to make myself a better person! The more I tried, the more I failed. Thank you for saving me from myself.

Personal Reflections

July 30

But I need something more*! For if I know the law but still can't keep it, and if the power of sin within me keeps sabotaging my best intentions, I obviously need help! I realize that I don't have what it takes. I can will it, but I can't do it. I decide to do good, but I don't really do it; I decide not to do bad, but then I do it anyway. My decisions, such as they are, don't result in actions. Something has gone wrong deep within me and gets the better of me every time.*

- Romans 7:17-20

This scripture shows that something is wrong deep within us and we don't have what it takes to live our lives. Most of us refuse to believe this truth about ourselves and keep beating our heads against the wall trying to figure out our problems and then try to improve ourselves. This verse highlights the fact that we need something more, not just in a vague, general way, but for each moment in time, for every moment of every day. The only one who can give us that kind of steady, guiding light is God Himself.

PRAYER: Lord, thank you for showing me clearly that I don't have what it takes. I feel tremendous relief after all these years of trying to belief in myself. I am glad I don't have to believe in myself anymore, because I have you to believe in. Although I don't have "what it takes" in life, I have "who it takes,"—my savior, the Lord Jesus Christ!

Personal Reflections

July 31

It happens so regularly that it's predictable. The moment I decide to do good, sin is there to trip me up. I truly delight in God's commands, but it's pretty obvious that not all of me joins in that delight. Parts of me covertly rebel, and just when I least expect it, they take charge.

- Romans 7:21-23

It would happen so regularly. When I was focused on myself and not God, I never expected sin to trip me up. I mistakenly thought I had everything under control. Now it seems obvious that there will always be parts of me that covertly rebel. It's obvious to me that no matter how much I try to obey God's commands, I will not be able to make myself do it. That clarity has only come from reading God's word, and God showing me what I am really like when I don't focus on Him and let Him live through me.

PRAYER: Thank you, Lord, that your word is sharper than a two-edged sword. Reading your word is like looking into a crystal-clear mirror "with bright lights" that reveals my helplessness to fix myself. This mirror clearly shows me that you are the only answer for my life. Plus, in this mirror, you write simple instructions in big, bold letters—instructions for how to follow you. Now I put my whole trust in you, for all my weaknesses are too much for me. Increase my delight in your commands and turn my focus towards you.

Personal Reflections

August 1

I've tried everything and nothing helps. I'm at the end of my rope. Is there no one who can do anything for me? Isn't that the real question?

The answer, thank God, is that Jesus Christ can and does. He acted to set things right in this life of contradictions where I want to serve God with all my heart and mind, but am pulled by the influence of sin to do something totally different.

- Romans 7:24-25

Many of us have felt that we are at the end of our rope and have tried everything and that nothing helps. We have also felt that there is no one who can do anything for us. At this point, we have been taught by our culture, and even the church, to try harder until we figure out the answers to our problems. This scripture instructs us to look upward (not inward) and discover the one and only solution, Jesus Christ. Only He was willing to die for us and do for us what we could never do for ourselves. Only He can enable us to serve God with our whole heart, mind, and strength. Only He is able to overcome the influence of sin in our lives by offering us something even more attractive and irresistible: Himself.

PRAYER: Finally, Lord, I looked up and found what I was never able to find looking inward. It seems so counter-intuitive to everything I have been taught until I read the clear instructions written in your word. Thank you from the bottom of my heart.

Personal Reflections

August 2

With the arrival of Jesus, the Messiah, that fateful dilemma is resolved. Those who enter into Christ's being-here-for-us no longer have to live under a continuous, low-lying black cloud. A new power is in operation. The Spirit of life in Christ, like a strong wind, has magnificently cleared the air, freeing you from a fated lifetime of brutal tyranny at the hands of sin and death.

- Romans 8:1-2

With the arrival of Jesus, God sent what was most precious to Him (His only son) as our focal point on how to live life. We can place our total focus on how Jesus lived his life and know for sure that Jesus would never steer us wrong. His life is an amazing example for us of how to live our lives every day. Jesus never took his eyes off his heavenly Father. He depended completely on God for every move he made. This spirit of life in Christ, like a strong wind, makes the air so clear. His Spirit clears our vision and frees us from the bondage of our former tyrannical masters: Sin and Death. Now our lives can be spent in thankfulness for the power of God's glory in us!

PRAYER: God, what a magnificent way to show us how to live. Your only Son is your glorious example of perfect love. We can give Him our full attention and never be given wrong directions. Through your Holy Spirit, hold onto us tightly— never let go. You are our only hope to get through this life.

Personal Reflections

August 3

God went for the jugular when he sent his own Son. He didn't deal with the problem as something remote and unimportant. In his Son, Jesus, he personally took on the human condition, entered the disordered mess of struggling humanity in order to set it right once and for all. The law code, weakened as it always was by fractured human nature . . . always ended up being used as a Band-Aid on sin instead of a deep healing of it. And now what the law code asked for but we couldn't deliver is accomplished as we, instead of redoubling our own efforts, simply embrace what the Spirit is doing in us.

- Romans 8:3-4

These verses describe so well how much God cares for us. God knew that the law was not enough to draw us close to Him. He went for the jugular when He sent His only son to earth to experience life as we do. Jesus experienced extreme pain and suffering in the form of physical torture, mental anguish, and emotional trauma. He knows what it feels like to be abused and neglected. He voluntarily died to save us, so He has personally felt the brutal impact of death. No one else could ever have compassion for us the way Jesus does.

PRAYER: Lord, thank you for showing me these verses. No one could ever possibly care for me as much as you do. I want to run to you and feel safe in your loving arms. I see now that I will never endure any hurt or pain that you cannot relate to and help me to bear.

Personal Reflections

August 4

Jesus said, "Put your sword back where it belongs. All who use swords are destroyed by swords. Don't you realize that I am able right now to call to my Father, and twelve companies—more, if I want them—of fighting angels would be here, battle-ready? But if I did that, how would the Scriptures come true that say this is the way it has to be?"

- Matthew 26:52-54

What is most phenomenal about all the suffering Christ endured is his choice to be lowered to our level, where we are unable to rescue ourselves from hurt and pain. He chose to endure what we endure without a supernatural rescue from fighting angels. He relates to how awful we feel when we are mistreated. He suffered an agonizing death and waited on his father to rescue him through his resurrection on the third day. Christ says, "I will wait with you and care for you—and your Heavenly Father will rescue you in the nick of time."

PRAYER: Lord, thank you for showing me such compassion that you were willing to suffer a cruel death just so I can be certain that there is nothing that can separate me from your love, not even death. Thank you for holding firm and refusing to accept the easy rescue. The fact that you could have called for help and ended your anguish at any time, but chose to endure to the end so that I might be rescued makes me love you even more.

Personal Reflections

August 5

God didn't put angels in charge of this business of salvation that we're dealing with here. It says in Scripture, "What is man and woman that you bother with them; why take a second look their way? You made them not quite as high as angels, bright with Eden's dawn light; Then you put them in charge of your entire handcrafted world. When God put them in charge of everything, nothing was excluded. But we don't see it yet, don't see everything under human jurisdiction. What we do see is Jesus, made "not quite as high as angels," and then, through the experience of death, crowned so much higher than any angel, with a glory "bright with Eden's dawn light." In that death, by God's grace, he fully experienced death in every person's place.

- Hebrews 2:5-9

Created in the image of God, we were born to reign over the earth, but we don't see everything under human jurisdiction yet. What we can see clearly is Jesus, made like us, a little lower than the angels, and then, through His sacrifice for our sins, crowned so much higher than any angel. Jesus's resurrection is a promise: we, too, will someday rise and reign with Him.

PRAYER: Lord, we will never stop thanking you for dying in our place. When we are in agony, remind us of your agony on the cross and how you suffer with us. Remind us of your promise that one day we, too, will be crowned in glory.

Personal Reflections

August 6

It makes good sense that the God who got everything started and keeps everything going now completes the work by making the Salvation Pioneer perfect through suffering as he leads all these people to glory. Since the One who saves and those who are saved have a common origin, Jesus doesn't hesitate to treat them as family, saying,

I'll tell my good friends, my brothers and sisters, all I know about you;
I'll join them in worship and praise to you.
Again, he puts himself in the same family circle when he says,
Even I live by placing my trust in God.
And yet again,
I'm here with the children God gave me.

- Hebrews 2:10-13

No wonder we are instructed to focus on Jesus and how he lived his life as an example of how to live our lives. He willingly placed his trust in God even to the point of dying on the cross. His reward was a glory "bright with Eden's dawn light." Now he will lead all who focus on him into glory. As we follow him, he joins us in worship and praise to God. He even puts himself in our same family circle as believers.

PRAYER: Lord, the words in this scripture give us such a beautiful picture of our journey of focus on you. We are the children God gave you. I am so grateful you want us in your family and call us your children.

Personal Reflections

August 7

So, my dear Christian friends, companions in following this call to the heights, take a good hard look at Jesus. He's the centerpiece of everything we believe, faithful in everything God gave him to do. Moses was also faithful, but Jesus gets far more honor. A builder is more valuable than a building any day. Every house has a builder, but the Builder behind them all is God. Moses did a good job in God's house, but it was all servant work, getting things ready for what was to come. Christ as Son is in charge of the house.

- Hebrews 3:1-6

This passage is yet another clear word picture with instructions to focus on the Builder rather than the building. The Builder is always the one to watch because He knows what He is doing and is the only one capable of teaching us how. The Builder holds the blueprints and shows us how to follow the instructions. All that we do is "servant work" under Him, getting things ready for the miraculous work of Jesus. Our lives are His masterpiece.

PRAYER: Lord, I am thankful that only you hold the blueprint for my life. For many years, I tried to make and follow my own blueprint and failed miserably. What a relief that you don't expect me to be my own builder. You long to build my life for me as I hold onto you.

Personal Reflections

August 8

How exquisite your love, O God!
  How eager we are to run under your wings,
To eat our fill at the banquet you spread
  as you fill our tankards with Eden spring water.
You're a fountain of cascading light,
  and you open our eyes to light.

                                                      - Psalm 36:7-9

God faithfully opens our eyes to light as we read His scriptures every day. I have become eager to run under His wings as He clears my vision more and more every day, showing how deeply He really does love me. This passage is such a beautiful description of God's love. Now I can't get enough of His love and want to discover new passages every day. His love is exquisite, like a deep draft of sparkling spring water, quenching my thirst to be loved. God Himself is like a fountain of cascading light, illuminating my life and bringing me deep joy.

PRAYER: Lord, you say in Proverbs that you are an acquired taste. I believe that more and more every day. I started off slow as I started reading these scriptures every day. Now I can't wait to read more of your word! I pray that everyone who reads these daily devotionals will experience the same acquired taste you have given me. Fill us all with the banquet that you spread for our delight. Open our eyes to your glorious beauty.

Personal Reflections

August 9

Dear friend, take my advice;
it will add years to your life.
I'm writing out clear directions to Wisdom Way,
I'm drawing a map to Righteous Road.
I don't want you ending up in blind alleys,
or wasting time making wrong turns.

- Proverbs 4:10-12

I am counting on the freedom of focus on God to add years to my life. Since I focus on God every day through His Word, I am learning over and over again that He writes out clear directions on how to live. He even draws a map for us so we don't waste our time making wrong turns and end up in blind alleys where we can't see Him. He is in the business of clearing our vision every moment of every day as we focus on Him.

PRAYER: Lord, I am especially thankful that you give me directions and draw things out on a map for me just so you can clear my vision for how to live. For years, I have felt learning disabled when it comes down to how to live life. Although your word has always been available to me, I often kept it on a shelf instead of having it right next to me all the time. I have always been prone to not using maps but trying to get to my destination without any directions. Thank you for showing me that my way never works. Now I open your word eagerly and let it tell me how to live.

Personal Reflections

August 10

*Dear friend, guard Clear Thinking and Common Sense
with your life;*
  don't for a minute lose sight of them.
They'll keep your soul alive and well,
  they'll keep you fit and attractive.
You'll travel safely,
  you'll neither tire nor trip.
You'll take afternoon naps without a worry,
  you'll enjoy a good night's sleep.
No need to panic over alarms or surprises,
  or predictions that doomsday's just around the corner,
Because GOD will be right there with you;
  he'll keep you safe and sound.

- Proverbs 3:21-26

This scripture starts with "guard Clear Thinking and Common Sense." These are part of God's essential Wisdom that He gives to everyone who asks for it (James 1:5). We can depend on this wisdom from God if we keep close watch over it. In the words of the scripture, we must "guard them with our life!" When we focus on God, He is right there with us to keep us safe. When we stay focused on His clear thinking and His common sense, we will neither tire nor trip.

PRAYER: Lord, this advice is better for getting rid of anxiety than taking a sleeping pill. When we live and breathe you, our focus on you replaces our worry. We don't need to panic over alarms or surprises and we can enjoy a good night's sleep. The reminder that you are right here with us is such a comfort. I have no need to be afraid of the twists and turns of life when you are keeping me safe and sound.

Personal Reflections

August 11

Believe me, before you know it Fear-of-GOD will be yours;
*   you'll have come upon the Knowledge of God.*
And here's why: GOD gives out Wisdom free,
*   is plainspoken in Knowledge and Understanding.*

- Proverbs 2:5-6

God's "Clear Thinking" and His "Common Sense" combine to be part of His "Wisdom," which He gives out for free to all who ask and focus on Him to see and hear His answers. We don't have to pay for His Wisdom—or for any of His gifts! He calls us to come get food for our aching hearts and drink for our parched souls, without any cost to us at all (Isaiah 55:1) That's how much He loves us. He even sent His son to die on the cross as payment in full so we could experience His love forever, completely free.

PRAYER: Lord, our lives are sometimes so confusing to us, and our weary hearts ache for just a crumb of clarity, a drop of understanding. The burden to be wise and make good decisions every day is too heavy for us to bear. Thank you for showing us that we are making it too hard on ourselves. Thank you for pouring out your clear thinking, common sense, and wisdom for free to all of us who just focus on you and ask you for it. You take all the pressure off to be wise on our own. Thank you for giving us the wisdom we need out of your sheer generosity, without finding fault.

Personal Reflections

August 12

Trust GOD from the bottom of your heart;
  don't try to figure out everything on your own.
Listen for GOD'S voice in everything you do, everywhere
you go;
  he's the one who will keep you on track.
Don't assume that you know it all.
  Run to GOD! Run from evil!
Your body will glow with health,
  your very bones will vibrate with life!

- Proverbs 3:5-8

I always thought it was my job to stay on track. I would try to figure out everything on my own. This scripture instructs not to try to have everything figured out—that would be trying to use our own thinking, our own common sense, our own wisdom. When I focus on my own thoughts, my own common sense, my own wisdom, that focus keeps me from focusing on God. God wants us to simply keep our complete focus on Him. He will do all the rest and He will keep us on track.

PRAYER: Lord, thank you so much for repeating the same message all through scripture. You made our brains to love repetition as your amazing way to keep us on track. Thank you for taking this responsibility in my life into your own hands because I failed over and over again trying to keep myself on track. Now I love to read your word every chance I get because it keeps me on track.

Personal Reflections

August 13

I've also concluded that whatever God does, that's the way it's going to be, always. No addition, no subtraction. God's done it and that's it. That's so we'll quit asking questions and simply worship in holy fear.

Whatever was, is.
Whatever will be, is.
That's how it always is with God.

- Ecclesiastes 3:14-15

Wow. Yesterday's scripture instructed us to stop trying to figure things out. Today's scripture instructs us to quit asking questions! Our culture teaches us to be analytical. Most therapies try to teach us to figure out our problems and come up with solutions, and we ourselves naturally ask questions as part of our self-analysis. However, our questions can interfere with our total focus on God. When we search within ourselves for answers, we will be continually frustrated—but God has all the answers and wants to share all His solutions on how to live life. He doesn't even need us to ask Him to share His answers! All we need is to focus on Him and He will reveal them to us.

PRAYER: Thank you, Lord, that my only part is to simply worship you. No debating, just thanking you over and over again that you love me unconditionally and freely show me how to live. Thank you that you have all the answers and that you love to show me the way when I am confused or uncertain of the right way to go. I don't want to seek for the answers inside myself anymore, because you have all the wisdom I need.

Personal Reflections

August 14

"Listen to me, family of Jacob,
everyone that's left of the family of Israel.
I've been carrying you on my back
from the day you were born,
And I'll keep on carrying you when you're old.
I'll be there, bearing you when you're old and gray.
I've done it and will keep on doing it,
carrying you on my back, saving you."

- Isaiah 46:3-4

Yesterday, the scripture instructed us not to ask questions as part of our total dependence on God. Today's promise says that God will carry us on His back from the time we are young until we are very old. In other words, we can depend on Him to carry us during our entire journey through life. He never makes us get off and walk. He does not expect anything from us other than to let Him carry us. When we are this dependent on Him, we have no need to ask Him questions. We are filled with praise and thanksgiving that He is willing to carry our entire load. There is no weight limit or any other conditions before He agrees to carry us. We just let Him!

PRAYER: Lord, this word-picture says it all. You literally want no effort from us! The best way for us to focus is to let you put us on your back and enjoy the ride. You are so gentle and understanding with us, even when we are weak and foolish. Thank you!

Personal Reflections

August 15

"So to whom will you compare me, the Incomparable?
Can you picture me without reducing me?
People with a lot of money
hire craftsmen to make them gods.
The artisan delivers the god,
and they kneel and worship it!
They carry it around in holy parades,
then take it home and put it on a shelf.
And there it sits, day in and day out,
a dependable god, always right where you put it.
Say anything you want to it, it never talks back.
Of course, it never does anything either!"

- Isaiah 46:5-7

Our natural tendency is to continually reduce God. All of our worries are about fear that God won't or can't take care of us. We feel everyone else has let us down so it is natural to feel God will, too. On our own, we are not capable of totally depending on Him. Our only hope is to focus on Him day and night to witness firsthand how God never abandons us. When we do feel abandoned by Him, it is only because we have turned our eyes away and don't see or feel Him carrying us on His back.

PRAYER: Lord, I am so grateful that you are not just another god on a shelf who never talks back. Thank you for talking to me in endless ways as I live and breathe you. Thank you for carrying me on your back and never letting me fall off.

Personal Reflections

August 16

And now, the Master, GOD, sends me and his Spirit
with this Message from GOD,
your Redeemer, The Holy of Israel:
"I am GOD, your God,
who teaches you how to live right and well.
I show you what to do, where to go.
If you had listened all along to what I told you,
your life would have flowed full like a river,
blessings rolling in like waves from the sea.
Children and grandchildren are like sand,
your progeny like grains of sand.
There would be no end of them,
no danger of losing touch with me."

- Isaiah 48:16-19

As we keep our eyes on God and feel Him carrying us, He shows us what to do and where to go. He will never carry us in the wrong direction. If you've ever given a piggyback ride to a small child, you know how tightly they cling to you, and how securely you hold them. Like children, we only get in trouble when we insist on getting down and wandering off on our own.

PRAYER: Lord, as I meditate on how you carry us, I get a sense of the closeness you desire in your relationship with me. You want my arms and legs wrapped around you, holding on tight. You want my face close to your head so you can feel my every breath. Thank you that you never want to lose touch with me.

Personal Reflections

August 17

The Master, GOD, has given me
a well-taught tongue,
So I know how to encourage tired people.
He wakes me up in the morning,
Wakes me up, opens my ears
to listen as one ready to take orders.
The Master, GOD, opened my ears,
and I didn't go back to sleep,
didn't pull the covers back over my head.

- Isaiah 50:4-5

Every one of us knows what it is to be tired to the depths of our spirits. This scripture offers us encouragement for when we are tired and don't know how to go on. When we allow Christ to carry us on His back He will do everything for us. He will wake us up in the morning, He will open our ears to be ready to listen to Him, and He will teach our tongue to speak words of encouragement to others. When we let Him carry us, He gives us the strength not to tire out, so that we don't pull the covers back over our head in weariness and discouragement. We don't go back to sleep, but instead encourage other tired people with the promise He has given us.

PRAYER: Lord, is there nothing you won't do for us when we allow you to take over our lives? The world is full of tired, stressed-out, performance-driven people. What a relief to know that we don't have to live that way anymore. Thank you for giving us the strength not only to wake up and listen to you, but also to stay alert and encourage others.

Personal Reflections

August 18

But it was our sins that did that to him,
    *that ripped and tore and crushed him—*our sins*!*
He took the punishment, and that made us whole.
    Through his bruises we get healed.
We're all like sheep who've wandered off and gotten lost.
    We've all done our own thing, gone our own way.
And God has piled all our sins, everything we've done wrong,
    on him, on him.

                         - Isaiah 53:5-6

Even after we have wandered off over and over again and gone our own way, Christ piles all of our weight on His back and carries us through life. He does everything for us so that our only part is to focus on Him. He carries the weight of our sins and struggles, so we don't have to focus on our own weight. He surrounds us with all of His creation so we can give Him our total attention and not be drawn to things of this world. He created us with five powerful senses so we can enjoy His creation. The world has all kinds of attractions to draw our senses to sin, but nothing can compare to how He draws us to Himself.

PRAYER: Lord, I am so thankful that nothing can compare to how you love us. You suffered a brutal death to show us that no one and nothing can come close to how much you care for us. You pour out your love in every way possible to show us that our only hope is your unending forgiveness.

Personal Reflections

August 19

"Hey there! All who are thirsty, come to the water!
Are you penniless? Come anyway—buy and eat!
Come, buy your drinks, buy wine and milk. Buy without
  money—everything's free!...
Pay attention, come close now, listen carefully to my
  life-giving, life-nourishing words.
I'm making a lasting covenant commitment with you,
  the same that I made with David: sure, solid, enduring
  love.

- Isaiah 55:1, 3

Not only does Christ carry our weight, He doesn't charge anything for it! He feeds our hungry souls and fills us with good things, all at no cost to us. Yet we often live as if we have to pay to follow Him. We doubt His unconditional love. We often get off His back, wander off, and then act as if we need to work off our sins and earn back His love before we can be carried again. This is such nonsense! All Christ desires is that we let Him lift us onto His back again. He wants us to cling closely around His neck like a little child and pay close attention to His nourishing, life-giving words.

PRAYER: Lord, we know our deep need for dependence on you. Although weakness is considered a terrible flaw in our performance-driven culture, you embrace us in our brokenness and desire to carry us as if we are little children. Thank you, Lord. We are weary and heavy laden. We want to come to you and rest in your love.

Personal Reflections

August 20

Seek GOD while he's here to be found,
pray to him while he's close at hand.
Let the wicked abandon their way of life
and the evil their way of thinking.
Let them come back to GOD, who is merciful,
come back to our God, who is lavish with forgiveness.

- Isaiah 55:6-7

In our culture, we have been taught that our logical thoughts are our only hope in life. We are taught not to pay attention to any distractions to this logical process. Counselors spend hours trying to teach clients to correct their erroneous or distorted thinking patterns. The truth is that neither we nor any counselor can correct our thinking. This scripture says to abandon our thinking and seek God's way of thinking. We do this when we come back to Him by allowing Him to lift us back up onto His back.

PRAYER: Lord, what a relief to abandon our way of thinking and listen to your thinking. Our thinking declines the longer we strive to figure out what to do with our lives. What a burden is lifted when we admit self-defeat and begin the journey of allowing you to carry us to victory. You are the hero. You are the star of the game. Our role is to keep our eyes on you as we watch you win the game of life for us. Our efforts are futile and get in the way of your success. Our only part is to encourage others to also look your way as we maintain our focus on you.

Personal Reflections

August 21

"I don't think the way you think.
The way you work isn't the way I work...
For as the sky soars high above earth,
so the way I work surpasses the way you work,
and the way I think is beyond the way you think."

- Isaiah 55:8-9

Thank goodness His way of thinking is beyond our way! He makes it so easy to know His thoughts because they are so different than our thoughts. Our thoughts insist that we have to work hard—that we have to struggle to do our best—that we have to find a way to please Him. As He shares in His word, God's thoughts clearly say that His work surpasses the way we work. In other words, nothing we could ever do for ourselves could come close to measuring up to what He can perform in our lives. So quit trying!

PRAYER: Lord, we are so grateful that your ways far surpass our futile efforts. They far surpass us as the sky soars high above the earth. Even though some churches continue to preach performance-based Christianity, you clearly show us in your word that it is your performance that saves us, and not our own efforts. The way you continually work in our lives, to change us and rescue us from ourselves surpasses our wildest imaginations. Continue to clear our vision everyday by pointing out that the secret to success is watching you perform in our lives.

Personal Reflections

August 22

Just as rain and snow descend from the skies
and don't go back until they've watered the earth,
Doing their work of making things grow and blossom,
producing seed for farmers and food for the hungry,
So will the words that come out of my mouth
not come back empty-handed.
They'll do the work I sent them to do,
they'll complete the assignment I gave them.

- Isaiah 55:10-11

God offers a guarantee that His words, His instruction, His performance will yield results in our lives. None of us can guarantee that our efforts will yield results. Yet our culture, especially our Christian culture promises us that God appreciates our efforts. No, He doesn't. He clearly says our effort—our striving for His approval—is not only a waste of time, but gets in the way of focus on Him. We can't even see His guaranteed success. Thank goodness we can simply go back to His word and be reminded of His promises. In the daily grind of life in our self-performance culture, we can count on daily reminders of His promises by focusing on the instructions in His word.

PRAYER: Lord, even though we are accustomed to reading your word as part of our futile attempts to win your approval, we are grateful that you show us that reading your word will get the focus off our efforts to please and draw our attention to how amazing you are. Reading your word yields passion, not striving.

Personal Reflections

August 23

"So you'll go out in joy,
you'll be led into a whole and complete life.
The mountains and hills will lead the parade,
bursting with song.
All the trees of the forest will join the procession,
exuberant with applause.
No more thistles, but giant sequoias,
no more thornbushes, but stately pines—
Monuments to me, to GOD,
living and lasting evidence of GOD."

- Isaiah 55:12-13

The passion He gives us as we read His word drives us to go out in joy to share His mighty work in our lives with others. We don't go out in obligation but bursting with songs about how He has lead us into a whole and complete life. We can't contain our excitement! Plus, God surrounds us with nature to inspire us. Giant sequoias and stately pines are monuments to God, living and lasting reminders of His handiwork that help sustain our passion.

PRAYER: Lord, thank you that we don't have to try to generate our own passion from within. Our own efforts to be joyful fail miserably, because we are not capable of creating our own joy. You supply our joy and fill us with passion as we focus on you and your amazing creation all around us. Thank you for carrying us on your back and leading us into a whole and complete life!

Personal Reflections

August 24

"I'm telling you these things while I'm still living with you. The Friend, the Holy Spirit whom the Father will send at my request, will make everything plain to you. He will remind you of all the things I have told you. I'm leaving you well and whole. That's my parting gift to you. Peace. I don't leave you the way you're used to being left—feeling abandoned, bereft. So don't be upset. Don't be distraught."

- John 14:25-27

Not only do we have God's word and God's beautiful nature to keep us focused on Him, we have His Holy Spirit to constantly remind us of all the things He has told us. The Holy Spirit provides us play-by-play instructions. We don't have to call any of our own plays. We don't need to improvise or even call an audible at the line of scrimmage. Our plays only lose yardage. God desires to make all our play calls for us and gives us a headset in the Holy Spirit to guide us throughout every play.

PRAYER: Lord, thank you that we don't need to depend on ourselves at all in the game of life. Life can be nerve-wracking sometimes, and I am so relieved to know that you are taking care of every little detail. Thank you that my only part is to keep my focus on you and listen closely to your every word. Thank you that you promise never to leave me abandoned or bereft, but that you give me peace to fill my mind and heart while you guide my every step.

Personal Reflections

August 25

GOD brings death and GOD brings life, brings down to the grave and raises up. GOD brings poverty and GOD brings wealth; he lowers, he also lifts up. He puts poor people on their feet again; he rekindles burned-out lives with fresh hope, restoring dignity and respect to their lives—a place in the sun! . . . He protectively cares for his faithful friends, step by step, but leaves the wicked to stumble in the dark. No one makes it in this life by sheer muscle!

- 1 Samuel 2:6-9

God controls everything in our lives, including money and life and death. Although His control means we are powerless over our own fate, I am now grateful my life is completely under His control. After many years of believing the falsehood that I controlled my own destiny, I learned this lesson the hard way: that the harder I tried, the more I screwed up my life. I no longer want to be in control. I want to be completely dependent on Him. I have also learned that He expects nothing from us but to acknowledge Him as our Savior and to simply focus on Him.

PRAYER: Lord, thank you for making your plan so simple that all of us can follow you. I am grateful that your plan does not expect any kind of perfect performance from me. That pressure burned me out years ago. I appreciate so much that you want to re-kindle our burned-out lives with fresh hope. Thank you.

Personal Reflections

August 26

Hannah prayed:

> *I'm bursting with GOD-news!*
> *I'm walking on air.*
> *I'm laughing at my rivals.*
> *I'm dancing my salvation.*

> *Nothing and no one is holy like GOD,*
> *no rock mountain like our God.*

> *- 1 Samuel 2:1-2*

God rekindles us with God-news! He tells us something that can only come from him. The way He tells leaves us with no doubts that He loves and deeply cares for us. His news is unexpected and something that no man can do. We burst with the energy and excitement that He gives us to accompany His news. He provides both the information and the feelings. We don't have to act surprised or pretend to be excited because our happy feelings come from Him. He gives us His thoughts and fresh feelings to replace our own negative thoughts and depressive feelings. God is our source for happiness.

PRAYER: Lord, I am so glad you repeat the same message over and over again in your word. Quite honestly, without your constant reminders, I too easily slip back into my old habits of feeling responsible for my own happiness. I can't make myself happy. I never could. I am so grateful that you make me happy and I no longer feel that awful pressure to perform.

Personal Reflections

August 27

Indeed, I've kept alert to GOD'S ways;
I haven't taken God for granted.
Every day I review the ways he works,
I try not to miss a trick.
I feel put back together,
and I'm watching my step.
GOD rewrote the text of my life
when I opened the book of my heart to his eyes.

- 2 Samuel 22:23-25

Here God reveals the secret to having His happiness inside us. When we keep alert to God and review the ways He works over and over again every day, He gives us the feeling of being put back together. He takes the old negative text of our life, the script full of guilt and shame and failure, and He rewrites that old script about us with His own script for our lives. When we open "the book of our heart," lay bare all of our thoughts, dreams, and feelings to Him, and finally allow ourselves to look in His eyes, we will find only love, compassion, and everlasting joy.

PRAYER: Thank you again, Lord, that our only part in our relationship with you is to open our heart to you and look into your eyes. As we focus on you with our deepest feelings and tap into our memories of your love, you rewrite our negative life script with positive thoughts and feelings that can only come from you. We are not just learning lines to a new movie— we are literally experiencing a new life in you.

Personal Reflections

August 28

GOD'S Spirit spoke through me, his words took shape on my tongue. The God of Israel spoke to me, Israel's Rock-Mountain said, 'Whoever governs fairly and well, who rules in the Fear-of-God, is like first light at daybreak without a cloud in the sky, like green grass carpeting earth, glistening under fresh rain.' And this is just how my regime has been, for God guaranteed his covenant with me, spelled it out plainly and kept every promised word—my entire salvation, my every desire.

- 2 Samuel 23:2-5

I often have counseled clients to change how they speak to their spouse or children. Likewise, God wants to change how all of us speak to others. As we focus on Him, He wants others to see His love in and through us. The only way that is possible is for Him to speak instead of us. While it is humanly impossible for us to keep our mouth shut while He speaks through us, God offers us the Holy Spirit to literally shape God's words on our mouth. We know for sure they are God's words because the thoughts he gives us to say out loud are new and clearly different than our own thoughts.

PRAYER: Lord, thank you that we don't have to come up with the words you want us to share on our own. I always thought it was my responsibility to come up with the words you wanted me to share, but this scripture clearly shows that you freely give us the words to say through your Holy Spirit. God you are amazing!

Personal Reflections

August 29

Blessed the man, blessed the woman, who listens to me,
awake and ready for me each morning,
alert and responsive as I start my day's work.
When you find me, you find life, real life,
to say nothing of GOD'S good pleasure.

- Proverbs 8:34-35

I have always been a morning person since my childhood days of getting up early to milk cows on the dairy farm. I have always felt alert and responsive as I started my day's work. This scripture describes how God instructs us to be as He starts His day's work in us. I find it so strange to shift from starting my work to focusing on God as He starts His day's work in me. I ask myself, am I listening? Are my senses awake and ready to respond to His instructions throughout the day? God promises that we will find real life when we are alert and responsive to him. As a bonus, we will feel His good pleasure!

PRAYER: Thank you, Lord, that you give us the gift of happiness when we discover you and hold onto you for dear life as you perform your day's work in us. As a tired, old performer in life, I am relieved to surrender my work and gladly receive your work in me.

Personal Reflections

August 30

"Are you confused about life, don't know what's going on?
Come with me, oh come, have dinner with me!
I've prepared a wonderful spread—fresh-baked bread,
roast lamb, carefully selected wines.
Leave your impoverished confusion and live!
Walk up the street to a life with meaning."

- Proverbs 9:4-6

For years, clients have come to my office hoping I could assist them in figuring out their confusion. For years I unsuccessfully tried my hardest to help them sort through their tangled emotions, memories, and thoughts. However, I no longer join clients in their "figuring out" efforts. I encourage them to leave their confusion, wake up and begin to live a new life with meaning. I tell them to wake up and focus on God. Living life this way is like eating a magnificent banquet, where God feeds us wonderful, nutritional meals full of His bountiful wisdom, love, and strength.

PRAYER: Lord, thank you that you supply all I need every day. You not only prepare and serve me great meals, you sit down and eat with me and enjoy talking with me. My old confusion that hung thickly about me whenever I tried to figure out my life is finally gone. Thank you for your wake-up call to begin living a life full of meaning with you.

Personal Reflections

August 31

If you don't know what you're doing, pray to the Father. He loves to help. You'll get his help, and won't be condescended to when you ask for it. Ask boldly, believingly, without a second thought. People who "worry their prayers" are like wind-whipped waves. Don't think you're going to get anything from the Master that way, adrift at sea, keeping all your options open.

- James 1:5-8

What a clear-cut, simple instruction, "If you don't know what you are doing, pray to the Father. He loves to help." This verse makes me feel so loved and cared for. In a do-it-yourself, performance-driven culture, we have lost touch with our need for dependence. We are expected to figure out life for ourselves and perform to a very high standard. We apologize when we need to ask for help. Our Savior says, "No need to apologize, just run to me, I love to take care of you." Our Savior takes so much better care of us than we take care of ourselves!

PRAYER: Lord, what a relief that I can run to you when I don't know what I am doing. The more I run to you, the more I see that I never know what I am doing and always need you to carry me on your back. You are never condescending or resentful when I need help. Quite frankly, I need you to help me get through every moment of every day.

Personal Reflections

September 1

May God, who puts all things together, makes all things whole, who made a lasting mark through the sacrifice of Jesus, the sacrifice of blood that sealed the eternal covenant, who led Jesus, our Great Shepherd, up and alive from the dead, now put you together, provide you with everything you need to please him, make us into what gives him most pleasure, by means of the sacrifice of Jesus, the Messiah. All glory to Jesus forever and always! Oh, yes, yes, yes.

- Hebrews 13:19-21

What a surprise to see that He provides us with everything we need to please Him! For many of us people-pleasers, our first and biggest job we assign ourselves is to try to please others. Of course, we would assume it is our job to please our Heavenly Father. But He says no, it is His job to give us what we need to please Him. What a relief to all people-pleasers who never feel able to measure up! Even though we can't measure up, God gives His love to us unconditionally. Our only part is to say yes to His love and share the joy He gives us.

PRAYER: Thank you, Lord, that you put all things together and provide for everything we need, even what we need to please you. You release us from the stress and anxiety that haunts our futile efforts to please others. Thank you for giving us a desire to be in your presence, a desire that grows daily as we focus on your love.

Personal Reflections

September 2

Post this at all the intersections, dear friends: Lead with your ears, follow up with your tongue, and let anger straggle along in the rear. God's righteousness doesn't grow from human anger. So throw all spoiled virtue and cancerous evil in the garbage. In simple humility, let our gardener, God, landscape you with the Word, making a salvation-garden of your life.

- James 1:19-21

We are never able to lead with our ears until we are humbled by God's amazing love and His desire to provide to give us even what we need to please Him. His love melts our anger. We stand in awe of His love with our mouths open and no words to even express the magnitude of His love. In the past, our tongues were too busy trying to perform, trying to figure things out, trying to prove we have the answers. Now, we are humbly grateful we no longer have to perform. We are relieved not to have to come up with answers. We are filled with joy as we experience Him giving us everything we need.

PRAYER: Lord, we want to watch you perform in our lives, focusing on you with all five of our senses, starting with our ears. You surround us with your presence and your handiwork. Your creation fully engages all of our five senses. Not one of them is left out!

Personal Reflections

September 3

Don't fool yourself into thinking that you are a listener when you are anything but, letting the Word go in one ear and out the other. Act on what you hear! Those who hear and don't act are like those who glance in the mirror, walk away, and two minutes later have no idea who they are, what they look like.

- James 1:22-24

No wonder we need to live and breathe God! No wonder we need to keep His word in plain view all the time. No wonder God makes it clear to always focus on Him. Without keeping our eyes on Him, within minutes we lose sight of who we are and what we look like. We quickly go back to thinking we need to perform. We quickly revert back to seeing ourselves in the old way, never feeling able to measure up. Only when we cast our eyes on Him and hold onto Him for dear life are we able to see ourselves as He sees us. Only when we let Him carry us are we able to know who we are as He defines us.

PRAYER: Lord, thank you for showing us we are your precious children, each of us special to you, each of us helpless without you. We are beautiful in your sight. We no longer want to focus on how we look in our own eyes. Please teach us how to view ourselves and others through your eyes of compassion and love.

Personal Reflections

September 4

My dear friends, don't let public opinion influence how you live out our glorious, Christ-originated faith. If a man enters your church wearing an expensive suit, and a street person wearing rags comes in right after him, and you say to the man in the suit, "Sit here, sir; this is the best seat in the house!" and either ignore the street person or say, "Better sit here in the back row," haven't you segregated God's children and proved that you are judges who can't be trusted?

- James 2:1-4

Our only hope is to keep our eyes fixed on Jesus so we can clearly see that our faith is Christ-originated. Whenever we look around at others, we are utterly incapable of resisting the urge to be swayed by public opinion. It is absurd to have faith in ourselves to use good judgment in living our lives. Our faith is not in ourselves or our abilities. In fact, our faith only originates because He is a faithful God. When we understand this, we can finally live out this faith freely, without self-consciousness, and without paying any attention to the fashions and customs of our world. We are finally free to love others and treat them impartially, as Jesus did.

PRAYER: Lord, thanks for another reminder in scripture that you originate and build our faith as we focus on you and witness your unconditional love. We are moved with your passion in us to share your love with anyone, regardless of what they look like.

Personal Reflections

September 5

Listen, dear friends. Isn't it clear by now that God operates quite differently? He chose the world's down-and-out as the kingdom's first citizens, with full rights and privileges. This kingdom is promised to anyone who loves God. And here you are abusing these same citizens! Isn't it the high and mighty who exploit you, who use the courts to rob you blind? Aren't they the ones who scorn the new name—"Christian"—used in your baptisms?

- James 2:5-7

I am so grateful that God acts so differently from the world's high and mighty people. If God decided to award Kingdom citizenship to people based on merit or wealth or ability, I would never make it in the door. But because God chooses the people who are at the end of their rope, desperate to depend on Him for their deliverance, I know I have a place in His glorious plan. Also, because all of us Kingdom citizens belong to the same God, I feel a kinship with others and a responsibility to protect them from those who would seek to discourage them.

PRAYER: Lord, thank you so, so much that you are not "high and mighty," but gentle and loving with us. We are all your people, the discouraged and downtrodden and desperate, in need of your grace and strength each day. Help me to help others see your goodness and mercy. Thank you for giving us the kingdom!

Personal Reflections

September 6

So roll up your sleeves, put your mind in gear, be totally ready to receive the gift that's coming when Jesus arrives. Don't lazily slip back into those old grooves of evil, doing just what you feel like doing. You didn't know any better then; you do now. As obedient children, let yourselves be pulled into a way of life shaped by God's life, a life energetic and blazing with holiness. God said, "I am holy; you be holy."

- 1 Peter 1:13-16

Although "roll up your sleeves" sounds like we need to start working really hard, the next phrase says "put your mind in gear, be totally ready to receive the gift." Children get so excited when they are about to receive gifts at Christmas. With the sensory side of their brain in full gear, they delight in the beautiful colors of the wrapping paper, touching, and shaking the gift as their thinking mind tries to guess what's inside. Filled with anticipation, they let themselves be pulled into a complete sensory and cognitive focus on what they are about to receive. No danger of minds wandering—both sides of their brain are totally engaged! This is the kind of complete focus that God desires from us as we let ourselves be pulled into a way of life shaped by His life.

PRAYER: Lord, at Christmas when we receive gifts, our minds blaze with energy as we anticipate and enjoy our gifts. We don't lazily let our minds wander. Please give us the same kind of anticipation when we think about the gift that is coming to us when you come back!

Personal Reflections

September 7

Your life is a journey you must travel with a deep consciousness of God. It cost God plenty to get you out of that dead-end, empty-headed life you grew up in. He paid with Christ's sacred blood, you know. He died like an unblemished, sacrificial lamb. And this was no afterthought. Even though it has only lately—at the end of the ages—become public knowledge, God always knew he was going to do this for you. It's because of this sacrificed Messiah, whom God then raised from the dead and glorified, that you trust God, that you know you have a future in God.

- 1 Peter 1:18-21

When we open a gift, we often ask the giver, "How did you know what I wanted? This is the perfect gift!" We deepen our enjoyment when we explore the thought behind the gift, knowing the giver sacrificed time and money to show us love. God pulled out all the stops with the gift of His Son's death on the cross. He pulled us out of a life that only led to death and gave us a life that never ends!

PRAYER: Lord, no wonder we trust you when we focus on what you were willing to give us and how much it cost you! Our heads are not empty now, but full of both thoughts and feelings about your incredible love. Both the sensory and thinking sides of our brains are fully engaged in our relationship with you. No room for falling back into old patterns of behavior!

Personal Reflections

September 8

Now that you've cleaned up your lives by following the truth, love one another as if your lives depended on it. Your new life is not like your old life. Your old birth came from mortal sperm; your new birth comes from God's living Word. Just think: a life conceived by God himself! That's why the prophet said, "The old life is a grass life, its beauty as short-lived as wildflowers; grass dries up, flowers droop, God's Word goes on and on forever. This is the Word that conceived the new life in you."

- 1 Peter 1:22-25

Brain imaging studies show that our brain literally has visible "grooves" that represent our patterns or habits of living. Unless we live with a "deep consciousness of God" (1 Peter 1:18-21), we will lazily slip back into our old behavioral patterns. However, God offers to implant a new groove in our brain through His living word. His word goes on and on forever, so we never have to worry that He won't give us a new daily portion of Himself to focus on. This new groove He implants in our brain is part of our new birth, conceived by God Himself!

PRAYER: Lord, thank you that none of our evil grooves (idols and addictions) can compare to the "new-birth groove" you implant in our brain. As long as we focus on you, we stay in your presence, which surrounds us, protects us, and draws us away from slipping back into our old grooves. Nothing can compare to the allure of your unconditional love!

Personal Reflections

September 9

So clean house! Make a clean sweep of malice and pretense, envy and hurtful talk. You've had a taste of God. Now, like infants at the breast, drink deep of God's pure kindness. Then you'll grow up mature and whole in God.

- 1 Peter 2:1-3

When we clean our house we focus on the dirt to make sure we do a good job. The Old Testament taught people to follow God the same way. The New Testament teaches us how to clean up our life in a new, totally different way. The traditional way of cleaning up our lives, focusing on the dirt, did not work for people in the days of the Old Testament. The new way to make a clean sweep of malice and pretense, envy and hurtful talk is not about focusing on the dirt in our lives, because God says we always fail when we try through human effort to clean ourselves up. God says the only way to get cleaned up is to drink deep of His pure kindness. Drinking deep of His pure kindness means full sensory attention to His love and mindful focus on His thoughts He shares in His word and through thoughts He gives us directly through the Holy Spirit He plants in us.

PRAYER: Lord, thank you so much that you clean up our dirt and vacuum out our house as we focus on you and dwell in your house. You make a clean sweep of our life house and transform our old house into a new home where we dwell with you.

Personal Reflections

September 10

For instance, we know that when these bodies of ours are taken down like tents and folded away, they will be replaced by resurrection bodies in heaven—God-made, not handmade—and we'll never have to relocate our "tents" again. Sometimes we can hardly wait to move— and so we cry out in frustration. Compared to what's coming, living conditions around here seem like a stopover in an unfurnished shack, and we're tired of it! We've been given a glimpse of the real thing, our true home, our resurrection bodies! The Spirit of God whets our appetite by giving us a taste of what's ahead. He puts a little of heaven in our hearts so that we'll never settle for less.

- 2 Corinthians 5:1-5

Not only does God clean up our house while we focus on Him, He is preparing a new home for us in heaven where we will spend eternity with Him. While on earth, He dwells in our hearts so we get a taste of how wonderful heaven will be. So wonderful that it makes our current earthly homes seem like unfurnished shacks. Even though it seems like waiting for His return is taking forever, once we are with Him in heaven, our stay here on earth will feel like a mere stopover.

PRAYER: Lord, there are times when we can hardly wait to move out of our earthly bodies and our current circumstances. Thank you that you will replace these "tents" with resurrection bodies in heaven that are no longer mortal and decaying, but eternal!

Personal Reflections

September 11

That's why we live with such good cheer. You won't see us drooping our heads or dragging our feet! Cramped conditions here don't get us down. They only remind us of the spacious living conditions ahead. It's what we trust in but don't yet see that keeps us going. Do you suppose a few ruts in the road or rocks in the path are going to stop us? When the time comes, we'll be plenty ready to exchange exile for homecoming.

- 2 Corinthians 5:6-8

God encourages us by suggesting that we just see our cramped conditions here on earth as simple reminders of our spacious living conditions ahead. In other words, don't focus our attention on our horrible conditions here on earth, because we will end up discouraged and depressed, with our heads dropping and our feet dragging. Rather than focus on these ugly conditions, we can choose to use them as prompts to switch our attention to our bright future in heaven. We can focus ahead by reading in God's word about the home our heavenly Father is building for us and praising Him for His wonderful love.

PRAYER: Lord, thank you for the powerful, glimpses you give us of our future lives with you. You created our brains to store vivid images of these glimpses you give us through your word and the Holy Spirit. Thank you that these images are sent to encourage us and to focus our attention on you when things on earth are hard. You are building our new home, and this world can hardly hold a candle to its brightness!

Personal Reflections

September 12

This is the kind of life you've been invited into, the kind of life Christ lived. He suffered everything that came his way so you would know that it could be done, and also know how to do it, step-by-step. He never did one thing wrong, not once said anything amiss. They called him every name in the book and he said nothing back. He suffered in silence, content to let God set things right. He used his servant body to carry our sins to the Cross so we could be rid of sin, free to live the right way. His wounds became your healing. You were lost sheep with no idea who you were or where you were going. Now you're named and kept for good by the Shepherd of your souls.

- 1 Peter 2:21-25

If we are going to totally focus and follow God, it's reassuring to know that He knows how to live life step-by-step, without ever doing one thing wrong. He suffered everything that came His way, just so we would know He has total understanding and compassion for our struggles. He wasn't some goody-two-shoes who lived an easy life. He was ridiculed and called every name in the book. He certainly can relate to all the junk we go through in life.

PRAYER: Lord, as lost sheep who have no idea who we are or where we are going, we thank you for inviting us into your fold, where we are safe and sound. We are grateful that we can depend on who you are and where you are going. Our identity is in you.

Personal Reflections

September 13

If with heart and soul you're doing good, do you think you can be stopped? Even if you suffer for it, you're still better off. Don't give the opposition a second thought. Through thick and thin, keep your hearts at attention, in adoration before Christ, your Master. Be ready to speak up and tell anyone who asks why you're living the way you are, and always with the utmost courtesy. Keep a clear conscience before God so that when people throw mud at you, none of it will stick. They'll end up realizing that they're the ones who need a bath.

- 1 Peter 3:13-16

For us to see the kind of life Christ lived, we are instructed to keep our hearts at full attention, in adoration of Jesus. Giving God our full sensory attention, with our eyes, ears, nose, mouth and hands, is how we experience God with our heart. We are at full focus, ready to receive His thoughts and His words of instruction. We drink deep of God's pure kindness and He shows us exactly how to follow Him, step by step. God's kindness that we drink in cannot be contained; we simply have to show the love we feel inside to others.

PRAYER: Lord, you instruct us step-by-step how to share with others what you do for us each day. What a relief not to have to figure this out on our own. You show us how to do everything—even how to witness to others. Thank goodness there is nothing you expect out of us on our own strength!

Personal Reflections

September 14

Everything in the world is about to be wrapped up, so take nothing for granted. Stay wide-awake in prayer. Most of all, love each other as if your life depended on it. Love makes up for practically anything. Be quick to give a meal to the hungry, a bed to the homeless—cheerfully. Be generous with the different things God gave you, passing them around so all get in on it: if words, let it be God's words; if help, let it be God's hearty help. That way, God's bright presence will be evident in everything through Jesus, and he'll get all the credit as the One mighty in everything—encores to the end of time. Oh, yes!.

- 1 Peter 4:7-11

These verses give us more step-by-step instructions on how to stay focused on God—by sharing God's hearty help through giving a meal to the hungry or a bed to the homeless. Another great way to stay focused on God is to pass His words around. These can be words from scriptures or words God gives us when we stay wide-awake in prayer. As we share God's words and His help, He gives us a strong feeling of love that makes up for practically anything.

PRAYER: Lord, sharing you makes it so easy to focus on you and not be distracted by all my own dirt. You clean my house as I stay focused on you, drinking deep from your pure kindness. I am so glad you do all the performing in me. I am so glad you get all the credit. I feel so relieved to have the monkey of performance-pressure off my back!

Personal Reflections

September 15

Since Jesus went through everything you're going through and more, learn to think like him. Think of your sufferings as a weaning from that old sinful habit of always expecting to get your own way. Then you'll be able to live out your days free to pursue what God wants instead of being tyrannized by what you want.

- 1 Peter 4:1-2

Expecting to get our way comes naturally for all of us. Our culture even promotes getting our own way. Yet, expectations cause anger, anxiety, and even depression when they aren't fulfilled. We automatically set ourselves up to feel bad. Feeling bad blocks our freedom to live out our days pursuing what God wants. Instead, we choose to live under the bondage and tyranny of what we want. These verses teach us to learn from how Jesus responded to sufferings. When we learn to expect sufferings, and when we respond to them as He did, following our risen Savior brings us His joy rather than anger or depression.

PRAYER: Lord, thank you for showing me in these verses how your teaching is the opposite of the world's teaching. The world teaches me to expect to get what I want, which yields bondage to anger, anxiety, and depression. You instruct me to expect sufferings, but comfort me with the promise that you will use them to change me and make me free to pursue you. Lord, give me constant reminders of how you think, so your thoughts become my thoughts.

Personal Reflections

September 16

Friends, when life gets really difficult, don't jump to the conclusion that God isn't on the job. Instead, be glad that you are in the very thick of what Christ experienced. This is a spiritual refining process, with glory just around the corner.

- 1 Peter 4:12-13

When life gets difficult, our natural tendency is to automatically feel abandoned by God and jump to the conclusion that He isn't on the job, or that He doesn't care about protecting us. From a human perspective, it is impossible to envision that glory is just around the corner. However, when we focus on Jesus, we see difficulties in life as a reminder that we are in the thick of what Christ experienced. He suffered it all long before us, and in the midst of our pain, He is with us, helping us bear it. He has not abandoned us. He always takes care of us in tangible ways that remind us that he is always close to us, especially in difficult times.

PRAYER: Lord, when life is easy, I want to praise you. When life is difficult, I will choose to praise you even more, because you are my only hope to get through life's difficulties. I know you don't expect me to fake being happy when life is difficult, but I also know that you bring me your joy when I acknowledge your presence. Thank you for never leaving or forsaking me, especially during difficult times. I will choose to believe that glory is just around the corner!

Personal Reflections

September 17

If you're abused because of Christ, count yourself fortunate. It's the Spirit of God and his glory in you that brought you to the notice of others. If they're on you because you broke the law or disturbed the peace, that's a different matter. But if it's because you're a Christian, don't give it a second thought. Be proud of the distinguished status reflected in that name!

- 1 Peter 4:14-16

How is it possible not to give it a second thought when we are abused because of Christ? It is not possible unless we focus on Him and stay in deep reflection of the distinguished status of His name. It is our continual focus on Him, and His spirit and glory in us, that brings us the notice of others in the first place. Some will notice and choose to follow Jesus. Others will choose to reject Him and pour out their rejection on us. When we see our abuse in that light, we are proud of whom we follow. That's the only way not to give our sufferings a second thought.

PRAYER: Lord, all of our earthly teachers have emphasized self-protection and have urged us to avoid putting ourselves in a position where we can be criticized and persecuted for our faith in you. Even in our churches, we tend to stay in the warmth and comfort of our modern, beautiful facilities, and not venture out into the cold, cruel dark world. Lord, we choose to follow you out there now, and we will rejoice in you even through rejection and pain.

Personal Reflections

September 18

I, Simon Peter, am a servant and apostle of Jesus Christ. I write this to you whose experience with God is as life-changing as ours, all due to our God's straight dealing and the intervention of our God and Savior, Jesus Christ. Grace and peace to you many times over as you deepen in your experience with God and Jesus, our Master. Everything that goes into a life of pleasing God has been miraculously given to us by getting to know, personally and intimately, the One who invited us to God. The best invitation we ever received! We were also given absolutely terrific promises to pass on to you— your tickets to participation in the life of God after you turned your back on a world corrupted by lust.

- 2 Peter 1:1-4

The peace and promises that God wants to pass on to us only begin when we focus on Him. This focus is impossible unless we turn our backs on a world corrupted by lust. There are many, many lusts that only fade into the past when we devote our eyes and our other senses to Christ. Nothing compares to His desirability, but desiring Him is an acquired taste that Christ can only give us, just as He miraculously gives us everything we need to please Him.

PRAYER: Lord, remind us over and over again of these steps to experiencing daily life-change. Thank you for the invitation to focus on you. Continue to show us how to deepen our experience Jesus, our Master.

Personal Reflections

September 19

Because the stakes are so high, even though you're up-to-date on all this truth and practice it inside and out, I'm not going to let up for a minute in calling you to attention before it. This is the post to which I've been assigned—keeping you alert with frequent reminders—and I'm sticking to it as long as I live. I know that I'm to die soon; the Master has made that quite clear to me. And so I am especially eager that you have all this down in black and white so that after I die, you'll have it for ready reference.

- 2 Peter 1:12-15

The purpose of the daily verses in Clear My Vision is to keep us all alert with frequent reminders about how we can focus on our Maker and Redeemer. A critical aspect of these daily reminders, of course, is that focusing on God is a simple choice we make, not a grueling effort we engage in to be holy. We are not able to earn God's favor through any efforts to perform. However, by giving Him the full attention of our thoughts and five senses, we prepare our hearts to be filled with His thoughts and feelings, which change us from the inside out!

PRAYER: Lord, thank you for Peter's example of eagerly wanting to put down his reminders in black and white so we all have ready reference to the instructions you give us on how to follow you. Lord, just as you gave Peter a clear vision, please clear our vision!

Personal Reflections

September 20

We weren't, you know, just wishing on a star when we laid the facts out before you regarding the powerful return of our Master, Jesus Christ. We were there for the preview! We saw it with our own eyes: Jesus resplendent with light from God the Father as the voice of Majestic Glory spoke: "This is my Son, marked by my love, focus of all my delight." We were there on the holy mountain with him. We heard the voice out of heaven with our very own ears.

- 2 Peter 1:16-18

Experiencing the wonder of Christ's unconditional love is not just wishing on a star. We often long for things and allow our imaginations to go wild until we realize that we were just engaging in wishful thinking. We hurt our own feelings and are filled with disappointment because our desires were left unfulfilled. However, experiencing Christ is not magical thinking or imagined feelings. He has revealed His splendor so that we see His magnificence with our own eyes and hear His voice with our very own ears. Our imaginations have not just gone wild. His love is real and we can feel Him with every fiber of our being.

PRAYER: Lord, we are so thankful that your love for us is not just something we imagine. How cruel it would be to discover that your love is not real. Sometimes your love is all we have to hang onto when times are very difficult, but you never leave or forsake us!

Personal Reflections

September 21

We couldn't be more sure of what we saw and heard—God's glory, God's voice. The prophetic Word was confirmed to us. You'll do well to keep focusing on it. It's the one light you have in a dark time as you wait for daybreak and the rising of the Morning Star in your hearts. The main thing to keep in mind here is that no prophecy of Scripture is a matter of private opinion. And why? Because it's not something concocted in the human heart. Prophecy resulted when the Holy Spirit prompted men and women to speak God's Word.

- 2 Peter 1:19-21

Sometimes we concoct voices or sounds in our minds. In the counseling field, these are called hallucinations or delusions. This Scripture clearly tells us that seeing God's glory and hearing His voice are definitely not human concoctions. Instead of ignoring what we see and hear, we are instructed to keep focusing. As we continue to focus, God promises that we will have one light we can fix our eyes on even in the darkest times and that He will show us the rise of the Morning Star at daybreak.

PRAYER: Lord, we are so afraid of the dark in our lives. When it is pitch black, we have absolutely nothing to focus on. Thank you that, even in the darkest times, you promise us one light so we can stay focused on you. Your light never grows dim or gets snuffed out; it shines the brightest when everything else in our lives is dark.

Personal Reflections

September 22

My dear friends, this is now the second time I've written to you, both letters reminders to hold your minds in a state of undistracted attention. Keep in mind what the holy prophets said, and the command of our Master and Savior that was passed on by your apostles. First off, you need to know that in the last days, mockers are going to have a heyday. Reducing everything to the level of their puny feelings, they'll mock, "So what's happened to the promise of his Coming?"

- 2 Peter 3:1-4

I can't even imagine how it is possible to stay in a state of undistracted attention. Even addicts sometimes take a break from focusing on their addictions! The good news is that God doesn't ask us to stay focused through our own efforts. His word offers continual reminders of His promise to someday return and make everything new. Even though mockers may have a heyday looking around at all the bad things in the world and claiming that His promises are false, we know that even when we feel alone, He is here, and He keeps His promises.

PRAYER: Lord, we are grateful that you provide us with continual reminders that bring us to a state of undivided attention on you with all of our thoughts and five senses. Our gratitude deepens as we are surrounded by mockers who try to draw our attention away from you. These mockers only remind us how much we desire to stay focused on you, and how much we look forward to your return.

Personal Reflections

September 23

Since everything here today might well be gone tomorrow, do you see how essential it is to live a holy life? Daily expect the Day of God, eager for its arrival. The galaxies will burn up and the elements melt down that day—but we'll hardly notice. We'll be looking the other way, ready for the promised new heavens and the promised new earth, all landscaped with righteousness.

- 2 Peter 3:11-13

When we read sentences like, "do you see how essential it is to live a holy life?" we tend to hang our heads in defeat because we know we cannot measure up. However, these verses show us that a holy life is not about performance or measuring up, but about eagerly anticipating the Day of God, His second coming. As we focus on the promised new heavens and the promised new earth, all landscaped with righteousness, we become filled with God-focus, our whole being waiting in anticipation for His return. When He comes, we will hardly notice the destruction of evil because we are looking the other way, focused on the kingdom of righteousness, our new home with Him. What a vivid description of Him holding our minds in a state of undivided attention!

PRAYER: Thank you, Lord! Over and over again, you remind us how to focus on you. Surely, as we continue to read these daily scriptures on how to focus, you are clearing our vision every day. We feel closer to you and to joining you in the Promised Land.

Personal Reflections

September 24

We saw it, we heard it, and now we're telling you so you can experience it along with us, this experience of communion with the Father and his Son, Jesus Christ. Our motive for writing is simply this: We want you to enjoy this, too. Your joy will double our joy!

- 1 John 1:3-4

We have been taught how to live a holy life through communion with the Father and His Son. We are promised this communion simply by accepting Christ as our Savior and giving Him our full attention. To focus on Him and have fellowship with Him is a choice we can make, one that does not require the effort of our own performance. In fact, any efforts on our part to be holy fail miserably, because focus on our own efforts serves only to distract us from focusing on and fellowshipping with our heavenly Father. What a relief to learn that living a holy life is not about human effort but about simple focus on our Savior!

PRAYER: Dear Lord, thank you for the constant reminders in your word to focus on you instead of on our human effort. We are so tired of the pressure to perform and of our incessant efforts to become holy on our own. Thank you for releasing us from this overwhelming, relentless pressure through your simple reminder to commune with you and your Son.

Personal Reflections

September 25

I write this, dear children, to guide you out of sin. But if anyone does sin, we have a Priest-Friend in the presence of the Father: Jesus Christ, righteous Jesus. When he served as a sacrifice for our sins, he solved the sin problem for good—not only ours, but the whole world's.

- 1 John 2:1-2

Many of us have been taught for years that stopping our sin is something we have to do on our own. These verses can lift a tremendous weight off our backs! Jesus Christ wants us to know that He solved the problem of our sin through His shed blood on the cross. He doesn't expect us to stop our sin on our own willpower. He wants us to focus on Him and His amazing love, and let Him guide us out of sin. Our focus is taken off our sin when we give Him our undivided attention. When He has all of our attention, the Lord clearly shows us that His unconditional love and care is far more attractive than any sin could ever possibly be.

PRAYER: Lord, thank you for teaching us that focus on you—not on our performance—guides us out of sin. Our efforts to pull ourselves out of sin only serve to keep us preoccupied with sin, and keeping our full attention on sin only makes that sin even more alluring to us. Thank you that when we simply choose to shift our focus to you and away from our sin, you work on our behalf to solve our sin problem.

Personal Reflections

September 26

I remind you, my dear children: Your sins are forgiven in Jesus' name. You veterans were in on the ground floor, and know the One who started all this; you newcomers have won a big victory over the Evil One... You veterans know the One who started it all; and you newcomers—such vitality and strength! God's word is so steady in you. Your fellowship with God enables you to gain a victory over the Evil One.

- 1 John 2:12-14

n these verses, we are given two reminders. One, we are forgiven in Jesus' name. Two, we know the Father from personal experience. Meditating on these two truths When we remember to ask God to remind us of these two truths, a great way to stay focused on Him. The secret to victory over the Evil One is our fellowship with Him, not our own human efforts to stop sinning. God's word is so steady in reminding us over and over again that our vitality and strength are gifts from God when we keep our eyes on Him!

PRAYER: Lord, I am thankful that your word keeps reminding me that you give us clear vision through focus on you. Thank you for your reminders. Thank you for your forgiveness. And thank you for the gift of focus. I am so relieved that I can finally be free of the burden of performance in my daily fellowship with you.

Personal Reflections

September 27

Don't love the world's ways. Don't love the world's goods. Love of the world squeezes out love for the Father. Practically everything that goes on in the world—wanting your own way, wanting everything for yourself, wanting to appear important—has nothing to do with the Father. It just isolates you from him. The world and all its wanting, wanting, wanting is on the way out—but whoever does what God wants is set for eternity.

- 1 John 2:15-17

What a drastic statement: "practically everything that goes on in the world . . . has nothing to do with the Father." Love for the world's ways occurs automatically when we focus on ourselves. This self-focus isolates us from our Father, who wants to show us His amazing love. He can give us a desire for Him that far surpasses all the worldly wants combined. All He asks is that we give Him all of our attention so that our focus on the world does not continue to squeeze out our love for Him.

PRAYER: Lord, thank you for more verses to remind us that focus on you is the only way to see how amazing you are. Nothing compares to how you singlehandedly draw us away from sin and love for the desires of the world. When you draw us to your love, our love of the world is left far behind in the dust.

Personal Reflections

September 28

Stay with what you heard from the beginning, the original message. Let it sink into your life. If what you heard from the beginning lives deeply in you, you will live deeply in both Son and Father. This is exactly what Christ promised: eternal life, real life!

- 1 John 2:24-25

These verses, and many others, make it clear that God's Word is the main course, the meat and potatoes, of focus on Him. These verses show us that by letting what we have heard from the beginning sink deep into our lives, we will live deeply in both Son and Father. Not only does that mean we will live for eternity, but living deeply in both Son and Father is our only protection from this world and its destruction. Christ's many promises to us never, ever fail. We will reign in eternity with Him; we will dwell in everlasting community with the Father, the Son, and the Spirit. Our new lives will be filled with glory, righteousness, and peace, as we bask in the glow of our Father's forever favor.

PRAYER: Lord, thank you for teaching us how to let your Word sink deeply into our lives through giving you the undivided attention of all our thoughts and feelings. The outcome is amazing! We will live deeply in both Son and Father! What a safe feeling from the ugliness of this world!

Personal Reflections

September 29

I've written to warn you about those who are trying to deceive you. But they're no match for what is embedded deeply within you—Christ's anointing, no less! You don't need any of their so-called teaching. Christ's anointing teaches you the truth on everything you need to know about yourself and him, uncontaminated by a single lie. Live deeply in what you were taught.

- 1 John 2:26-27

Part of living deeply in both Son and Father is that we experience His teachings embedded deep inside us in surround sound and high-definition color. His teachings are not just head knowledge, but are alive inside our hearts. With every breath we take, we experience His anointing. Anyone who tries to deceive us is no match for what is embedded deeply within us. When we live deeply in what Christ is teaching us, we are not confused by false teaching. We exult in God's truth about ourselves and the world, and we love His truth, which is uncontaminated by even a single lie.

PRAYER: Lord, thank you for making your teaching so clear that there is no way to confuse your instructions with false teaching. Thank you for not ever putting us in a position where we need to debate or figure out your teaching. You make your "how to manual for dummies" so all we have to do is focus and follow your simple step-by-step instructions.

Personal Reflections

September 30

But friends, that's exactly who we are: children of God. And that's only the beginning. Who knows how we'll end up! What we know is that when Christ is openly revealed, we'll see him—and in seeing him, become like him. All of us who look forward to his Coming stay ready, with the glistening purity of Jesus' life as a model for our own.

- 1 John 3:2-3

Isn't this verse incredible? We are children of God! Think of it—that's beyond our comprehension, and yet it is only the beginning. We are promised that when we live deeply in both Son and Father we will become like Him, simply by seeing Him. Again, amazing results in our lives from simply focusing on Him and staying ready for His Coming. Simply by focusing on Jesus' life, we will begin to reflect His glistening purity.

PRAYER: Lord, we never miss seeing something that glistens. Thank you so much that your life glistens so brightly that we cannot miss you as we turn our eyes toward you. We turn the eyes of our heart to you and you open them. You open all of our feelings to see you, smell you, hear you, touch you and even taste your goodness through your wonderful creation. Thank you that you are daily transforming our bodies and our minds to reflect your perfection.

Personal Reflections

October 1

All who indulge in a sinful life are dangerously lawless, for sin is a major disruption of God's order. Surely you know that Christ showed up in order to get rid of sin. There is no sin in him, and sin is not part of his program. No one who lives deeply in Christ makes a practice of sin. None of those who do practice sin have taken a good look at Christ. They've got him all backward.

- 1 John 3:4-6

Christ showed up in order to get rid of sin. As we give God our full undivided attention, we begin to imitate His sinless nature. The more we look at Him, the more we are changed into His likeness. That's how He gets rid of our sin—by enabling us to be like Him and get off the sin program. Anyone who stays focused on Him and lives deeply in Christ will not make a practice of sin. If we are making a practice of sin, that simply means we got Him all backwards. We are focused on our sins and not on Him.

PRAYER: Lord, thank you so much for this teaching. We are so glad that, by keeping our eyes on you, you get rid of our sin by not letting it in your program. By focusing on you, our sin gets left behind. All we need to do is not turn about and try to fix our own sin. You already dealt with our sin on the cross, and our messed-up efforts to clean up our lives and perform better only make our sin worse. We simply need to focus on You and leave our sin in your hands.

Personal Reflections

October 2

*From the very first day, we were there, taking it all in—
we heard it with our own ears, saw it with our own eyes,
verified it with our own hands. The Word of Life
appeared right before our eyes; we saw it happen! And
now we're telling you in most sober prose that what we
witnessed was, incredibly, this: The infinite Life of God
himself took shape before us.*

- 1 John 1:1-2

These verses spell out how the early disciples experienced communion with God through His Son from the very first day they began to follow Jesus in Galilee. Though we do not have Jesus embodied in front of us, our experience echoes the disciples in some ways. When we accept Jesus into our life, a whole new world opens up to us. We take it all in with all our thoughts and five senses. We hear the Word with our own ears. We see its power in our lives with our own eyes. Because we have given God our full attention with both sides of our brain, our thoughts as well as our senses, what we witness is incredible.

PRAYER: Thank you, Lord, that you are a God whose powers of attraction are infinitely more alluring than the power of addictions. As we give you all of our thought and sensory focus, you captivate us and draw us into a deep relationship with you. Our relationships with addictions fade into the darkness and get left behind as we fall deeper and deeper in love with you.

Personal Reflections

October 3

This, in essence, is the message we heard from Christ and are passing on to you: God is light, pure light; there's not a trace of darkness in him. If we claim that we experience a shared life with him and continue to stumble around in the dark, we're obviously lying through our teeth—we're not living what we claim. But if we walk in the light, God himself being the light, we also experience a shared life with one another, as the sacrificed blood of Jesus, God's Son, purges all our sin.

- 1 John 1:5-7

These verses teach us how to walk in the light. We walk in the light through a shared experience with God Himself, who is the light. With the sacrificed blood of Jesus purging all our sin, we are free to walk in the light, to leave our old life of stumbling around in the dark. Our part is to give God the full attention of all our thoughts and feelings. Since God Himself is the light, all of us who focus on Him stay in the light and experience a shared life with others who focus on Him.

PRAYER: Lord, thank you that you are pure light without a trace of darkness. Thank you that when we choose to focus on you, you give us a shared life with others who are also focused on you. Your light shines on all of us. Thank you for giving us the discernment to know when others around us are stumbling around in the dark, even when they claim to know you.

Personal Reflections

October 4

If we claim that we're free of sin, we're only fooling ourselves. A claim like that is errant nonsense. On the other hand, if we admit our sins—make a clean breast of them—he won't let us down; he'll be true to himself. He'll forgive our sins and purge us of all wrongdoing. If we claim that we've never sinned, we out-and-out contradict God—make a liar out of him. A claim like that only shows off our ignorance of God.

- 1 John 1:8-10

It is so interesting that these verses are written right after the verses on walking in the light. The only way we are able to admit our sins is by walking in the light. As we walk in the light, God's light shines on our sin. His light is the only way our vision is clear to see and confess our sin. Otherwise, if we stay in the dark, we stumble around, fool ourselves, and claim that we're free of sin. However, anyone who stands in the light can clearly see their own sin. If we were sinless, we would not even need a Savior to depend on, but as it is, we need Him desperately.

PRAYER: Lord, we are learning that we are totally dependent on you to show us our sin. Thank you—because we have a natural tendency to deny our sin in our efforts to be perfect. What a relief to have the pressure to perform lifted off our backs. You want to carry us everywhere, even up to the mirror to show us our sin just so you can let us know that you see us— and that you forgive us. You hold us even tighter, just to show us your love is unconditional.

Personal Reflections

October 5

So, my dear children, don't let anyone divert you from the truth. It's the person who acts right who is right, just as we see it lived out in our righteous Messiah. Those who make a practice of sin are straight from the Devil, the pioneer in the practice of sin. The Son of God entered the scene to abolish the Devil's ways.

- 1 John 3:7-8

When it comes to our focus on the Lord, we all seem to have ADHD because we are so easily distracted. Jesus came into our lives with His unconditional love and caring to draw our attention to Him away from our sinful living. Although He promises us that His love is far more attractive than the sins in our lives, we have to give Him a chance to fulfill this promise. Being attracted to His love is an acquired taste because we have been so used to the taste of sin. We give him a chance when we give Him our full attention so He can draw us to himself.

PRAYER: Thank you, Lord, that you simply ask for our full attention rather than demand a high standard of performance from us. We can choose to give you our full attention. That is a choice all of us are able to make. None of us have ever been able to measure up to your goodness. Thank you for your permission to stop trying. Thank you for your power to live rightly as we look to you.

Personal Reflections

October 6

People conceived and brought into life by God don't make a practice of sin. How could they? God's seed is deep within them, making them who they are. It's not in the nature of the God-begotten to practice and parade sin. Here's how you tell the difference between God's children and the Devil's children: The one who won't practice righteous ways isn't from God, nor is the one who won't love brother or sister. A simple test. For this is the original message we heard: We should love each other.

- 1 John 3:9-11

God's seed deep within us makes us who we are. Only when we focus on Him can His seed begin to grow within us and mature us into glorious God-children. As we give Him the full attention of our thoughts and feelings, our desire to sin fades into the background and is left behind. Instead, God fills us with a desire to love, which spills over into our feelings and actions towards others. This new, deep love is a simple test or measure of our focus on God, and a reflection of His life in us.

PRAYER: Lord, I realize now that this focus on you is the secret to leaving my sinful desires behind. When I choose to turn my heart away from my sins and my self-help salvation, I am free to give you my full attention. And as I look in awe at your goodness, I am filled with a new desire to love you and share your love with others.

Personal Reflections

October 7

My dear children, let's not just talk about love; let's practice real love. This is the only way we'll know we're living truly, living in God's reality. It's also the way to shut down debilitating self-criticism, even when there is something to it. For God is greater than our worried hearts and knows more about us than we do ourselves.

- 1 John 3:18-20

If we are merely talking about love and not feeling love or showing it, that's a reliable indicator that we're not focusing on our Lord. The only way we really know we are totally focused on Him is when we practice real love. That tells us for sure that we're living, truly living. Through focus on Him and practicing real love, God shuts down our self-criticism and worry, even when we have good reason to be self-critical or worried from a human perspective. We do mess up and fail ourselves and others, but God's love encourages us to take the hand He offers us, get back up again, and focus on Him instead of on our failures.

PRAYER: Lord, you have shown us through these verses how the desire to love is the outcome of focus on you. What an amazing motivator to want to focus on you. We all want the passion to love and feel loved. Many of us have struggled in our efforts to feel love for many years. To learn that love comes from focusing on you with all our thoughts and feelings renews our belief in the power of love.

Personal Reflections

October 8

And friends, once that's taken care of and we're no longer accusing or condemning ourselves, we're bold and free before God! We're able to stretch our hands out and receive what we asked for because we're doing what he said, doing what pleases him. Again, this is God's command: to believe in his personally named Son, Jesus Christ. He told us to love each other, in line with the original command. As we keep his commands, we live deeply and surely in him, and he lives in us. And this is how we experience his deep and abiding presence in us: by the Spirit he gave us.

- 1 John 3:21-24

Christians don't usually debate the importance of keeping God's commands. What we often do debate is how we are to keep His commands. It seems the more human effort we put into obedience, the worse we get at obeying. Fixated on our performance, we turn self-focus into a self-salvation method that fails miserably every time. This is why turning our eyes toward God and away from ourselves is the first step towards becoming like Him. Fixing our focus on Him is the only way to stop our endless cycle of condemning and trying to save ourselves.

PRAYER: Lord, thank you that not only do you give us your Word as a tool to focus on you, but you love us so much that you give us an internal focus tool in your Spirit. Thank you for the help and counsel of your Spirit, who helps us to focus on you and be in tune with you every moment of the day.

Personal Reflections

October 9

My dear children, you come from God and belong to God. You have already won a big victory over those false teachers, for the Spirit in you is far stronger than anything in the world. These people belong to the Christ-denying world. They talk the world's language and the world eats it up. But we come from God and belong to God. Anyone who knows God understands us and listens. The person who has nothing to do with God will, of course, not listen to us. This is another test for telling the Spirit of Truth from the spirit of deception.

- 1 John 4:4-6

When we chose to focus on God through the Spirit in us, no earthly attraction even comes close in comparison to how God makes us feel. Because of His deep and abiding presence, we feel a sense of belonging that the Christ-denying world will never experience. God gives us a heart-felt understanding of His love and we want to listen to Him. That's another test of how intent our focus is: do we desire to listen to God?

PRAYER: Lord, thank you for these tests of my focus on you. Thank you for showing me that the desire to love and listen do not depend on my efforts to feel but from my choice to give you the full attention of my thoughts and five senses. When we try in our own strength to love and listen, we fail miserably. When we simply choose to focus on you, you fill us with the gift of desire to both love you and listen to you.

Personal Reflections

October 10

This is how we know we're living steadily and deeply in him, and he in us: He's given us life from his life, from his very own Spirit. Also, we've seen for ourselves and continue to state openly that the Father sent his Son as Savior of the world. Everyone who confesses that Jesus is God's Son participates continuously in an intimate relationship with God. We know it so well, we've embraced it heart and soul, this love that comes from God.

- 1 John 4:13-16

What a relief that God has shown us that genuine love is a gift from Him, and not a feeling we have to strive for through our own human efforts. Striving to love never results in feeling the desire to love. Thankfully, He not only gives us the knowledge of His love but the feeling of His love. We've embraced His love with heart and soul. As we focus on Him, we live steadily and deeply in Him. Our focus serves as a channel for God to give us life from His life, through His very own Spirit.

PRAYER: Thank you, Lord, that all of us who continue to confess you, and state openly that you sent your Son as the Savior of the world, participate continuously in an intimate relationship with you—with Love Itself. Thank you that you choose to breathe your very life into us through your Spirit, and that we can live steadily and deeply in you as we embrace your love with all our heart.

Personal Reflections

October 11

God is love. When we take up permanent residence in a life of love, we live in God and God lives in us. This way, love has the run of the house, becomes at home and mature in us, so that we're free of worry on Judgment Day—our standing in the world is identical with Christ's. There is no room in love for fear. Well-formed love banishes fear. Since fear is crippling, a fearful life—fear of death, fear of judgment—is one not yet fully formed in love.

- 1 John 4:17-18

What amazing results God gives us when we focus on Him! We live in God and God lives in us. This love has the run of the house. This love becomes at home and mature in us! This love grows as God continually keeps the valve open so His love can flow into us. As it becomes well-formed, this love banishes fear. Yes! Our crippling fears get left behind the longer we choose to keep our thoughts and five senses focused on Him.

PRAYER: Thank you so much, Lord, that you don't expect me to get rid of my own fear, because the more I focus on my own efforts not to be afraid, the more afraid I feel. As I continue to focus on you and not on my fear, your love crowds out my fear and it gets left behind. Only when I turn around to look at it does my fear creep back into my heart. Thank you for your patience in graciously showing me that a return of fear is simply a reminder to refocus on you.

Personal Reflections

October 12

We, though, are going to love—love and be loved. First we were loved, now we love. He loved us first. If anyone boasts, "I love God," and goes right on hating his brother or sister, thinking nothing of it, he is a liar. If he won't love the person he can see, how can he love the God he can't see? The command we have from Christ is blunt: Loving God includes loving people. You've got to love both.

- 1 John 4:19-21

Loving God is not about what we say, but what we feel and what we do. These verses say that it's impossible to feel love for God and still hate your brother or sister. It's also impossible to fall in love with God if we ignore Him to focus on our own efforts. Loving God does not come out of our efforts to feel, but out of our choice to focus on Him. When we focus on an addiction, we fall in love with it, but when we focus on God, we fall in love with Him! The best part is that God promises that the satisfaction we get from Him far exceeds any gratification from earthly desires.

PRAYER: Lord, we know that when we choose an addiction, we become a different person. Thank you that when we choose you, we also become different—in a radical, amazing way! As we are transformed into your likeness, we love like we've never loved before. We share your love with others, no matter who they are. That's how loving you includes loving people—we can't help ourselves!

Personal Reflections

October 13

Every person who believes that Jesus is, in fact, the Messiah, is God-begotten. If we love the One who conceives the child, we'll surely love the child who was conceived. The reality test on whether or not we love God's children is this: Do we love God? Do we keep his commands? The proof that we love God comes when we keep his commandments and they are not at all troublesome.

- 1 John 5:1-3

Most of us have heard that "we love God when we keep His commandments," and most of us have taken this verse to mean that we need to try harder and perform better. The problem is, when we try harder, all the effort burdens and troubles us. So how is it possible to discover that keeping His commandments is "not at all troublesome"? The only way is to focus on God and fall in love with Him. When we are falling in love with Him more and more each day, we want to obey His commandments—and they are not troublesome.

PRAYER: Lord, you leave us with no doubt that love is the outcome and measure of our focus on you. Finally, we understand what you mean when you tell us that our performance can't save us. Only you can. We obey you because you give us the desire to please you out of love. We no longer feel the pressure to perform and be perfect to earn your favor. You showered favor on us when you made us your children!

Personal Reflections

October 14

I can't tell you how happy I am to learn that many members of your congregation are diligent in living out the Truth, exactly as commanded by the Father. But permit me a reminder, friends, and this is not a new commandment but simply a repetition of our original and basic charter: that we love each other. Love means following his commandments, and his unifying commandment is that you conduct your lives in love. This is the first thing you heard, and nothing has changed.

- 2 John 1:4-6

These verses are all loaded with focus words! Words like "reminder" and "repetition" are terms that constitute focus aids. John intends to emphasize the importance of conducting our lives in love, so he makes sure we know that to love is to obey the commandments, and that the most essential command is the command to love. Our obedience to God's commandments comes from the desire He gives us to love Him and each other.

PRAYER: Lord, always remind me that my love comes from you as I fix my eyes on you. If I credit myself when others feel your love flowing through me, the attention to myself throws me off track and I forget my focus on you. As soon as I look to myself, I find that self-focus means that your love cannot continue to flow through me, and I feel all the weight of guilt for failing to perform on my own. Thank you for your love that reminds me to lift up my eyes to you again.

Personal Reflections

October 15

And be very careful around them so you don't lose out on what we've worked so diligently in together; I want you to get every reward you have coming to you. Anyone who gets so progressive in his thinking that he walks out on the teaching of Christ, walks out on God. But whoever stays with the teaching, stays faithful to both the Father and the Son.

- 2 John 1:8-9

According to these verses, we remain faithful by staying with the teaching, completely focused on God and His word. No performance is required, no figuring out, no debating, no struggling, no evaluating, no effort of any kind. We simply choose to give Him our undivided attention. Anyone who tries to "get progressive" in his thinking walks out on the teaching of Christ because he gets fixated on his own ideas. There is nothing to "figure out" or "struggle over" in God's Word. His teaching is clear, plain, and simple. As we give Him our attention, He clears our vision so we see the simplicity of His Word.

PRAYER: Lord, we are grateful that our faithfulness is not based on our performance. We can only depend on you to keep us faithful, because our efforts always result in failure. Lord, our culture is so full of performance expectations. Thank you that you don't want us to perform in our relationship with you. You simply want to pick us up and carry us everywhere on your back while you do all the performing in us.

Personal Reflections

October 16

But you, dear friends, carefully build yourselves up in this most holy faith by praying in the Holy Spirit, staying right at the center of God's love, keeping your arms open and outstretched, ready for the mercy of our Master, Jesus Christ. This is the unending life, the real life!

- Jude 1:20-21

When verses begin with performance-type words like "build," the stage is set for a surprise. This verse gives us instructions on how to build which have nothing to do with our performance, but rather our choice to focus on God's performance. How we build ourselves up is not at all about human effort, but about the choice to focus right at the center of God's love, keeping our arms open and outstretched, ready for the mercy of Jesus. Don't you see? God is doing the performing in us, through the Holy Spirit's prayers, and the abundant mercy of Christ that transforms our hearts in love for Him!

PRAYER: Lord, these verses really take away the pressure to perform! Thank you that the actions in this verse are simple choices to focus and are not at all effort-based. You simply instruct us to look to the center of your love, keep our arms open and outstretched, and be ready to receive your actions in us. Thank you for your amazing actions in us—your Holy Spirit and your mercy!

Personal Reflections

October 17

And now to him who can keep you on your feet, standing tall in his bright presence, fresh and celebrating—to our one God, our only Savior, through Jesus Christ, our Master, be glory, majesty, strength, and rule before all time, and now, and to the end of all time. Yes.

- Jude 1:24-25

Once again, we have verses that start with performance words: "on your feet." Once again, these are not instructions for us to try to stay on our feet or "stand tall" on our own. God clearly shows us that He performs in us to keep us on our feet. When we celebrate our one God, our only Savior, His bright presence keeps us standing tall. When we give our Lord the full attention of our thoughts and five senses, He shines so bright. We see His glory, His majesty and His strength, which is everlasting from before the beginning of time. And this amazing God is the one holding us up!

PRAYER: Lord, you have taught us that our thanks and celebration of you activates your joy in us. We know that the joy of the Lord is our strength. Now we see that your strength keeps us on our feet. Your presence is so bright and glorious, and it energizes us to love you and care for others. Thank you for keeping us standing tall before you, as we focus on your majesty and goodness in our lives.

Personal Reflections

October 18

My purpose in writing is simply this: that you who believe in God's Son will know beyond the shadow of a doubt that you have eternal life, the reality and not the illusion. And how bold and free we then become in his presence, freely asking according to his will, sure that he's listening. And if we're confident that he's listening, we know that what we've asked for is as good as ours.

- 1 John 5:13-15

How often we have tried and tried to be confident! Yet the more effort we put into trying, the more unsure of ourselves we feel. Over time, we grow less and less confident that God is really listening. Fortunately, possessing true confidence in God has nothing to do with our human efforts to be confident. Of course, trying to be confident doesn't work! Our failure is simply a reminder that we are totally dependent on Him to build our confidence through His faithfulness to listen. Every time we choose to focus on Him, He shows us that what we ask for is ours. He continually raises our level of confidence the more we focus on Him.

PRAYER: Thank you, Lord, that our confidence in having eternal life with you is based on our choice to make you the focus of our lives, and not our own human efforts to feel worthy of your gifts. Simply through giving you our undivided attention (and not trying to figure out why we doubt) you clearly show us that you are a reality and not an illusion.

Personal Reflections

October 19

Dear friends, I've dropped everything to write you about this life of salvation that we have in common. I have to write insisting—begging!—that you fight with everything you have in you for this faith entrusted to us as a gift to guard and cherish. What has happened is that some people have infiltrated our ranks (our Scriptures warned us this would happen), who beneath their pious skin are shameless scoundrels. Their design is to replace the sheer grace of our God with sheer license—which means doing away with Jesus Christ, our one and only Master.

- Jude 1:3-4

The words "guard" and "cherish" in this passage remind us of the concentrated focus we must have towards God and His gifts of grace and faith. When we guard a gift, we don't take our eyes off the gift. The more we keep our eyes on the gift, the more we fall in love with the gift and come to cherish it. The gift becomes a treasure that we hang onto for dear life.

PRAYER: Lord, thank you for warning us that the shameless scoundrels who try to steal our most precious gift often look the most pious on the outside. Showcasing their own accomplishments, they try to convince us that our performance is the secret to this life of salvation. Others insist that your gift of grace means we can do whatever we want with our lives, taking our eyes off you, valuing your gifts cheaply. We don't want to fall into either camp.

Personal Reflections

October 20

Go easy on those who hesitate in the faith. Go after those who take the wrong way. Be tender with sinners, but not soft on sin. The sin itself stinks to high heaven.

- Jude 1:22-23

Many of us have been brutal on ourselves when we hesitate in the faith, and we often judge others harshly because of our own failed efforts. However, God has clearly shown us that our relationship with Him is all about His faithfulness—not ours. What a relief to read that we are to "go easy" when anyone hesitates in the faith. Hesitancy simply means we have taken our focus off Him. We all choose not to focus many times, so we can reach out to others in humility and simply encourage them to refocus on Him. These verses instruct us to really seek out and be especially tender with those who are looking the wrong way. We can get upset at the sin and still be gentle with the sinner. Instructing us to seek out opportunities to share with those focused on sin is one of the amazing ways God keeps us focused on Him.

PRAYER: Lord, thank you for giving us the ability to be gentle with those who have lost their focus on you. The more we seek to follow you and encourage others to follow you, the more focus on you becomes a way of daily living and sin starts to get left behind. As we desire you more and more every day, the desire to sin loses its appeal. Thank you that sin fades away in the distance as we draw nearer to you.

Personal Reflections

October 21

I, John, with you all the way in the trial and the Kingdom and the passion of patience in Jesus, was on the island called Patmos because of God's Word, the witness of Jesus. It was Sunday and I was in the Spirit, praying. I heard a loud voice behind me, trumpet-clear and piercing: "Write what you see into a book. Send it to the seven churches: to Ephesus, Smyrna, Pergamum, Thyatira, Sardis, Philadelphia, Laodicea."

- Revelation 1:9-11

Clear My Vision would not be complete without including some reflections on Revelation, which literally means "the vision." Revelation is all about focus. The colorful language engages all of our five senses, capturing our thoughts and imagination. Just feel these resounding words: "I heard a loud voice behind me, trumpet-clear and piercing." Notice, too, the instructions the Voice gave John: "write down what you see." There are no instructions that say, "figure it out" or "try to decipher what I am saying." Just as in the case of the writer John, our part in God's revelation to us is simply to be in the Spirit with all our thoughts and senses focused on God.

PRAYER: Lord, thank you that our "passion of patience in Jesus" flourishes when we are in very difficult circumstances. Your unconditional love blasts its way through what seems to be unbearable and gives us the energy to care and love like never before. You rescue us and give us new life when we are at our lowest and raise us to new heights of passion for you.

Personal Reflections

October 22

I saw this and fainted dead at his feet. His right hand pulled me upright, his voice reassured me: "Don't fear: I am First, I am Last, I'm Alive. I died, but I came to life, and my life is now forever. See these keys in my hand? They open and lock Death's doors, they open and lock Hell's gates. Now write down everything you see: things that are, things about to be. The Seven Stars you saw in my right hand and the seven-branched gold menorah—do you want to know what's behind them? The Seven Stars are the Angels of the seven churches; the menorah's seven branches are the seven churches.".

- Revelation 1:16-20

These verses are so descriptive of God's performance and our response when we focus on Him. What He says or does can be so powerful that we may even faint! Fainting symbolizes our condition of total helplessness—we are incapable of any effort. God does all the performing through His hand pulling us upright and His voice reassuring us. His voice proclaims powerful, clear, concise words of His ultimate authority in our lives.

PRAYER: Lord, only you can pick us up when we reach the point of total helplessness. Only you can revive us and save us from eternal damnation. In your unconditional love, you tell us exactly what to do. There is no question that you desire that none should perish. Our only part is to cast our eyes on you and have the headsets you give each of us turned on so you can call every play in the game of life.

Personal Reflections

October 23

"Come!" say the Spirit and the Bride.
Whoever hears, echo, "Come!"
Is anyone thirsty? Come!
All who will, come and drink,
Drink freely of the Water of Life!

- Revelation 22:17

This is a very brief verse that is loaded with meaning. "Anyone who is thirsty"—everyone who is hurting or tired or lonely—is invited to come to Jesus. Absolutely no one who reaches out will be turned away. Jesus will reach out and touch anyone who reaches out to Him. "Drink freely"—there is no cost to focus on Him, no effort demanded, just a simple choice to reach out and receive the free gift of God taking over our life now and eventually taking us to heaven to live with Him forever. And all of us who focus on Him can echo His words, inviting anyone else who is hurting to receive this free gift just as we did. Inviting others keeps us thirsty to continue drinking freely of the "water of life," the true Source of satisfaction.

PRAYER: Lord, thank you for showing me that receiving your gift requires no effort—and neither does inviting others. I don't have to talk anyone into buying anything—your gift is free! All those people who told me how much effort it was to be your child, and how much effort was involved in witnessing to others—they were so wrong! Your love is warm and inviting, and I can't wait to let others know about it.

Personal Reflections

October 24

*God's readiness to give and forgive is now public.
Salvation's available for everyone! We're being shown
how to turn our backs on a godless, indulgent life, and
how to take on a God-filled, God-honoring life. This
new life is starting right now, and is whetting our
appetites for the glorious day when our great God and
Savior, Jesus Christ, appears. He offered himself as a
sacrifice to free us from a dark, rebellious life into this
good, pure life, making us a people he can be proud of,
energetic in goodness.*

- Titus 2:11-14

These verses remind us that the news is already public that God
gives and forgives, and salvation is available for everyone. We
have been shown how to turn our backs on a godless, indulgent
life, and how to take on a God-filled, God-honoring life, simply
by choosing to focus on Him. Our new life starts as soon as we
give Him our full attention. The rewards of focus include God
energizing us in goodness and whetting our appetites for when
we see Him in heaven. He also gives us that unbelievable
feeling of freedom from our dark rebellious life.

*PRAYER: Lord, thank you for giving us the feeling of freedom
that comes with this good, pure life. What frees us more than
anything is that this good life is a gift from you, simply because
we have chosen to make you our focus. We no longer feel the
bondage that comes with performance pressure or the need to
measure up.*

Personal Reflections

October 25

It wasn't so long ago that we ourselves were stupid and stubborn, dupes of sin, ordered every which way by our glands, going around with a chip on our shoulder, hated and hating back. But when God, our kind and loving Savior God, stepped in, he saved us from all that.

- Titus 3:3-5

Just as the choice to focus on God is not about effort, neither is the choice to take our focus off Him. When we are completely honest, most of us have to admit that it is often not very long ago that we lost focus on Him—a few minutes ago, a few hours, days, or weeks ago. All of us still have moments of stupidity, moments of sin, of being "ordered around by our glands," having a chip on our shoulder, of feeling hated, or hating back. All of us can be caring and patient with anyone who is not on the focus path with God, because we've been in their shoes. Fortunately for all of us, in our moments of taking our focus off God, He continually gives us simple reminders to choose to refocus on Him.

PRAYER: Thank you, Lord that our focus lapses are no longer excuses to ridicule or condemn ourselves or others. They are simply reminders to refocus on you, reminders of how desperately we want and need to totally depend on you. We feel free from our pressure to perform. Our focus lapses keep us in constant touch with our inability to take care of ourselves. We are leaving behind our tendency to give ourselves credit for all you do in us.

Personal Reflections

October 26

It was all his doing; we had nothing to do with it. He gave us a good bath, and we came out of it new people, washed inside and out by the Holy Spirit. Our Savior Jesus poured out new life so generously. God's gift has restored our relationship with him and given us back our lives. And there's more life to come—an eternity of life! You can count on this.

- Titus 3:6-7

These verses are clear reminders that we had nothing to do with being saved from all that. God did everything. He gets total credit. He gets all the credit for giving us a good bath, washing us inside and out, pouring out new life and making us new. As a free gift, He restored our relationship with Him and gave us back our lives. Our only part is to focus on Him, so He can do all the work to clean us up and make us new people. The reality is that we don't have to plead "Jesus, take the wheel," as the country song suggests. He already has the wheel. We simply need to take our hands off.

PRAYER: Lord, we are so grateful for all the hard work you put into each of us. We thankfully give up and take our hands off the wheel. Our efforts only get in the way as we travel this road to heaven, the road on which you are taking us. Thank you that your hands are strong and steady on the wheel, and that we can trust you to get us to our destination.

Personal Reflections

October 27

I want you to put your foot down. Take a firm stand on these matters so that those who have put their trust in God will concentrate on the essentials that are good for everyone. Stay away from mindless, pointless quarreling over genealogies and fine print in the law code. That gets you nowhere. Warn a quarrelsome person once or twice, but then be done with him. It's obvious that such a person is out of line, rebellious against God. By persisting in divisiveness he cuts himself off.

- Titus 3:8-11

"I want you to put your foot down" may sound hard and performance-based, because in our American culture these words imply we should be tough. However, in context, they simply mean "make the choice to stay away" from pointless quarreling, and focus only on the essentials that are good for everyone. Even the word "concentrate" is not a performance word, but a focus word—a simple choice to devote all of our thoughts and five senses to focus on the essentials of God.

PRAYER: Lord, one of my favorite prayers now begins with "remind me." I trust that your Holy Spirit inside me will bring me reminders at exactly the right moment. Relying on your reminders is much better than relying on my own memory (and even better than using sticky notes, because I constantly forget where I put them!) Thank you for your faithfulness to remind me continually of your truth, especially right when I need it most.

Personal Reflections

October 28

Every time your name comes up in my prayers, I say, "Oh, thank you, God!" I keep hearing of the love and faith you have for the Master Jesus, which brims over to other believers. And I keep praying that this faith we hold in common keeps showing up in the good things we do, and that people recognize Christ in all of it. Friend, you have no idea how good your love makes me feel, doubly so when I see your hospitality to fellow believers.

- Philemon 1:4-7

Over the years, many of us have not experienced how good God's love can make us feel. Many of us were told by our Christian leaders that feelings were wrong or bad, and certainly did not apply in our relationship with Christ. Supposedly, His love was about our knowledge of Him and not about our "fickle" feelings. Nowhere in God's word is there a basis for this false teaching. On the contrary, Christ's love for us is intended to give us such an intense love for Him that we never want to take our eyes off Him and we can't hold ourselves back from sharing this love with others.

PRAYER: Lord, thank you that when we observe others who love you so much that they can't stop sharing, our hearts overflow with thanks to you. We feel doubly good inside when someone we have shared with shows compassion to fellow believers. No addiction can compare to how good you make us feel.

Personal Reflections

October 29

I'm sure that won't happen to you, friends. I have better things in mind for you—salvation things! God doesn't miss anything. He knows perfectly well all the love you've shown him by helping needy Christians, and that you keep at it. And now I want each of you to extend that same intensity toward a full-bodied hope, and keep at it till the finish. Don't drag your feet. Be like those who stay the course with committed faith and then get everything promised to them.

- Hebrews 6:9-12

God loves it when we show Him our love through helping the needy. He urges us not to "drag our feet." Many would interpret those words by saying we need to push ourselves to do more. Certainly, church leaders often pressure church members to do more and try harder. Fortunately, God's word to us is not "try harder," but "I do all the performing in you." As we choose to continue our focus on Him and continue to thank Him, He supplies us with the joy of the Lord, which is our strength—the endless supply of love that fills our hearts. Our passion, not our efforts, keeps us staying the course.

PRAYER: Lord, thank you once again for giving us verses that remind us how this journey with you works. You show us so clearly "how" to stay the course. You want us to receive all the promises and riches in glory that you have told us about. We want to keep sharing your good news. That's how good you have made us feel inside!

Personal Reflections

October 30

So come on, let's leave the preschool fingerpainting exercises on Christ and get on with the grand work of art. Grow up in Christ. The basic foundational truths are in place: turning your back on "salvation by self-help" and turning in trust toward God; baptismal instructions; laying on of hands; resurrection of the dead; eternal judgment. God helping us, we'll stay true to all that. But there's so much more. Let's get on with it!

- Hebrews 6:1-3

The challenge to "leave preschool" could definitely feed our obsession with pushing ourselves to try harder. However, the phrase "grand work of art" paints the real picture of what these words mean. We are to turn our backs on our self-help efforts! When we choose to focus on Him by "turning in trust toward God," God can get on with helping us and teaching us as if we are going all the way from preschool to a post-graduate education. He wants to perform in and through our lives as a master artist. He wants to craft us into a refined, finished masterpiece work of art.

PRAYER: Lord, I am thankful and relieved that you do not expect us to do "salvation by self-help." I have started and restarted my attempts at crafting myself into a masterpiece of art so many times without success. Lord, I give up that futile effort now. From now on, I want to watch you do the artwork in my life. Teach me to see your handiwork. Clear my vision.

Personal Reflections

October 31

We who have run for our very lives to God have every reason to grab the promised hope with both hands and never let go. It's an unbreakable spiritual lifeline, reaching past all appearances right to the very presence of God where Jesus, running on ahead of us, has taken up his permanent post as high priest for us, in the order of Melchizedek.

- Hebrews 6:18-20

What a word-picture of how to focus on God: "We who have run for our very lives to God." Broken and defeated in our own efforts to make our lives work, we ran to Him in our despair, and now cling onto Him for dear life. We are totally dependent on Him, which goes totally against our natural tendency for independence. God shows us (to our total surprise) that He has wanted us all along to run to Him. When we cling to Him, He provides us with an unbreakable spiritual lifeline that reaches all the way to the very presence of God—"where Jesus, running on ahead of us, has taken up his permanent post as high priest for us."

PRAYER: Lord, after reading these verses, I am so inspired to focus on you . . . No earthly addiction or relationship can come remotely close to promising me an unbreakable lifeline. No one else can promise me a Savior who has taken up a permanent post as high priest on my behalf. I truly have every reason to grab this promise with both hands, and never let go!

Personal Reflections

November 1

So now we have a high priest who perfectly fits our needs: completely holy, uncompromised by sin, with authority extending as high as God's presence in heaven itself. Unlike the other high priests, he doesn't have to offer sacrifices for his own sins every day before he can get around to us and our sins. He's done it, once and for all: offered up himself *as the sacrifice. . .the Son, who is absolutely, eternally perfect.*

- Hebrews 7:26-28

Despite our best efforts, we have never been able to find someone who perfectly fits our need for a Savior. Even the high priests in the Old Testament weren't sinless. But unlike other high priests, Jesus has authority extending as high as God's presence in heaven itself. He doesn't have to offer sacrifices every day for Himself, because He has no sin. Instead, He offered Himself as the ultimate sacrifice for our sins, once and for all. He is willing and able to perform in us to perfection and meet all our needs—for free! All He needs from us is the choice to believe in His saving power and make Him the focus of our lives. He doesn't want any effort from us. He simply wants our undivided attention.

PRAYER: Jesus, when we really focus on your word and receive what you offer us in these verses, you become irresistible. What you offer "shoots adrenaline into our souls" (Hebrews 12:3). We can't contain our wild enthusiasm to share your offer with others!

Personal Reflections

November 2

May God himself, the God who makes everything holy and whole, make you holy and whole, put you together—spirit, soul, and body—and keep you fit for the coming of our Master, Jesus Christ. The One who called you is completely dependable. If he said it, he'll do it!

- 1 Thessalonians 5:23-24

Once again, verses that clearly remind us that God does all the performing and work in our lives. God Himself, who put us together, makes us holy and whole and keeps us fit for the coming of our Master, Jesus Christ. He doesn't just keep us fit in one area of our lives. He covers every area—spirit, soul, and body. He simply asks us to show up every day, cast our eyes on Him and let Him do his job. He is completely dependable. He never misses a day's work. Unlike any boss we have ever had, God always does what He says. He gives us a headset to put on everyday so we don't miss a single instruction. Our only part is to choose to keep the headset turned on!

PRAYER: Lord, the more we discover verses on focus, the more freedom we feel. The pressure to perform is gone. We feel totally confident in you, and feel relieved that we no longer have to try to build our own confidence. What you ask of us is so clear and simple without any need on our part to figure life out. All of us can follow. To follow you is to be free.

Personal Reflections

November 3

Watch out for people who try to dazzle you with big words and intellectual double-talk. They want to drag you off into endless arguments that never amount to anything. They spread their ideas through the empty traditions of human beings and the empty superstitions of spirit beings. But that's not the way of Christ. Everything of God gets expressed in him, so you can see and hear him clearly. You don't need a telescope, a microscope, or a horoscope to realize the fullness of Christ, and the emptiness of the universe without him. When you come to him, that fullness comes together for you, too. His power extends over everything.

- Colossians 2:8-10

We don't need a telescope, microscope, or horoscope to see that some ideas are not of God. If anything adds to what God says, claiming things He never claimed, this is not of God. If anything makes what God has said smaller, squeezing Him into a box, this is not of God. Fancy words are not needed to understand God's simple offer: "Come to me, fix your eyes on me, and you will have a life that overflows in joy to those around you."

PRAYER: Lord, many of us have tried to be perfect for years, focused on what we think you are saying in your Word. Typically, we end up focusing on what we have to do to take care of ourselves. We quickly forget that you want to take care of everything in our lives.

Personal Reflections

November 4

Going under the water was a burial of your old life; coming up out of it was a resurrection, God raising you from the dead as he did Christ. When you were stuck in your old sin-dead life, you were incapable of responding to God. God brought you alive—right along with Christ! Think of it! All sins forgiven, the slate wiped clean, that old arrest warrant canceled and nailed to Christ's cross.

- Colossians 2:12-14

God brought us alive—right along with Christ! Before that, it was impossible for us to focus on Him. We were stuck in our old sin-dead life. All we were able to do was focus on our sin and try to figure out our own problems. None of our efforts could bring us into the fullness of Christ. Only Christ's perfect performance on earth and His gruesome sacrifice on the cross raised us from the dead—just like God raised Christ from the dead. Our sin slate was wiped clean. His work brought us to life so we can focus on Him and begin to live a life of fullness in relationship with Him. That is His only desire for us.

PRAYER: Lord, these verses give such a clear picture of why our performance efforts never work. We have been dead and unable to figure anything out or achieve any results. Only your actions on the cross brought us to life. Thank you that we are no longer stuck in sin, where we had no choice but to focus on ourselves. Thank you so much for canceling our old arrest warrant and giving us new life.

Personal Reflections

November 5

So don't put up with anyone pressuring you in details of diet, worship services, or holy days. All those things are mere shadows cast before what was to come; the substance is Christ. Don't tolerate people who try to run your life, ordering you to bow and scrape, insisting that you join their obsession with angels and that you seek out visions. They're a lot of hot air, that's all they are. They're completely out of touch with the source of life, Christ, who puts us together in one piece, whose very breath and blood flow through us. He is the Head and we are the body. We can grow up healthy in God only as he nourishes us.

- Colossians 2:16-19

Many of us not only put a lot of pressure on ourselves to perform in life—we also get a lot of pressure put on us by others. These verses remind us that those who pressure us are just a lot of hot air—out of touch with the source of life, Christ. We no longer want to focus on their pressure on us to perform, any more than we focus on our own efforts. Only God is completely safe to focus on. He does all the work. We can rest and relax in Him while He nourishes us to grow up healthy.

PRAYER: Lord, once again, thank you for verses that give us a feeling of freedom from the pressure to perform. Whether we pressure ourselves or allow others to pressure us, you instruct us to choose to focus on you. You are the only source of life, after all!

Personal Reflections

November 6

So, then, if with Christ you've put all that pretentious and infantile religion behind you, why do you let yourselves be bullied by it? "Don't touch this! Don't taste that! Don't go near this!" Do you think things that are here today and gone tomorrow are worth that kind of attention? Such things sound impressive if said in a deep enough voice. They even give the illusion of being pious and humble and ascetic. But they're just another way of showing off, making yourselves look important.

- Colossians 2:20-23

Why do we let ourselves be bullied by pretentious religion? We may easily get distracted by a speaker's impressive qualities like a deep voice or a charming smile, especially if the speaker champions performance-based illusions of something spiritual, humble, or ascetic. We long for someone to tell us exactly what to do. God designed us to need someone to run our lives, to need someone to focus on, yet His desire is not that we be bullied into enslavement to a set of do's and don'ts. His design is simply that we be totally dependent on Him.

PRAYER: Lord, even though we are easily distracted, you are more attractive than anything or anyone here on earth. No one and nothing here on earth is the least bit comparable to your wisdom. All you ask is that we choose to focus on you, so you can show us how nothing can compare to how impressive you are.

Personal Reflections

November 7

So if you're serious about living this new resurrection life with Christ, act *like it. Pursue the things over which Christ presides. Don't shuffle along, eyes to the ground, absorbed with the things right in front of you. Look up, and be alert to what is going on around Christ—that's where the action is. See things from* his *perspective.*

- Colossians 3:1-2

These verses sound a little bit like they are ordering us around. Many pious people can give orders like this without showing us how to act serious. However, like so many other verses in scripture, instructions are given that clearly show us what acting serious looks like. We are instructed to pursue the things over which Christ presides. How do we pursue? We pursue by simply looking up, not keeping our eyes on the ground and just shuffling our feet along. By simply choosing to look up, we are alert to what is going on around Christ—that's where the action is. Looking up allows us to see things from His perspective.

PRAYER: Lord, we are so relieved that "acting serious" requires shifting our focus to you, not rigorous performance. We have spent our whole lives trying to be so serious about obeying you through our own efforts, and we have failed so many times that we do just shuffle along in discouragement with our eyes to the ground. We are so weary in our failures to perform. Finally, we see clearly that all we need to do is "look up" and you take care of all the work.

Personal Reflections

November 8

Your old life is dead. Your new life, which is your real *life—even though invisible to spectators—is with Christ in God. He is your life. When Christ (your real life, remember) shows up again on this earth, you'll show up, too—the real you, the glorious you. Meanwhile, be content with obscurity, like Christ.*

- Colossians 3:3-4

When we stay focused on God, He becomes our real life. Consequently, we become dead to our old life—it falls off the back of the truck and is left behind. It only gets revived when we look in the rear view mirror, turn the truck around, go back and pick it up. Fortunately, since Christ died for our sins once and for all, we are now free to quickly refocus on Him after we do try to revive our old selves. Through keeping our sights on God, we will show up, too, the real us in Christ, when He returns again on this earth.

PRAYER: Lord, we are glad to be rid of our old lives and to have you be our new, real Life. As we stay focused on you and our old life dies off, we start to notice how bad it looks and smells and tastes. Our senses remind us how attractive you are to our senses and how unattractive our old self is. Thank you for the many ways you remind us to leave our old, dead life behind us in the dust.

Personal Reflections

November 9

Don't lie to one another. You're done with that old life. It's like a filthy set of ill-fitting clothes you've stripped off and put in the fire. Now you're dressed in a new wardrobe. Every item of your new way of life is custom-made by the Creator, with his label on it. All the old fashions are now obsolete. Words like Jewish and non-Jewish, religious and irreligious, insider and outsider, uncivilized and uncouth, slave and free, mean nothing. From now on everyone is defined by Christ, everyone is included in Christ.

- Colossians 3:9-11

As part of our focus on God and Him being our new life, He has custom-made a whole new wardrobe for each of us. He has stripped off our old, filthy, ill-fitting fashions and burned them in the fire. Our old clothes and our old identities are now obsolete and mean nothing. From now on, all of us who believe in Him and follow Him are defined by Christ, and included in Christ. Isn't that a strangely wonderful and liberating thought? No longer do we need to be judged by an external pattern of righteousness, because we are all equal in Jesus's sight, and are free do what He tells us to do.

PRAYER: Lord, thank you for showing us in these verses that everything about our new selves, including our new wardrobe, is custom-made by you. We gladly put on each piece of the new wardrobe you have designed for us. We are relieved that you have burned our old clothes, so the only thing that anyone sees in us when they look is you.

Personal Reflections

November 10

Let the peace of Christ keep you in tune with each other, in step with each other. None of this going off and doing your own thing. And cultivate thankfulness. Let the Word of Christ—the Message—have the run of the house. Give it plenty of room in your lives. Instruct and direct one another using good common sense. And sing, sing your hearts out to God! Let every detail in your lives—words, actions, whatever—be done in the name of the Master, Jesus, thanking God the Father every step of the way.

- Colossians 3:15-17

As we focus on God, He keeps us in tune and in step with each other. We are like a band marching in unison. No one goes off and does his own thing. The band director keeps us stepping to the beat with his baton as he mouths instructions to us. God's instructions are the Word of Christ. As we give His Message room in our lives, we are able to encourage and help each other out when one of us is having difficulty seeing the director. We also join each other in singing our hearts out to cheer each other on. We are all filled with such desire for Him that everything we say and do is in the name of Jesus.

PRAYER: Lord, we chant "thank you, thank you" each step of the way as we march in sync with the clear vision you are giving us as we focus on you. The more our band practices giving you the undivided attention you deserve, the more every detail of our lives reflects your love for us and our love for you and others.

Personal Reflections

November 11

Regarding life together and getting along with each other, you don't need me to tell you what to do. You're God-taught in these matters. Just love one another! You're already good at it; your friends all over the province of Macedonia are the evidence. Keep it up; get better and better at it.

- 1 Thessalonians 4:9-10

All of us who maintain our focus on God are all in the same band. The more our focus band marches together, the more we get along with each other. Getting along is a direct result of our focus on Him. The more we practice focus, the "better and better" aware at getting along we become, not because we try on our own strength to get along, but because we simply choose to keep practicing our focus. With our focus on Him, we thank Him. He fills us with His joy. The joy of The Lord is our strength, and this strength is the source for loving one another.

PRAYER: Lord, through all these daily verses on focus, you are showing us all in a very simple, concise way how this new life in you works. These verses can be stated in this very clear formula-like fashion that doesn't need any human tinkering. All year long, you have been repeating these same things over and over again. Thank you so much for clearing our vision.

Personal Reflections

November 12

And then this: We can tell you with complete confidence—we have the Master's word on it—that when the Master comes again to get us, those of us who are still alive will not get a jump on the dead and leave them behind. In actual fact, they'll be ahead of us. The Master himself will give the command. Archangel thunder! God's trumpet blast! He'll come down from heaven and the dead in Christ will rise—they'll go first. Then the rest of us who are still alive at the time will be caught up with them into the clouds to meet the Master. Oh, we'll be walking on air! And then there will be one huge family reunion with the Master. So reassure one another with these words.

- 1 Thessalonians 4:15-18

Our continual "focus practice" here on earth is simply a marathon rehearsal for the day of Christ's return. What a day of clear vision that will be! We will be walking on air with other loving followers of Christ. We will be caught up into the clouds with the dead in Christ who will rise first. All of us will meet the Master and enjoy one huge family reunion in the clear, brilliant skies. We will all form one gigantic picture with the Master. We will be surrounded by His glory: absolutely no distractions, only His beauty to behold.

PRAYER: Jesus, thank you for these verses that give us a vision of the future that makes our continual choices to focus so rewarding. Thank you that you will give us perfect 20/20 vision to behold you in all your glory.

Personal Reflections

November 13

Do everything readily and cheerfully—no bickering, no second-guessing allowed! Go out into the world uncorrupted, a breath of fresh air in this squalid and polluted society. Provide people with a glimpse of good living and of the living God. Carry the light-giving Message into the night so I'll have good cause to be proud of you on the day that Christ returns. You'll be living proof that I didn't go to all this work for nothing.

- Philippians 2:14-16

When we focus and carry God's light-giving Message into the night, we are living proof that God is faithful and that His work in us has not been in vain. When we focus, His light shines through us into the dark and provides a breath of fresh air in our squalid and polluted society. When we focus, what we do does not require any effort. We do everything readily and cheerfully without any bickering or second-guessing.

PRAYER: Lord, thank you for showing us how to carry your message into the night. When we simply focus on you, we walk around full of your joy. We feel no pressure at all to perform and no worry that we will disappoint you. You are doing all the work! We are simply the grateful vessels carrying you around inside us.

Personal Reflections

November 14

Steer clear of the barking dogs, those religious busybodies, all bark and no bite. All they're interested in is appearances—knife-happy circumcisers, I call them. The real *believers are the ones the Spirit of God leads to work away at this ministry, filling the air with Christ's praise as we do it. We couldn't carry this off by our own efforts, and we know it—even though we can list what many might think are impressive credentials.*

- Philippians 3:2-5

These verses give us permission not to feel any pressure to hang around religious busybodies who are only interested in appearances and are knife-happy circumcisers. When we focus on God, we don't even have to worry about picking them out. God takes care of steering us clear of them. When we stay focused on Him, He clearly shows us that they are not in His field of vision. When we focus on Him, the Spirit of God leads us, with other focused, real believers, to work away at His ministry. This work does not require any effort because we are filling the air with Christ's praise out of pure joy, without any desire to show off our credentials.

PRAYER: Lord, thank you so much that the only qualification there is to be a real believer is choosing to follow you. Even better, thank you so much that you show us the simple plan of how to follow you. We choose to focus on you and you do all the rest. You do all the work in and through us as you carry us.

Personal Reflections

November 15

As long as I'm alive in this body, there is good work for me to do. If I had to choose right now, I hardly know which I'd choose. Hard choice! The desire to break camp here and be with Christ is powerful. Some days I can think of nothing better. But most days, because of what you are going through, I am sure that it's better for me to stick it out here. So I plan to be around awhile, companion to you as your growth and joy in this life of trusting God continues. You can start looking forward to a great reunion when I come visit you again. We'll be praising Christ, enjoying each other.

- Philippians 1:22-26

When we choose to focus on Christ, God puts us in a win-win position in life. Whenever God decides to take us to heaven, we are eager to be with Him in eternity. Through our focus on Him, He has shown us that there will be no greater joy than when He takes us home to be with Him forever. However, as long as we focus on Him here on earth, we are full of joy as we praise Christ together. We are in a win-win experience, either here or in heaven, because we feel His joy.

PRAYER: Lord, we have spent most of our lives feeling like we are in a lose-lose situation. When we focus on earthly pleasures, we end up feeling miserable. When we try to clean up our act and perform for God, we are still miserable and constantly feel we can't measure up. Only when we focus on you, can we experience your joy as you perform in us.

Personal Reflections

November 16

Think of yourselves the way Christ Jesus thought of himself. He had equal status with God but didn't think so much of himself that he had to cling to the advantages of that status no matter what. Not at all. When the time came, he set aside the privileges of deity and took on the status of a slave, became human! *Having become human, he stayed human. It was an incredibly humbling process. He didn't claim special privileges. Instead, he lived a selfless, obedient life and then died a selfless, obedient death—and the worst kind of death at that—a crucifixion.*

- Philippians 2:5-8

When we focus on God, it is a very humbling process. Through our focus on Him, God shows us how to live a selfless, obedient life. We don't claim any special status or privileges, we take on the status as His servant, a slave. We give up our right to our own decisions and simply say and do whatever we are instructed by God. We totally give up any independence and simply follow Him. This humbling process transforms us into life in Him where we no longer desire to be independent.

PRAYER: Lord, thank you for giving us the desire to become more and more dependent on you. When we choose to become your servant or slave, you set us free. You give us freedom from being enslaved to our own sin. Our focus on you releases us from the power and control of our sin.

Personal Reflections

November 17

If I have to "brag" about myself, I'll brag about the humiliations that make me like Jesus. The eternal and blessed God and Father of our Master Jesus knows I'm not lying. Remember the time I was in Damascus and the governor of King Aretas posted guards at the city gates to arrest me? I crawled through a window in the wall, was let down in a basket, and had to run for my life.

- 2 Corinthians 11:30-33

Before we made the choice of a lifetime to focus on God, we would often brag about our performance efforts—a natural outcome of self-focus. Now that we focus on God, we feel uncomfortable drawing attention to ourselves. We credit God for all His performance in us, and any attention we receive as a result. We want to shout His praises, not our own. We may be mocked or taken advantage of for being like Jesus, because being like Him is not popular in our culture. We don't typically brag when we are ridiculed, but the writer of this passage is trying to tell us that while focusing on God may get us some unwanted attention, in God's eyes, it's a badge of honor.

PRAYER: Lord, although it is not fun when others ridicule us or take advantage of us because we follow you, this mistreatment simply reminds us that we are focused on you. As we focus on you, some people may not like what they see, and we may be vulnerable to attack. Despite this unwanted attention, however, we long to share your love every chance we get.

Personal Reflections

November 18

If I had a mind to brag a little, I could probably do it without looking ridiculous, and I'd still be speaking plain truth all the way. But I'll spare you. I don't want anyone imagining me as anything other than the fool you'd encounter if you saw me on the street or heard me talk.

- 2 Corinthians 12:6

Again, Paul is talking about bragging, but not in a way that we draw attention to ourselves. Paul says speaking the plain truth can easily draw attention, but he prefers to be seen as any fool on the street that doesn't get noticed by the crowd. Paul simply did not want to risk people glorifying him instead of Christ. As we focus on God, we gratefully defer any praise to others seeing only Christ. We want Him to get all the praise.

PRAYER: Jesus, many of us have only felt more pressure to perform when others praise our efforts. When we focus on you, we know for certain that all efforts are yours, not ours. We are even embarrassed when others give us praise because we know that we have done nothing, and that you have done all the performing. So, we say a simple "thank you" and give you all the credit. We take the praise as an opportunity to emphasize how you deserve all the glory for anything good they see in us.

Personal Reflections

November 19

That convinced them. They called the apostles back in. After giving them a thorough whipping, they warned them not to speak in Jesus' name and sent them off. The apostles went out of the High Council overjoyed because they had been given the honor of being dishonored on account of the Name. Every day they were in the Temple and homes, teaching and preaching Christ Jesus, not letting up for a minute.

- Acts 5:40-42

When we focus on God, we lose our desire for personal attention. We don't want to let up for a minute in our focus on Him, or in sharing His love and caring for others. His joy in us when we show love and caring energizes us never to let up. Sometimes when we speak in Jesus' name, we get extreme, undesirable attention, like a thorough whipping. However, like the apostles, we still experience His overflowing joy, because we feel honored to be dishonored on account of His name.

PRAYER: Jesus, thank you for taking care of us as we focus on you and share your love and caring with others. You not only take care of us, you also give us your joy so we can even endure persecution by those who don't follow you. Please energize us to continue to speak your truth and love to those around us, no matter what they may do to us or say about us.

Personal Reflections

November 20

That stirred up the people, the religious leaders, and religion scholars. They grabbed Stephen and took him before the High Council. They put forward their bribed witnesses to testify: "This man talks nonstop against this Holy Place and God's Law. We even heard him say that Jesus of Nazareth would tear this place down and throw out all the customs Moses gave us." As all those who sat on the High Council looked at Stephen, they found they couldn't take their eyes off him—his face was like the face of an angel!

- Acts 6:12-15

Stephen was so focused on God and filled with His Spirit that even when his enemies looked at him, they saw the face of an angel. We can also be filled with the Spirit when we make Jesus the center of our lives. When God gives us His joy, we are "brimming with God's grace and energy" (Acts 6:8). Now that we don't want attention for ourselves anymore, we start to get noticed. Fortunately, God has clearly shown us that we are only getting attention because of Him in us.

PRAYER: Lord, we used to strive to get attention and praise for our efforts, to be successful. Now, we only want to focus on you and watch as you do all the work in and through us. We don't even want credit for results. When others see our radiant faces, we only want to give you all the praise for how happy you have made us by pouring out your love on our hearts.

Personal Reflections

November 21

"But then those 'fathers,' burning up with jealousy, sent Joseph off to Egypt as a slave. God was right there with him, though—he not only rescued him from all his troubles but brought him to the attention of Pharaoh, king of Egypt. He was so impressed with Joseph that he put him in charge of the whole country, including his own personal affairs."

- Acts 7:9-10

Joseph was sold into slavery by his own brothers! Even though they sent him to Egypt, God was right there with Joseph. God rescued Joseph—brought him to the attention of the king, who put Joseph in charge of the whole country. Later, God used Joseph's good standing with the king to save the entire country from famine. When we focus on God, we volunteer to be His slave, to do everything He shows and tells us to do without questioning His authority. When we invite His control over our lives, God treats us like royalty—just like the king treated Joseph. Even though we are slaves for the Lord, we feel free for the first time in our lives because of the way He treats His followers in such a loving and caring way.

PRAYER: Lord, thank you for taking such good care of us. We want to stay completely focused, dependent on you. You make us feel like royalty. Just like you were with Joseph, you are always right there with us to protect us. You not only rescue us from all our troubles, you lead us into places of prominence where we can reach others for your kingdom.

Personal Reflections

November 22

At that point they went wild, a rioting mob of catcalls and whistles and invective. But Stephen, full of the Holy Spirit, hardly noticed—he only had eyes for God, whom he saw in all his glory with Jesus standing at his side. He said, "Oh! I see heaven wide open and the Son of Man standing at God's side!"

- Acts 7:54-56

What a description of pure focus! Despite a rioting mob, Stephen hardly noticed—he only had eyes for God. He even saw God in all His glory with Jesus standing at His side. He saw heaven wide open. This level of focus was only possible because God filled Stephen with the Holy Spirit. These verses give us an intense picture of what God can do simply through our focus on Him. We do have to choose to focus with all of our thoughts and five senses, but it is God who fills us with the Holy Spirit and does all the rest.

PRAYER: Lord, it is hard to imagine that simply focus can result in only having eyes for you even when our life is being threatened. We know that we could ever do this through our own efforts to concentrate. Thankfully, you don't make focus about our effort. Focus is simply about our choice and your effort. Through filling us with your Holy Spirit and showing us your glory, you carry us through many hardships, including death encounters.

Personal Reflections

November 23

Yelling and hissing, the mob drowned [Stephen] out. Now in full stampede, they dragged him out of town and pelted him with rocks. The ringleaders took off their coats and asked a young man named Saul to watch them.

- Acts 7:57-58

God can use focus in many ways. Stephen's focus on God was used by God to fill him with the Holy Spirit and to show him heaven when he was about to be stoned. Because of this, Stephen had a glimpse of his reward and was able to endure a very painful death. On the other side of the equation, the mob ringleaders wanted young Saul to focus on their coats while they stoned Stephen, but God used this situation to give Saul his first glimpse of God's wonders through Stephen's death. Even though Saul's radical conversion experience came later, God never misses an opportunity to begin the journey that brings us to making the choice of a lifetime to focus on Him.

PRAYER: Lord, looking back, we can now see the many times you showed up in our lives as you prepared us to come to a place where we choose to focus on you. You were preparing us to finally give up on our own efforts to perform. Through our many failed attempts to succeed in life, you patiently waited for us to come to the end of ourselves. We thought giving up was the end, but it was only the beginning of an amazing journey of focus on you.

Personal Reflections

November 24

As the rocks rained down, Stephen prayed, "Master Jesus, take my life." Then he knelt down, praying loud enough for everyone to hear, "Master, don't blame them for this sin"—his last words. Then he died.

- Acts 7:59-60

When Stephen was being stoned, he wanted to die so he could go to be with Master Jesus. He even knelt in reverence, praying loudly, as a witness to everyone, including Saul. Even though Saul congratulated the killers, the seed had been planted. In our own lives, even while facing death, we can focus on our heavenly Father. Our focus is a final testimonial to our Lord and Savior. We do not fear death, because we will get to see God in person. What a joy to all of us who have chosen to focus on Him! Our confidence paints a vivid picture of our most precious relationship with God. What a testimony to unbelievers of His amazing love!

PRAYER: Lord, although we fear the physical and emotional pain of facing death, we long to be in heaven with you. You have loved us so unconditionally. You have performed endless miracles in our lives. We can't thank you enough. What an amazing day that will be when we get to thank you in person! Please fill our hearts with longing for you and sharpen our desire to meet you face-to-face.

Personal Reflections

November 25

Previous to Philip's arrival, a certain Simon had practiced magic in the city, posing as a famous man and dazzling all the Samaritans with his wizardry. He had them all, from little children to old men, eating out of his hand. They all thought he had supernatural powers, and called him "the Great Wizard." He had been around a long time and everyone was more or less in awe of him.

- Acts 8:9-11

There are lots of modern day Simon's in our culture, even in our churches, who are dazzling everyone. Those of us who keep our eyes on God are grateful that none of these "magicians" comes even close to rivaling our miracle-working God. These famous posers are all about promoting themselves and not giving honor to God. When we maintain our focus on God, He clearly shows us how and why to stay clear of these performers and imposters. While many stand in awe of these people, those of us who focus on God are not drawn to their attention-seeking antics.

PRAYER: Lord, we thank you for not letting us become confused when we encounter attractive imposters who have others eating out of their hand. You make sure that they do not even enter our field of vision when we focus on you. We readily admit we can't sort out the good from the bad very well on our own. We are grateful that you keep us away from the influence of imposters as we give you our undivided attention.

Personal Reflections

November 26

But when Philip came to town announcing the news of God's kingdom and proclaiming the name of Jesus Christ, they forgot Simon and were baptized, becoming believers right and left! Even Simon himself believed and was baptized. From that moment he was like Philip's shadow, so fascinated with all the God-signs and miracles that he wouldn't leave Philip's side.

- Acts 8:12-13

Nothing can come even close to comparing to the news of God's kingdom and the proclamation of the name of Jesus. People left and right quickly forget about the famous Simon's of the world. All we need is for someone to draw our attention to all the God-signs and miracles. As we focus, we become fascinated with God and soon want to share our fascination with others. That is the beauty of the simple choice to focus on God. Even someone as charismatic as Simon stopped focusing on himself and believed in Christ and was baptized.

PRAYER: Lord, these verses clearly show us that even impressive people are more impressed with you when humble servants and slaves of the King announce your good news and proclaim the name of Jesus. All we have to do is simply draw attention to you and not ourselves. You do all the rest. No fancy words out of our mouths or sophisticated explanations are required. In fact, they just get in the way of our focus on you.

Personal Reflections

November 27

All this time Saul was breathing down the necks of the Master's disciples, out for the kill. He went to the Chief Priest and got arrest warrants to take to the meeting places in Damascus so that if he found anyone there belonging to the Way, whether men or women, he could arrest them and bring them to Jerusalem.

- Acts 9:1-2

Saul was hyper-focused on hunting down followers of Christ. He was constantly breathing down their necks, and was prepared in advance to make arrests. In today's culture, many of us experience first-hand how it feels to be hyper-focused, on careers or relationships or any kind of addiction imaginable. We know how to focus; we choose to focus every day on addictions to food, sex, drugs, shopping, gaming, or gambling. We make these choices continually, so that when we wake up each morning, our mental movie camera has our obsession in clear view and we are ready for "lights, camera, action!"

PRAYER: Lord, my desire is to have so much practice at focusing on you that you are the image that is in my mind when I go to sleep at night and when I wake up each morning. I am filled with excitement when I remember that as I give you my undivided attention, I will progressively become hyper-focused on you. I always thought that hyper focus was bad, but this kind of focus on you will be amazing!

Personal Reflections

November 28

He set off. When he got to the outskirts of Damascus, he was suddenly dazed by a blinding flash of light. As he fell to the ground, he heard a voice: "Saul, Saul, why are you out to get me?"

- Acts 9:3-4

God is well aware of the power of addictions. He is the creator of our brains and He knew that it would take a sudden jolt to get Saul's hyper-focus off capturing followers of Christ. Saul was obsessed with his passion to arrest the Master's disciples, but Saul's story shows that no hyper-focus on anything can compare to the power that God has to get our attention. Just think about it—a blinding flash of light that knocks you to the ground and a voice that calls out your name—wouldn't that throw you off-course? Wouldn't that have the power to make you re-think everything? God knows exactly what each of us needs, and He has the power to do anything to change our focus from our own misguided pursuits to a joyful focus on Him, even if it takes a blinding flash of light!

PRAYER: Lord, I am so glad that you will go to any length to get our attention. I love how creative and persistent you are! I am so amazed at how you got Saul's attention and changed him from Saul the persecutor into Paul the apostle. Paul's writing in your Word has been so instrumental in showing me how to focus on you. Thank you for your amazing power to transform hearts, even in a case as hopeless as Saul's life.

Personal Reflections

November 29

He said, "Who are you, Master?"

"I am Jesus, the One you're hunting down. I want you to get up and enter the city. In the city you'll be told what to do next."

- Acts 9:5-6

When Saul experienced his encounter with God, he clearly heard God's voice and heard exactly what God said. I find it amazing that even as Saul asked God who He was, Saul already knew whoever was addressing him was his Master. When we have an encounter with God, we experience what Saul went through. We have given up on ourselves and our ability to succeed. We long for someone to take care of us and to tell us what to do. God always answers our desperate plea in a powerful, commanding way. We readily follow Him and listen to His instructions. God gives simple, precise orders, like He gave to Saul: "I want you to get up and enter the city. In the city you'll be told what to do next."

PRAYER: Lord, thank you for setting the tone for how to focus during our first intense encounter with you. When we are dazed and don't know what to do, we pray that you will do whatever it takes to get our attention back on you, even if that means you have to knock us to the ground and blind us with your radiant light. Please continue to tell us exactly what to do, step by step as we do what we are told. You show us clearly that you are the master and our only role is to give you our undivided attention.

Personal Reflections

November 30

His companions stood there dumbstruck—they could hear the sound, but couldn't see anyone—while Saul, picking himself up off the ground, found himself stone-blind. They had to take him by the hand and lead him into Damascus. He continued blind for three days. He ate nothing, drank nothing.

- Acts 9:7-9

Very often, God so clearly shows us what to do when we first encounter Him; we simply pick ourselves up off the ground, allow God to take us by the hand, and blindly follow wherever He goes. During this intense encounter with God, we have no doubt He is now our Master. We don't ask questions—we don't want to. We don't even try to figure things out; we are tired of thinking all the time. We simply want to follow Him as He gently takes us by the hand. Even better, the Lord wants us to let Him hold our hand forever as we simply follow Him.

PRAYER: Lord, please continue to clear our vision even in times of darkness. We've lost our way and no longer know where we're going, but we feel like little children again as we hold onto your hand. We don't want to run our own lives anymore. We are thankful that you have volunteered to lead and guide us. We are glad to be called your servants and listen only to you.

Personal Reflections

December 1

There was a disciple in Damascus by the name of Ananias. The Master spoke to him in a vision: "Ananias."

"Yes, Master?" he answered.

"Get up and go over to Straight Avenue. Ask at the house of Judas for a man from Tarsus. His name is Saul. He's there praying. He has just had a dream in which he saw a man named Ananias enter the house and lay hands on him so he could see again.".

- Acts 9:10-12

Once again, God is straightforward and clear with His instructions. In fact, our Master "orders us around." He tells us what to do and instructs us as any master would instruct his servants. He doesn't expect us to give Him any input or come up with an opinion. Although we are trained in our culture and churches to give input and share our opinions, God simply wants us to follow Him without any hesitation. We acquire a taste for becoming God's true servants as we choose to focus on Him. The more we focus on Him, the more we see how amazing He is, and eventually we want nothing more than to be simple servants of our Master.

PRAYER: Lord, although it feels unnatural at first, we feel a sense of freedom in becoming your true servants that we never felt before. We thought we were independent, but we have found out we were in bondage to our own thoughts and actions, actions which lead to self-destruction. Now, in becoming your slave, we have been freed from our own personal bondage.

Personal Reflections

December 2

Ananias protested, "Master, you can't be serious. Everybody's talking about this man and the terrible things he's been doing, his reign of terror against your people in Jerusalem! And now he's shown up here with papers from the Chief Priest that give him license to do the same to us."

But the Master said, "Don't argue. Go! I have picked him as my personal representative to non-Jews and kings and Jews. And now I'm about to show him what he's in for—the hard suffering that goes with this job."

- Acts 9:13-16

Our Master's instructions are simple and direct and leave no room for discussion. Many times, the Lord tells us to do things that don't make sense to the human mind. In these verses, Ananias was protesting that everyone was talking about Saul doing terrible things. Saul even had papers from the Chief Priest that gave him license to do more terrible things. From a human perspective, Ananias argument made perfect sense. However, God sees things from a supernatural perspective. God made a radical change in Saul in an instant with a blinding, flashing light. God doesn't ask us to logically understand how He changes us or others. He only asks us to focus and follow.

PRAYER: Lord, thank you for showing us that the only way to receive your supernatural actions is to watch you at work. We don't figure you out in order to believe. We watch you and experience your supernatural power in our lives and the lives of others.

Personal Reflections

December 3

So Ananias went and found the house, placed his hands on blind Saul, and said, "Brother Saul, the Master sent me, the same Jesus you saw on your way here. He sent me so you could see again and be filled with the Holy Spirit." No sooner were the words out of his mouth than something like scales fell from Saul's eyes—he could see again! He got to his feet, was baptized, and sat down with them to a hearty meal.

- Acts 9:17-19

When we are self-absorbed in some form of addiction, we are blind to what Christ wants to do in our lives. We put endless effort into attempting to see how to live—but the harder we try the blinder we become. Our scales only fall off when we choose to focus on our Master and trust Him to guide our lives. When Saul stopped pursuing his own journey of destruction and chose to sit quietly and wait on the Lord, God sent Ananias to heal his blindness and filled him with the Holy Spirit. When we accept Christ as our Master and choose to focus on Him instead of our own schemes for living, He fills us with the Holy Spirit and heals our own spiritual blindness.

PRAYER: Lord, the harder we try to see clearly, the cloudier our vision becomes. We just get more and more confused and frustrated, trying and failing to find the answers to living. Only you can make us see. We are thankful that physical and spiritual healing comes from you.

Personal Reflections

December 4

Saul spent a few days getting acquainted with the Damascus disciples, but then went right to work, wasting no time, preaching in the meeting places that this Jesus was the Son of God. They were caught off guard by this and, not at all sure they could trust him, they kept saying, "Isn't this the man who wreaked havoc in Jerusalem among the believers? And didn't he come here to do the same thing—arrest us and drag us off to jail in Jerusalem for sentencing by the high priests?"

- Acts 9:19-21

Once we choose to focus on our Master, He doesn't waste any time showing us what to do to spread His good news. Spreading the good news is a great way to grow in Christ, because it helps to keep our focus on Him. God put Saul to work so fast that people were caught off guard and doubted that they could trust him. The same thing is true today. People may not trust us when we tell them about our focus on God, because they struggle to accept that Christ does all the effort for us. Many people continue to try to practice "self-help salvation," even though it fails every time.

PRAYER: Lord, just like Saul, we have been determined for years to make our relationship with you based on performance. When we finally accept that our only part is to focus on your performance in us, others are sometimes not sure they can trust this truth. Thank you for being so patient with all of us.

Personal Reflections

December 5

But their suspicions didn't slow Saul down for even a minute. His momentum was up now and he plowed straight into the opposition, disarming the Damascus Jews and trying to show them that this Jesus was the Messiah.

- Acts 9:22

Despite people not trusting Saul's preaching, Saul did not slow down—even for a minute! He was not concerned what people thought of him. He simply wanted to show people that Jesus was the Messiah. The same is true today. When we are focused on Christ and His glory, we are not concerned what people think of us or our message about the grace of God. God will show others how He wants to free them from their performance-centered lives—just like He showed us. We simply want to share with others what God showed us. Nothing else matters. We can be patient with others, because it took us a long, long time to accept what God wanted us to see. Now that God has given us clear vision on this issue, we are free to live in Him.

PRAYER: Lord, remind us over and over again that we don't need to slow down, even for a minute, just because others are slow to respond to your calling that we simply choose to focus on you. Our sharing is in response to you showing what to say and do every minute of every day. We do not have to react to others' doubts and suspicions. We simply thank you that you don't expect us to try to overcome their doubts. You do that work. We simply share what you showed us.

Personal Reflections

December 6

Peter went off on a mission to visit all the churches. In the course of his travels he arrived in Lydda and met with the believers there. He came across a man—his name was Aeneas—who had been in bed eight years paralyzed. Peter said, "Aeneas, Jesus Christ heals you. Get up and make your bed!" And he did it—jumped right out of bed. Everybody who lived in Lydda and Sharon saw him walking around and woke up to the fact that God was alive and active among them.

- Acts 9:32-35

At various times, all of us have lived like God is not really alive and active in our circumstances. When we wake up to the fact that God is living and moving in our lives, present with us, we want to share our amazing discovery. God does not expect us to overcome others' doubts when we share that Jesus is our Master. He takes care of doubts with His miracles in our lives—like making a paralyzed man walk again. God has endless ways of showing people how amazing He is. We are simply delighted to be a part of what God is showing everyone.

PRAYER: Lord, when you overcome others' doubts, we are even more attracted to focusing on you. Everything you do inspires us to continue our focus and to continue to share you with others.

Personal Reflections

December 7

When the church in Jerusalem got wind of this, they sent Barnabas to Antioch to check on things. As soon as he arrived, he saw that God was behind and in it all. He threw himself in with them, got behind them, urging them to stay with it the rest of their lives. He was a good man that way, enthusiastic and confident in the Holy Spirit's ways. The community grew large and strong in the Master.

- Acts 11:22-24

As we see God overcoming the resistance in others choosing to focus on Him, our desire to focus on Him becomes more and more of a permanent passion. Unlike earthly passions which come and go, our passion to focus only grows stronger and stronger. We become more and more enthusiastic and confident in the ways of the Holy Spirit. Like Barnabas, we will make it our business to throw our support behind others who are following hard after God. Together, we can be used by God to strengthen our communities in His truth.

PRAYER: Lord, we are grateful that you grow our desire to focus on you more and more every day. The more we focus on you, the more we want to focus on you. What you show us in our thoughts and through our five senses, continually encourages us not to take our eyes off you. The more we watch you work, the more we thank you because you show us what you are doing for us and for others. The more we thank you, the more we experience the joy of the Lord.

Personal Reflections

December 8

Then Barnabas went on to Tarsus to look for Saul. He found him and brought him back to Antioch. They were there a whole year, meeting with the church and teaching a lot of people. It was in Antioch that the disciples were for the first time called Christians.

- Acts 11:25-26

As we learned in previous verses in Acts, once the scales fell from Saul's eyes, he went right to work. He wasted no time preaching in the meeting places. In these verses, once Barnabas found Saul, he took Saul back to Antioch and started teaching a lot of people. When God shows us how to focus on Him and we learn that He doesn't require us to perform to earn His favor, we eagerly start sharing what God is showing us. He shows us so clearly that we simply want to share what God is teaching us. We don't need years of trying to figure out or analyze what God is telling us. We are simply messengers and have no need to expand or fine tune what He is saying.

PRAYER: Lord, thank you for making your message on focus so crystal clear that we simply repeat what you are showing us. Just like the apostles, we have no need for fancy language or interpretation. We simply want to spread the amazing news what you have done for us after years and years of wandering around in the wilderness of self-performance. Thank you that we can shine the light everywhere we go!

Personal Reflections

December 9

Suddenly there was an angel at his side and light flooding the room. The angel shook Peter and got him up: "Hurry!" The handcuffs fell off his wrists. The angel said, "Get dressed. Put on your shoes." Peter did it. Then, "Grab your coat and let's get out of here." Peter followed him, but didn't believe it was really an angel—he thought he was dreaming.

- Acts 12:7-9

Peter was in prison, awaiting almost certain death at the hands of people who hated Jesus. God sent His angel to shake Peter awake, break off the handcuffs, and lead Peter out of jail. The angel spoke clear words of instruction—Peter didn't need any time or effort to figure out or interpret what the angel was saying to him. Even though he thought it was a dream, Peter followed the angel because God's messenger was so obviously in control of the situation. Peter had nothing to do but follow him—he didn't waste time in reluctance or questions.

PRAYER: Lord, you long to show us your supernatural actions in our lives. You simply ask us to give you our undivided attention, so we actually notice you. When we simply focus on you, we are amazed at how you are taking care of us. Your instructions are so simple and direct that we can't mess them up. When we just choose to follow you, we are shown what to do, and amazing things happen. We may have to pinch ourselves to make sure we aren't dreaming!

Personal Reflections

December 10

Past the first guard and then the second, they came to the iron gate that led into the city. It swung open before them on its own, and they were out on the street, free as the breeze. At the first intersection the angel left him, going his own way. That's when Peter realized it was no dream. "I can't believe it—this really happened! The Master sent his angel and rescued me from Herod's vicious little production and the spectacle the Jewish mob was looking forward to."

- Acts 12:10-11

The Lord loves to remind us over and over again of His supernatural actions. After causing handcuffs to fall off Peter's wrists, the Lord then swung open a gate "on its own." The Lord knows we need His ongoing supernatural actions to keep our attention on Him. He knows how quickly we tend to give ourselves credit for what is happening in our lives. He wants to continually amaze us, and show us what He can do for us that we could never do for ourselves. The Lord also knows our faith is small, so He constantly has His ways of showing us that "this really happened."

PRAYER: Lord, we are not embarrassed to admit we want your constant supernatural actions in our daily lives to remind us to keep our eyes on you. We feel no shame in confessing this dependency and in needing your frequent reminders to keep our focus on you. We love to thank you and are happy to admit that we clearly see we cannot depend on ourselves.

Personal Reflections

December 11

Still shaking his head, amazed, he went to Mary's house, the Mary who was John Mark's mother. The house was packed with praying friends. When he knocked on the door to the courtyard, a young woman named Rhoda came to see who it was. But when she recognized his voice—Peter's voice!—she was so excited and eager to tell everyone Peter was there that she forgot to open the door and left him standing in the street.

- Acts 12:12-14

When we focus on Him, so many times we just continually shake our heads in amazement at God's supernatural actions in our lives. We get so excited we even lose our "common sense," like Rhoda, who forgot to open the door and left Peter standing in the street! Fortunately, when we give God the full attention of our thoughts and five senses, He doesn't need our common sense to help Him do His God-thing. He simply wants our desire to be totally dependent on Him. We gladly see our common sense as "nonsense" compared to His supernatural sense.

PRAYER: Lord, like Rhoda, most of us have experienced the embarrassment of being so excited that we forget something obvious. Even then, in our embarrassment, we can't thank you enough for how amazing you are. We are relieved that you do not depend on our common sense to do your work in us. You only need and desire our choice to focus on you.

Personal Reflections

December 12

But they wouldn't believe her, dismissing her, dismissing her report. "You're crazy," they said. She stuck by her story, insisting. They still wouldn't believe her and said, "It must be his angel." All this time poor Peter was standing out in the street, knocking away.

- Acts 12:15-16

Even though Rhoda forgot to open the door for Peter, she did not forget she heard Peter's voice. Even when she was dismissed and called crazy, she still did not doubt what she heard and stuck to her story. We are so fortunate that God is so clear in His supernatural actions in our lives that we don't have to depend on others for confirmation. We get excited when we receive confirmation, but we are not dependent on the validation of others. God is more than capable of handling His job in our lives completely on His own. He knows what to do and shows us that He alone performs everything in our lives.

PRAYER: Lord, thank you for these verses that remind us that you and you alone are capable of showing us everything that you do in our lives. We place all our confidence in you, not ourselves or anyone else. We give you our full attention, because only you are completely faithful and trustworthy. Sharing and receiving confirmation from other followers is a bonus, not something we need to see you clearly. We give you total credit for clearing our vision.

Personal Reflections

December 13

Finally they opened up and saw him—and went wild! Peter put his hands up and calmed them down. He described how the Master had gotten him out of jail, then said, "Tell James and the brothers what's happened." He left them and went off to another place.

- Acts 12:16-17

All of us can relate to the word "finally." We "finally" made the simple choice to open up and see God just like these people finally opened up and saw Peter. God created us with a brain that is designed to "go wild." When we focus on God with our thoughts and five senses, He gives us lots to go wild about! Forget the religious crowd that says our relationship with Him is not about our feelings. God created our brains so that our relationship with Him is full of feeling. We feel awful without Him; we go wild when we see Him. We react the same way Rhoda and everyone else reacted when they saw Peter.

PRAYER: Jesus, thank you that these verses clearly confirm the importance of our emotions in our relationship with you. When we focus on ourselves, our emotions get us in lots of trouble. When we focus on you, emotions help us experience thankfulness for your gifts, energy in your joy, and delight in your love in our lives. Our emotions are the driving force behind our drive to share with others. When we are focused on you, our emotions work for us, not against us.

Personal Reflections

December 14

When the service was over, Paul and Barnabas were invited back to preach again the next Sabbath. As the meeting broke up, a good many Jews and converts to Judaism went along with Paul and Barnabas, who urged them in long conversations to stick with what they'd started, this living in and by God's grace.

- Acts 13:42-43

Paul and Barnabas took time for long conversations with new converts, in order to urge them to stick with the new life they had begun in Christ. When God initially shows us our part in our relationship with Him—simply choosing to focus on Him and living by His grace—this new living is totally out of character for us. We are used to doing things on our own and not depending on anyone. This new life of focus can be like a new vehicle we are not used to driving. Having someone in the car with us to guide us can be so helpful, and long conversations with a more experienced believer can really help us to keep our focus on God.

PRAYER: Lord, thank you for giving us countless verses on how to focus throughout this entire year to guide us in our new way of God-attentive living. We are so grateful that our old way of living is completely out of the picture in your field of vision. The more we focus on you, the more our old life gets left behind to die. May all of our glances in the rear view mirror at our old life be only glances to remind us to keep our eyes straight, focused on you.

Personal Reflections

December 15

When the next Sabbath came around, practically the whole city showed up to hear the Word of God. Some of the Jews, seeing the crowds, went wild with jealousy and tore into Paul, contradicting everything he was saying, making an ugly scene.

- Acts 13:44-45

Focusing on God and living in His grace is such an attractive message to discouraged and disheartened people. However, the pious crowd will always feel threatened by this message, because they have received many accolades for their self-righteous works in the name of religion. This crowd tore into Paul, especially since he was once one of them. The same jealousy still exists in today's world. People who have gained self-acclaim for their religious works in the name of Jesus consider anti-performance teaching to be almost heresy. They can't imagine that our only part in the Christian life is the simple choice to focus, or that God does all the work for us. They want credit for all the effort and hard work they've part into being good Christians.

PRAYER: Lord, we are thankful you showed us clearly that we are total failures as "good Christians" and that our only hope is complete focus and total dependency on you. We are grateful that you want us to quit trying to do good works because we are sick and tired of failing on our own efforts. It feels amazing to be finally free of the pressure to perform.

Personal Reflections

December 16

But Paul and Barnabas didn't back down. Standing their ground they said, "It was required that God's Word be spoken first of all to you, the Jews. But seeing that you want no part of it—you've made it quite clear that you have no taste or inclination for eternal life— the door is open to all the outsiders. And we're on our way through it, following orders, doing what God commanded when he said,

I've set you up as light to all nations. You'll proclaim salvation to the four winds and seven seas!"

- Acts 13:46-47

Despite heavy resistance from the religious crowd, Paul and Silas did not back down. Once again, "not backing down" appears to be a self-performance or effort-based phrase, but this was born of deep desire for them, not duty. They witnessed the whole city showing up, wanting new life. They witnessed God opening the door wide for everyone who wanted to join this new life in Christ. It was an irresistible movement of God, welcoming anyone who desired to listen to come and hear the good news. Paul and Silas were simply following God's orders, sharing what God showed them. They had no need to turn it into a performance!

PRAYER: Lord, during this year, I've seen what you say in your Word about focus. Thank you for the privilege to share these verses. I wake up every day with your desire deep in my soul to share more. I love you for taking away my burden to perform.

Personal Reflections

December 17

When the non-Jewish outsiders heard this, they could hardly believe their good fortune. All who were marked out for real life *put their trust in God—they honored God's Word by receiving that life. And this Message of salvation spread like wildfire all through the region.*

- Acts 13:48-49

Despite strong resistance from the religious crowd, the message that Paul and Barnabas shared spread like wildfire. This is what happens when we simply share what God is doing instead of trying to do the work on our own. Simply sharing what God says about focus on Him and how to let go of our own efforts spreads like wildfire. God is working day and night to connect followers of His Word. God has opened doors all over and people everywhere want to hear the message. For all of us who focus on Him, God is putting us in strategic places and giving us amazing opportunities to share what He has shown us. People are leaving the performing religious crowd to join in with other followers of this message.

PRAYER: Lord, we want to share your love with others out of our new-found joy that we have received from focusing on you. We are so happy we simply want to share with everyone who will listen. Our sharing is not even work to us! We feel free to share like never before. Thank you that your ministry in us is exploding because of all the work you are doing.

Personal Reflections

December 18

*Some of the Jews convinced the most respected women
and leading men of the town that their precious way of
life was about to be destroyed. Alarmed, they turned on
Paul and Barnabas and forced them to leave. Paul and
Barnabas shrugged their shoulders and went on to the
next town, Iconium, brimming with joy and the Holy
Spirit, two happy disciples.*

- Acts 13:50-52

Even after respected women and leading men turned against
Paul and Silas and forced them to leave, they simply shrugged
their shoulders and moved on to the next town, happy and
"brimming with joy." When people do not approve of our
actions, we tend to react in a very negative and defensive way,
especially if the disapproval comes from a respected, well-
known source. We often end up focusing on winning
acceptance, but Paul and Silas didn't care about these things.
The only way it was possible for Paul and Silas to simply move
on, brimming with joy, was to remain totally focused on
following God. This focus kept them from being distracted by
the opinions of important people, or by their own desire to be
liked and accepted.

*PRAYER: Lord, thank you for teaching us how to deal with our
need to be liked, especially by respected people. You don't
expect us to overcome our insecurities; you simply tell us to
keep our eyes on you. When we listen to you and refuse to focus
on the way others are treating us, we are able to shrug our
shoulders and move on. Your joy fills our hearts to the brim!*

Personal Reflections

December 19

Then some Jews from Antioch and Iconium caught up with them and turned the fickle crowd against them. They beat Paul unconscious, dragged him outside the town and left him for dead. But as the disciples gathered around him, he came to and got up. He went back into town and the next day left with Barnabas for Derbe.

- Acts 14:19-20

The fanatical religious crowd hunted Paul from one city to another. They hated him so much they wanted him dead, and even resorted to mob violence on multiple occasions. Yet even when Paul's enemies had beat him and left him for dead, God raised him up and sent him on to Derbe so he could proclaim the Message of God's salvation there. Sometimes, we can feel emotionally beat up—like our spirit has been battered unconscious. The pain is so bad that we become afraid to feel, and the only way we know how to handle this pain is to leave our feelings for dead. Trying to overcome our fear of emotion only makes us feel more dead inside. However, when we choose to focus on God, His love breathes life back into our feelings.

PRAYER: Lord, thank you so much for doing for us what we could never do for ourselves. Just like you picked Paul up, renewed his spirit, and sent him onto the next town to continue to spread your message, you pick us up, revive our hearts, and give us your joy which is our energy source to continue to share your love.

Personal Reflections

December 20

After proclaiming the Message in Derbe and establishing a strong core of disciples, they retraced their steps to Lystra, then Iconium, and then Antioch, putting muscle and sinew in the lives of the disciples, urging them to stick with what they had begun to believe and not quit, making it clear to them that it wouldn't be easy: "Anyone signing up for the kingdom of God has to go through plenty of hard times."

- Acts 14:21-22

When we hear words like "muscle" and "sinew," we think of hard, physical exertion, like struggling to lift weights. In their proper context, these action words simply mean to stick with the Message, and be reminded of the truth by retracing what we have already heard. Reminders are a critical part of our focus on God's grace-performance in us. Without constant reminders, hard times will definitely distract us. When Paul retraced his steps to Antioch and Iconium, we can be sure that this took him back to the painfully hard time when he was beaten and left for dead. However, Paul kept his focus on God, and used the time to strengthen other believers, tracing and retracing the grace of Jesus in their lives.

PRAYER: Lord, just like our physical muscles are built through the repetition of lifting weights, you build up spiritual muscle in us through constant reminders of your grace performing in us. When we experience hard times, we begin to see them simply as reminders that we are totally dependent on you.

Personal Reflections

December 21

"So why are you now trying to out-god God, loading these new believers down with rules that crushed our ancestors and crushed us, too? Don't we believe that we are saved because the Master Jesus amazingly and out of sheer generosity moved to save us just as he did those from beyond our nation? So what are we arguing about?"

- Acts 15:10-11

Every time we take our focus off God and take life into our own hands, we are making an attempt to "out-god God." Many of us have lived most of our lives by crying out to God in times of crisis—only to take matters into our own hands once it feels like the crisis is over. We go back to performing life on our own and essentially let God know that we can do a better job of running our lives than He does. Even church leaders fall into cycles of crushing their congregations with lots of rules and forget that the Master Jesus, out of sheer generosity, amazingly spared us of any requirement to perform. We do not need to do anything in order to earn God's favor or our own salvation. God's favor rests on us now, because we belong to Christ.

PRAYER: Lord, how thankful we are to feel free of the burden to perform and feel free from the struggle to meet requirements that we have never been able to achieve on our own. Thank you for clearing showing us your Message is so plain and simple there is absolutely no need to even argue about any details.

Personal Reflections

December 22

There was dead silence. No one said a word. With the room quiet, Barnabas and Paul reported matter-of-factly on the miracles and wonders God had done among the other nations through their ministry. The silence deepened; you could hear a pin drop.

- Acts 15:12-13

Only when we stop focusing on rules and regulations can our minds quiet down enough to shift our attention to God and what He is doing in our world. When we recall all the miracles and wonders that God has done, we can hear a pin drop in our minds as we quietly soak in the sheer generosity of God in saving us just as He did our ancestors. We are speechless as we give the total focus of our thoughts and five senses to our amazing Savior. As an added bonus, when our focus shifts away from us and how we want to shape the world, we can finally can stop arguing with other believers about the "right way" to follow God. All of a sudden, our man-made rules disappear, and God is the only things that matters.

PRAYER: Lord, thank you that you made us with such amazing minds that are able to receive and soak in your miracles and wonders. You created our brains with the incredible capacity to simply focus on you so you can fill our quiet minds with all the wonderful thoughts and feelings you have generated for us to replace our own side-show distractions.

Personal Reflections

December 23

As they traveled from town to town, they presented the simple guidelines the Jerusalem apostles and leaders had come up with. That turned out to be most helpful. Day after day the congregations became stronger in faith and larger in size.

— Acts 16:4-5

This whole year, these verses have shown us the simple of focusing on God. Like the simple guidelines given to the early church, these "focus guidelines" have been so helpful to me, and I pray they will be helpful to all who choose to follow them. Day after day, we who have turned our eyes to God and given up on old methods of self-salvation have become stronger in faith. Just like the congregations of early Christians, we grow when we depend on God. God strengthens us both emotionally and spiritually as we choose to focus on Him each and every day.

PRAYER: Lord, thank you for the constant reminders we have seen through these verses all year. We have found freedom in these many reminders that you don't want us to try to strengthen ourselves. You simply desire our total dependence on you each moment of every day. Thank you for teaching us that your performance in us is all we need, and that our only part is to make the simple choice day after day to focus on you, turn our eyes to you, and keep you at the center of our lives.

Personal Reflections

December 24

They went to Phrygia, and then on through the region of Galatia. Their plan was to turn west into Asia province, but the Holy Spirit blocked that route. So they went to Mysia and tried to go north to Bithynia, but the Spirit of Jesus wouldn't let them go there either. Proceeding on through Mysia, they went down to the seaport Troas.

- Acts 16:6-8

What is so amazing about our choice to focus on God is how He so clearly directs each step of our lives. When we follow Him, God clearly shows us where to go and where not to go. He will literally block the path if it would take us in the wrong direction. He blocked two routes back-to-back in these verses! God sees ahead on our behalf because we can't see the future. Some people get upset when God blocks a road, but we must remember that He sees all the potential pitfalls clearly, and we cannot predict where a blocked path would have taken us. When God redirects us, we can be so thankful, because it takes the pressure off us to figure out the right direction. He does that job for us, giving us the freedom to simply depend on Him.

PRAYER: Lord, many times we have worried endlessly about what to do and which way to go in our lives. We tend to get confused, even about small decisions we feel we should be able to handle. Thank you that you love us so much that you freely give each of us your undivided attention in every decision, big and small.

Personal Reflections

December 25

That night Paul had a dream: A Macedonian stood on the far shore and called across the sea, "Come over to Macedonia and help us!" The dream gave Paul his map. We went to work at once getting things ready to cross over to Macedonia. All the pieces had come together. We knew now for sure that God had called us to preach the good news to the Europeans.

- Acts 16:9-10

When we choose to focus on God, He has countless ways to clearly show us the path to follow Him. In these verses, God showed Paul through a dream. God made the dream so clear that it gave Paul his map. A map is detailed and gives exact directions. Nothing is more clear than a map! As a result of this clarity, Paul knew for sure that God had called him and his companions to preach the good news to the Europeans. Today, God wants to show us which way to go, just as clearly as He showed Paul. He wants us to know how He performs for us.

PRAYER: Lord, we are so glad that you love us so much that you want us to see clearly how you work in our lives. You don't want us to miss a single detail. You brilliantly created our brains to be able to choose to focus all our thoughts and feelings on you. You created us with the choice to focus that does not require any pressure to perform or effort to achieve. You simply desire that we follow you in every detail of our lives while you perform all your work in us.

Personal Reflections

December 26

The judges went along with the mob, had Paul and Silas's clothes ripped off and ordered a public beating. After beating them black-and-blue, they threw them into jail, telling the jailkeeper to put them under heavy guard so there would be no chance of escape. He did just that—threw them into the maximum security cell in the jail and clamped leg irons on them.

- Acts 16:22-24

No wonder God created us with such an amazing ability to focus on Him! Otherwise, Paul and Silas could have never made it through a black-and-blue beating. Even today, people are still getting black-and-blue beatings every day. Some of the beatings are physical. Others are emotional. Both kinds of beatings hurt, often beyond what we are capable of handling on our own. Only through the ability God gave us to focus on Him with all our thoughts and feelings is He able to draw our attention to Him, away from such intense pain.

PRAYER: Lord, we are so thankful that you created us with the thought and sensory capacity to simply choose to give you our undivided attention. We certainly enjoy this thought and sensory ability when we praise and worship you. However, the brain capacity you created in us also works in an unbelievable way during times of intense pain and hardship. Thank you that you are always only a "focus" away no matter how dark things may seem.

Personal Reflections

December 27

> *Along about midnight, Paul and Silas were at prayer and singing a robust hymn to God. The other prisoners couldn't believe their ears. Then, without warning, a huge earthquake! The jailhouse tottered, every door flew open, all the prisoners were loose.*
>
> — Acts 16:25-26

Paul and Silas were beaten black-and-blue and thrown in a maximum-security cell, with irons clamped on their legs. You would think they would be moaning and groaning. Instead, they were praying and singing—loudly! No wonder the other prisoners couldn't believe their ears! This story shows the capacity to focus the beautiful mind that God gave us. Paul and Silas were so confident that God was in control, and so focused on praising Him, that they astonished everyone around them. God honored their faithfulness by sending a huge earthquake, literally shaking the prison to its core and causing all the doors to fly open!

PRAYER: Lord, I am beginning to really see your power, and how my focus on you can overcome my bondage and set me free. In these verses, you sent an earthquake to draw everyone's attention to you and free Paul and Silas. Whether you send an earthquake or a little raindrop to show us your love, we are so thankful that you never stop drawing our attention to you through ways big and small. Whether your words come to us as loud as thunder or as soft as a whisper, the love behind those words is irresistible.

Personal Reflections

December 28

Startled from sleep, the jailer saw all the doors swinging loose on their hinges. Assuming that all the prisoners had escaped, he pulled out his sword and was about to do himself in, figuring he was as good as dead anyway, when Paul stopped him: "Don't do that! We're all still here! Nobody's run away!".

- Acts 16:27-28

These verses describe an unbelievable scene. There are many, many stories and movies of prison escapes. I have never come across a story about a non-escape! The jailer was so certain (like all of us would be) that all the prisoners had escaped that he was about to kill himself. How many of us have come to a time in our lives where we feel we are "as good as dead anyway"? This is when God always responds: "I'm still here!" God never leaves or forsakes us, especially when we are at the end of our rope. He simply calls us to give our total focus to Him and let Him perform a miracle in our lives that saves us from total disaster in the nick of time.

PRAYER: Lord, although we typically refuse to turn our full attention to you until the last second, you desire that we focus on you all the time, not just in the midst of a crisis. You desire to guide us with your love every single moment. Following you each moment of every day is total focus. That is when we feel real freedom in our relationship with you—we don't even desire to go back to our self-performance after a crisis is past.

Personal Reflections

December 29

The jailer got a torch and ran inside. Badly shaken, he collapsed in front of Paul and Silas. He led them out of the jail and asked, "Sirs, what do I have to do to be saved, to really live?" They said, "Put your entire trust in the Master Jesus. Then you'll live as you were meant to live—and everyone in your house included!".

- Acts 16:29-31

The jailer in these verses was badly shaken by the events he witnessed at the jail. He was so badly shaken that he collapsed. He was immediately ready to be rescued—ready to follow Jesus. All of us who are focused on God have had a defining moment in our lives, where we were so badly shaken that we completely gave up on ourselves. In desperation, we were ready to let go of our own performance agendas. Any desire to run our own lives was gone—we embraced total dependence on God. Although we occasionally have lapses of taking over control again, our lapses are only reminders of how glad we are that God now has full rein over our lives.

PRAYER: Lord, thank you for reminders of how ready we were to give you total control over our lives when we experienced those life-defining moments of personal disaster. These vivid reminders help to keep us focused on you, to completely depend on you, and follow you closely. We remember our emotional collapses like they only happened yesterday and give you thanks for those times where you rescued us from our despair.

Personal Reflections

December 30

They went on to spell out in detail the story of the Master—the entire family got in on this part. They never did get to bed that night. The jailer made them feel at home, dressed their wounds, and then—he couldn't wait till morning!—was baptized, he and everyone in his family. There in his home, he had food set out for a festive meal. It was a night to remember: He and his entire family had put their trust in God; everyone in the house was in on the celebration.

- Acts 16:32-34

Once the jailer made the simple choice to follow Jesus, Paul and Silas went on to spell out in detail the whole story of Jesus. This turned into a big celebration that lasted all night long! Often, when we run to Jesus to hang onto for dear life, God gives us a night to remember like this one. What a starting point to a new life of choosing to focus on Him and never letting Him out of our sight! He desires that we celebrate our life with Him every day for the rest of our lives.

PRAYER: Lord, our night to remember launches is into a new life of focus on you. As we follow you with all our thoughts and five senses, we see a whole new world—a whole new field of vision, which excludes all the idols and addictions we have focused on in the past. These old lovers that have so repeatedly seduced and betrayed us fade away, as we continue to gaze into your eyes and give you our undivided attention.

Personal Reflections

December 31

"The God who made the world and everything in it, this Master of sky and land. . .he made the entire human race and made the earth hospitable, with plenty of time and space for living so we could seek after God, and not just grope around in the dark but actually find him. He doesn't play hide-and-seek with us. He's not remote; he's near. We live and move in him, can't get away from him! One of your poets said it well: 'We're the God-created.' Well, if we are the God-created, it doesn't make a lot of sense to think we could hire a sculptor to chisel a god out of stone for us, does it?"

- Acts 17:24-28

Just as God starts our life of focus with a night to remember, He gives us new, vivid memories every day as we live and move in Him. The new field of vision He lays out before us as we focus on Him includes "the earth hospitable, with plenty of time and space for living so we could seek after God, and not just grope around in the dark but actually find Him." What a miraculous vision He gives us to focus on, especially in our earthly world of strife and envy, competition, crowding, and lack of free time. God creates new time and space for us for our journey of focus on Him.

PRAYER: Lord, as we close out this year of focus verses, we marvel at what you have shown us. We marvel at how specific and practical your instructions are for living a focused life. We marvel at how you have given us this glorious gift of sight. Continue to clear our vision from now until eternity, as we choose every day to devote our focus to only you and you alone.

Personal Reflections

About the Author

David Heebner, LPC, has had a broad and successful career of more than 30 years working in the field of mental healthcare; from helping individual clients with clinical or behavioral addiction issues to running treatment centers that aid people in recovering from addictions of all kinds. Currently, David manages his own private practice in northern Virginia. He provides outpatient services to individuals, couples, parents, and children from his offices in Chantilly and Ashburn, and worldwide via FaceTime. In 2012, David began to develop the FocusChoice Therapy model, which draws on spiritual principles and neuroscientific discoveries to bring peace and freedom to people who live imprisoned by performance-based thinking. He is also the author of *Overcoming Depression God's Way*, *The Bible and the Brain*, and *Heavenly Addiction: Overcoming Earthly Addictions God's Way*.